ONE

PARADISE IN MALIBU, HELL IN HARTFORD

Bob Dylan answered George Harrison's phone call after only one ring. Harrison was surprised because his calls to Dylan usually ended up in voicemail. George asked Bob if he could stop by to use his home studio to record a B side for a German twelve-inch single of "This Is Love," the second single promoting his new album *Cloud Nine*. Bob said yes. How could he deny a friend, and a former Beatle, in his time of recording need?

Harrison's producer, Jeff Lynne of Electric Light Orchestra fame, was rolling with Harrison for the session. The two Brits decided to give Roy Orbison a call and invite him to Bob's Point Dume estate. Orbison, who had been recording a comeback album with Lynne, joined the gang. Harrison needed to get a guitar that he had stashed at Tom Petty's place, and since Petty hand no plans for April 3, 1988, he elatedly joined the posse headed towards Malibu.

Although Dylan moaned about having to feed his musical comrades, he was an amiable host. Harrison had already worked out the basic chord progression for the song he needed to record. Now they had to come up with words and a title. As the five of them were strumming acoustic guitars and tossing around ideas, Harrison looked into Dylan's garage and saw a road case that read, "Handle with Care." A song was born.

It was mostly Harrison's baby, but everybody pitched in lyrics, and the group decided to add a "lonely" bit to showcase Orbison's distinctive operatic voice. Orbison was the oldest member of this impromptu group, and the others had idolized Roy for years before they became stars. Praising Orbison's voice in *Chronicles*, Dylan writes, "He could sound mean and nasty on one line and sing in a falsetto voice like Frankie Valli in the next. With Roy, you didn't know if you were listening to mariachi or opera . . . He sounded like he was singing from an Olympian mountaintop and he meant business."

"Handle with Care" materialized swiftly and the tune was recorded that night. There's an optimistic sweep to the beginning of the song as Harrison sings the first two verses. The tune develops with relaxed swagger, sounding like a Harrison number that could have found a home on a Beatles album like *Rubber Soul* or *Revolver*. Suddenly, Orbison's voice jerks the song out of cruise control: "I'm so tired of being lonely. I've still got some love to give. Won't you show me someone who really cares?" Orbison's improbable crooning creates tension that demands resolution.

Singing as one, the vocals are strong and melodious as a bridge is built to Harrison's next verse, but the standout voice belongs to Dylan— "Everybody, got somebody, to leeeeeann on. Put your body, next to mine, and dreeeeeeamm on." Dylan's rumbling growl anchors the song, and his voice is the ideal counterpoint to Orbison's. In the first half of "Handle with Care," Harrison, Orbison, and Dylan, the three members of this gathering who were already in the Rock and Roll Hall of Fame, placed their iconic stamps on the tune as they created a distinct group sound. The Traveling Wilburys had arrived.

During a radio interview, Harrison talked about starting a band called the Trembling Wilburys, a moniker he later modified. Harrison's dream group had materialized, at least for one day. When the record execs heard "Handle With Care," they realized they had a track too good to be squandered as simply B side filler material. Motivated by the positive vibe of the egoless "Handle With Care" session, the Wilburys agreed to reconvene for an album that had to be written and completed before Dylan's upcoming tour in June. In early May, the *Traveling Wilburys Volume 1* was completed in ten days. Each member of the group took on a nickname and the surname Wilbury. Dylan was Lucky Wilbury, George was Nelson, Jeff was Otis, Roy was Lefty, and Tom was Charlie T.

DYLAN

& THE

GRATEFUL DEAD

A TALE OF TWISTED FATE

Howard F. Weiner

CONTENTS

The last verse of "Handle with Care" concludes as Harrison sings, "Oh the sweet smell of success, handle me with care." He sings with the satisfaction of someone who has recently tasted success, and can sense it in the moment. The sweet smell of success line was written by Petty, and Harrison was pleased with it. The overdubbed instrumental outro is the final notch on this masterpiece. Dylan wails into his harmonica as Harrison's guitar knifes in underneath—two iconic sounds dance in unison to the melody. For the fadeout line, all that's left are acoustic guitars, a drum beat, and a delicious Dylan harp blast, visceral, and ultimately, beautiful. There might be 1,000 more technically skilled harp players than Dylan, but Bob blows the right stuff, instinctively delivering the unforgettable.

Creative rebirth was in the air for the solo careers of the Wilburys. After his five-year hiatus from recording, Harrison's *Cloud Nine*, released in 1987, climbed to the eighth position on the album charts and spawned the number one hit, "Got My Mind Set on You." A finely polished production, *Cloud Nine* flows with a coherent sound and a pleasing mix of songs that effectively display Harrison's voice and guitar virtuosity. It lacks the adventurism of *All Things Must Pass*, but Harrison was back in the limelight and inspired. His enthusiasm spilled into the birth of the Traveling Wilburys, a project that would not have happened if it weren't for his infectious personality and ability to bring musicians together, as he did when he arranged the Concert for Bangladesh. Not one to horde enthusiasm or success, Harrison sought to share his blessings with his peers.

Following a succession of superb albums, Electric Light Orchestra ran out of steam in the '80s, and Jeff Lynne focused his efforts on producing and collaborating. Heavily influenced by the Beatles, Lynne was thrilled to produce *Cloud Nine* and assist in Harrison's comeback. Lynne was also producing Orbison's comeback album, *Mystery Girl*, which was released after Roy's fatal heart attack on December 6, 1988. It was a cruel twist of fate for a legend in the thick of a surprising renaissance.

After an impressive run of hit singles during the JFK and LBJ administrations, and establishing himself as one of the most distinctive voices of his time, Orbison suffered a string of personal tragedies and his career went into decline. If you searched for Roy on the radio in the '70s and early '80s, you'd only find him on oldies stations. If absence makes the heart grow fonder, that might explain the Orbison resurgence that materialized around 1987, when he was inducted into the Rock and Roll Hall of Fame and released *In Dreams: The Greatest Hits*, a re-recording of his older hits. Roy was relevant again, and this Wilburys project would help turn a new generation on to "The Big O."

Tom Petty, the youngest Wilbury, had a solid run of albums with his band, the Heartbreakers, for six years until they staggered into a creative malaise around 1983. Tours featuring Petty and the Heartbreakers backing Dylan on the same bill with the Grateful Dead introduced his music to a more eclectic audience. Although his early albums sold well and yielded tunes that received radio play, his canon was missing the masterpiece that would vault him into the revered stratosphere of his traveling siblings. The missing jewel was already recorded by the time the Wilburys convened in Malibu. Thanks to production and collaboration assistance from Lynne, Petty had recorded all the tracks to *Full Moon Fever*. Released six months after the *Traveling Wilburys Volume 1*, *Full Moon Fever* was a monster, going 5x platinum in the United States. (Jeff) Lynnesanity was running wild in Southern California.

Dylan was the Wilbury who didn't have much of a connection to Lynne prior to the Port Dume Summit. If Harrison's phone call on 4-3-88 had slipped into Dylan's voice mail, there probably would have been no Traveling Wilburys. Harrison and Lynne would have cut their B side track elsewhere. However, Dylan answered destiny's call. His latest album, *Knocked Out Loaded*, was a commercial disaster. Dylan was stuck in a funk, during which he still managed to write and record enough brilliant songs to put just about any other songwriter to shame. But, after touring with the Grateful Dead, and then Tom Petty and the Heartbreakers as his backing bands, Dylan had a revelation: Performing his songs for the public was his mission and salvation. The Wilbury powwow was another spark, and confirmation, that Lucky Wilbury was back on the right track as he readied for his upcoming tour, the one that would forever change him as a performing artist.

This was the beginning of what would become known as Dylan's Never Ending Tour, which was influenced by the Grateful Dead, who built a legacy based on their thirty years of live performances. As the Traveling Wilburys convened for the first time, Jerry Garcia, the guitar guru of the Grateful Dead, was finishing off an East Coast tour in Hartford, Connecticut. Back in 1973, when Garcia was playing with his side project bluegrass band Old and In the Way, his nickname was Spud Boy. If Garcia weren't tangled up with hippies in Hartford, he would have loved to have received an invitation to Dylan's Malibu rendezvous. Spud Wilbury has a nice ring to it. Garcia was a group guy all the way—a little heartfelt crooning, steel pedal guitar, or banjo—whatever the song called for, Spud Boy would have accommodated, just like he had for Jefferson Airplane and CSNY back in the day.

I was with Garcia and the Deadheads in the Hartford Civic Center on April 3, 1988; and unfortunately, the next two nights. These were awful performances on the heels of a heartwarming comeback saga. After decades of chemical overindulgence, Garcia lapsed into a near fatal coma soon after a 1986 Dead gig with Dylan and Petty in RFK Stadium. The heat and humidity turned Washington, DC into a pizza oven on that weekend. Close to death after turning forty-four, Garcia's ensuing comeback was somewhat miraculous. In less than two months, he was back on stage with the Jerry Garcia Band, and Grateful Dead gigs resumed two months after that. In 1987, the band recorded their first studio album in seven years, *In the Dark*, which produced their first hit song, "Touch of Grey," which was accompanied by a popular MTV video. Hearing Garcia sing the "I will survive" chorus brought tears of joy to his devotees. The band's popularity soared throughout the '80s, but after "Touch of Grey," going to a Dead show was becoming a rite of passage for curious American college kids—baseball, hot dogs, apple pie, and Grateful Dead.

Garcia had lost weight and appeared happier and more active on stage than he had in years. Initially, the coma had stripped Garcia of his guitar virtuosity. It took months of hard work to return to form, and at times, his playing was spectacular. The Dead also fulfilled a group fantasy when they performed as Dylan's backing band at six stadium shows in July. There was a palpable sense of optimism in the Grateful Dead universe. Maybe the band was headed towards a new golden age. I'd seen approximately 140 Grateful Dead shows by the time I headed south to see the band kick off their East Coast spring 1988 tour in Atlanta, and then I headed to the next stop, Hampton, Virginia. There were inspirational moments, but I was also aware of flat segments that suggested that Garcia was gassed. The non-stop strain of playing all those shows with the Dead and Jerry Garcia Band, as if he had never been sick, was not in his best interest.

While Dylan and friends were barbequing assorted meats and relying upon their collective muse to create "Handle With Care," a tune that would bring joy to millions, Garcia and his mates dumped a carcass of Dead songs upon a sold-out crowd of sycophants in the Hartford Civic Center. Garcia's shredded voice indicated he was suffering from a cold, but that didn't stop him, or the band, from performing two stellar shows on their previous stop in Brendan Byrne Arena. The inventive set lists and momentous jamming made up for any vocal hiccups.

In Hartford, usually a hotbed for inspired performances, the band was exhausted. The first set of 4-3-88 ended with a lazy "Don't Ease Me In," a tune that doesn't require much improvisation. When Garcia was on a roll, they usually ended the set with an up-tempo tune with room to jam, like "Deal," "The Music Never Stopped," or "Let it Grow." When the band played "Don't Ease Me In" again to close the set the following night, this was a clear sign of Garcia's mental and physical fatigue. Since 1978, the Grateful Dead never played the same song two nights in a row unless they were developing a new composition, and even when that was the case, it was unusual.

During the three-night Hartford run, the Dead skipped playing the popular song combinations that best defined their sound: Scarlet Begonias > Fire on the Mountain, and Estimated Prophet > Eyes of the World. Also missing in action was "Morning Dew," the revered spiritual anthem and Holy Grail for Deadheads. It was a depressing run; the worst I'd ever seen. Inconsistent performances would plague the Grateful Dead for the remainder of their days.

The fate of Dylan and the Dead intertwined in the late '80s, and after their close encounters, they seemingly reversed roles and destinies. Fame became an albatross and curse to Dylan as he was anointed the prophet, savoir, and poet laureate of his generation. As he tried to shed these annoying tags, his mystique maintained. After winging it through the '80s as if he were the busboy of his generation, Dylan's popularity flattened out. And as many times as he tried to reinvent himself, the legend of who he was could never fade.

The Grateful Dead were counterculture American heroes, part of a freewheeling caravan of hedonistic pranksters who shunned commercialism, embraced mind-altering substances, and created their own musical universe. Year after year their cult expanded, and after a decade or two, they became big business. Continued success in America will inevitably do that to you. By the time they had the honor of playing with Dylan, the Grateful Dead were the bigger concert draw. This is where the wheel reversed. Inspired by what he witnessed with the Grateful Dead, Dylan began his Never Ending Tour, and slowly reinvented himself as a traveling troubadour over the next thirty years. Dylan received every award, degree, and honor an artist can receive, from a lifetime Grammy Award to a Nobel Prize for Literature. But the defining artistic statement of the second half of his career is the Never Ending Tour, which is still rolling strong.

Dylan had the freedom to run and hide from fame and reinvent himself. Jerry Garcia was a sitting duck as the Dead became commercial behemoths. In 1994, the Grateful Dead grossed over $49,000,000 dollars in ticket sales, even though, creatively, the band was a shell of what it used to be. Money and fame were now hounding Garcia, yet he was loyal to the core; he never let his family down, all the people who had come to make a living off the Grateful Dead. There were long periods when Garcia was so lost in a haze of heroin and Persian smoke that he completely tuned out the rest of his mates. But he never quit the band or divorced himself from his kingdom.

Dylan is the ultimate survivor, and a lone wolf all the way. On the surface, Bob and Jerry may seem as different as any two icons from the same era could be, but a closer look will reveal that they were brothers in spirit, two peas from the same pod, and the same time and place in American history.

TWO

MAKING IT COME ALIVE

R obert Allen Zimmerman, the oldest son of Abe and Beatty
Zimmerman, was born on May 24, 1941, in Duluth, Minnesota,
an iron ore shipping town on the shores of Lake Superior. When Bob
was four, Beatty gave birth to Bob's only sibling, David. After Abe was
stricken with polio, the family moved to Hibbing, Minnesota, a town
built on the Mesabi Iron Range. The Zimmermans were part of a significant Jewish community in Duluth. There were few Jews in Hibbing,
but Abe's brothers lived there, and they provided employment for Abe
at their hardware store. Displaying a natural flair for showmanship at
the age of four, Bob sang at family gatherings and received enthusiastic
applause for his rendition of "Accentuate the Positive." Beatty encouraged her sons to get involved in music and bought a piano in hopes that
Bob and David would learn to play.

Jerome John Garcia was born on August 1, 1942, at Children's
Hospital in San Francisco. Jerry's father, Jose Garcia (everyone called
him Joe), was an accomplished saxophone and clarinet player, and
his mother, Ruth, played piano. Jerry's only sibling, Clifford "Tiff"
Garcia was born five years before Jerry. There was always music in
the Garcia residence on 121 Amazon Street. The Garcia clan was nom-
inally Catholic, and their ancestors were of Spanish descent. Due to
lack of work and issues with the music union, Joe Garcia and a partner
opened Garcia's, a bar/hotel on the waterfront, in 1937. The watering
hole was in a seedy part of town, and the patrons were mostly sailors.
Jerry experienced a much more diverse cultural scene than young Bob
Zimmerman did in Duluth and Hibbing.

Jerry endured two life-altering tragedies at a very young age. When he was four, he was chopping wood with Tiff. Jerry was placing the kindling and Tiff was swinging the ax. They had a rhythm going until Jerry left his middle finger there a split-second too long. His finger wasn't severed, but by the time they got Jerry to the hospital, the finger had to be amputated. Growing up without a middle finger must have been a source of some insecurity. Although looking back on it, Garcia said, "I got a lot of mileage out of having a missing finger when I was a kid."

Garcia is still getting plenty of mileage out of it. His handprint with the missing finger is probably the most famous handprint in the world, a symbol indelibly attached to one of the most beloved guitarists of his time. And missing the middle finger on his right hand never hindered his guitar virtuosity. In fact, learning how to compensate for the amputated finger on his strumming hand may have made him a better player. The other tragic event from his childhood would leave deeper emotional scars.

Joe and Ruth took five-year-old Jerry on a fishing trip to Willow Creek on August 24, 1947. While Joe was fishing in the Trinity River, he slipped off a rock and was swept away by the furious force of the raging river. Joe was a good swimmer but he never had a chance. Three fishermen arrived on the scene and pulled Joe from the waters. An ambulance arrived and tried to resuscitate Jerry's father for several hours, but their efforts were in vain.

In an interview, Jerry claimed to have witnessed his father's drowning, but most eyewitness accounts of the accident contradict that. It's possible Jerry's recollection is a learned memory from having heard the story retold throughout his childhood, although, either way, it was a traumatic event that turned his young world upside down. His relatives tried their best to shelter Jerry from the death, and a lot of pain was suppressed. Deadheads would often be moved to tears when they would hear Garcia's angelic voice sing "The Night They Drove Old Dixie Down," or achingly belt out a line like, "Nothing's for certain. It can always go wrong." Garcia's ability to summon such deep emotion while singing can likely be linked back to all the heartache that had been stored away from his childhood.

Following Joe Garcia's passing, Tiff was sent to live with his aunt and uncle, and Jerry lived with Ruth for a short time. Ruth decided to buy out her partner and focus on running the bar, Garcia's, so she chose to send Jerry and Tiff to live with her parents, Bill and Tillie Clifford. Jerry adored Grandma Tillie, a free-spirited woman who used to play a four-string banjo-ukulele. Jerry and Tiff's grandparents weren't disciplinarians, and consequently, the Garcia boys took full advantage of the freedom.

This liberal upbringing shaped Garcia's life philosophies and fortified his distaste for rules, in both social and musical realms. Jerry's relationship with his grandparents would come to resemble the relationship that his fans would have with him. Deadheads viewed Garcia as a cool grandfatherly figure who encouraged them to be themselves and do as they please. There was mutual respect with limited rules, regulations, or expectations. It was an amiable coexistence, a million miles away from the tumultuous relationship Bob Dylan would have with his admirers.

Dylan's childhood was stable in comparison to the upheaval and shifting scenery that Garcia experienced. Beatty Zimmerman was a loving mother who pampered her oldest son without spoiling him. However, young Bob was stuck in Hibbing with the North Country Blues. Listening to music turned him on to the vast world outside of his closed-off, small-town existence—an alternate reality that was nothing like Hibbing. Talking about Bill Monroe's "Drifting Too Far from the Shore" in the Martin Scorsese documentary *No Direction Home*, Dylan says, "The sound of the record made me feel like I was somebody else…I was maybe not even born to the right parents or something."

This tune had a sound and message that introduced young Bob to another time and place—Kentucky-style banjo and mandolin strumming accompanied by rural voices. The lyrics introduced Bob to another realm of spirituality: *Come to Jesus today, let him show you the way. You're drifting too far from the shore.* It would be many years before

Bob would turn to Christianity in a time of crisis, but he would always be intrigued and influenced by a broader sense of religion that went beyond Judaism. Although it's coincidental, the titles of two later-day Dylan albums, *Tempest* and *Oh Mercy*, are contained within the lyrics of Monroe's song, and Dylan wrote his own "Drifting Too Far From Shore" for his 1986 album *Knocked Out Loaded*.

Bob fell hard for the moaning, lovesick, country blues of Hank Williams. Hank's voice made the songs come alive. He could hear a robin weeping when he listened to "I'm So Lonesome I Could Cry." Dylan was attracted to the distinctive, heartfelt crooning of Williams, and in *Chronicles*, he praises his songwriting prowess. "In Hank's recorded songs were the archetype rules of poetic songwriting...Even his words—all of his syllables are divided up so they make perfect mathematical sense."

Listening to radio way past the midnight hour in his pocket-sized second-floor bedroom in Hibbing, Bob picked up blues and country stations in Chicago, Little Rock, and up and down and all around Highway 61. Before Elvis Presley, Chuck Berry, and the rock and roll explosion, Dylan was hip to legendary bluesmen like Muddy Waters, Howlin' Wolf, and Jimmy Reed. Bob also had a strong predilection for the music of Johnny Ray, and was drawn to the eclectic tone and style of John Jacob Niles. Absorbing it all like a sponge, Bob was making his moves and banging out his ideas and dreams on a baby grand in the living room. Bob and David received some piano lessons. David was the better student in the eyes of his teacher. Bob had other plans. Inspired by the music in his mind, he taught himself how to play piano and acoustic guitar as he blazed down an untrodden musical path.

Jerry Garcia dabbled in several artistic endeavors. He enjoyed painting, and wasn't solely fixated on music. In addition to listening to radio, Jerry amassed a healthy and diverse collection of 45s from the jukebox in his mom's bar. Tiff and Jerry moved back in with their mother when she remarried, and when Jerry turned fifteen, Ruth gave him an accordion for his birthday. Having been infected with the rock and roll fever sweeping over America in the summer of 1956, Jerry pleaded with her for an electric guitar. Ruth promptly went to a pawnshop and traded the accordion for an electric guitar and a small amp.

Jerry's early guitar heroes were Chuck Berry, Eddie Cochran, Bo Diddley, and an emerging star, Buddy Holly. Jerry's stepfather had shown him how to play some guitar chords in an open tuning, but he didn't know anyone who had an electric guitar. Just like Dylan on the piano, Jerry taught himself how to play. Garcia would study photos of guitar players and emulate the positioning of the chords they were playing.

Jerry discovered the joys of smoking marijuana at fifteen. Pot wasn't easy to find in 1956 America, but Jerry and his friend Grant Laird would score fifty-cent joints here and there. As a rebellious teenager, Garcia didn't take to drinking wine or beer, and throughout his life he was never a boozer. However, Jerry loved experimenting with drugs—uppers, downers, stimulants, and tranquilizers, of all forms, shapes, and potencies.

Due to his apathy for homework, schedules, and the tedious curriculum, Jerry was a horrible student. Envisioning a possible future as an artist, Jerry enrolled in the California School of Fine Arts in 1958. This part of San Francisco had become a Bohemian hub, and there was a great infatuation with Beat writers and poets: Allen Ginsberg, Lawrence Ferlinghetti, Gary Snyder, Michael McClure, etc.

An avid reader, one of Jerry's favorite novels in high school was George Orwell's *1984*. Garcia may have imagined what life would be like in the future, but he never could have dreamed up the nightmare and strangeness of his own predicament in 1984. He was grossly overweight, hopelessly addicted to Persian (a refined form of heroin), and he had isolated himself from his bandmates. At the same time, he was one of the greatest performing guitarists in the world, beloved and worshipped by hundreds of thousands of fans. It was a bizarre scenario. When he was at the California School of Fine Arts, Garcia devoured Jack Kerouac's *On the Road*—his circle of friends looked upon it as a mystical text. Once again, Garcia could never have envisioned that he would be the leader of a band that would inspire a massive group of devotees to follow him across America and get their kicks on the road like Kerouac and Neal Cassady.

On the Road was like a bible to Dylan until he was in hot pursuit of Woody Guthrie. Although he could no longer relate to the ideology of the book, he would always be awed by the brilliant bop poetry that flowed from Kerouac's pen, and many of his best songs would have dynamic flow and phrasing reminiscent of the Beats. Another huge novel for Bob was John Steinbeck's *Grapes of Wrath*. He wrote a fifteen-page essay on the book for his English class. A decade later, the names of a few *Grapes of Wrath* characters would end up in Dylan's 1966 masterpiece "Stuck Inside of Mobile with the Memphis Blues Again." There was the preacher, Ruthie, and a grandpa who died and was buried in the rocks.

Dylan's environment may have been culturally limited, but he had the blessing of attending Hibbing High School, a majestic monument of education that cost four million dollars to build in 1920 money. After World War I, the former town of Hibbing was moved two miles south so vast deposits of iron ore could be mined, and the high school was part of the payoff from the mining company. The exquisite architecture of the building contains marble busts, brass rails, decorative ceilings, and painted murals. The auditorium is a stunning venue unto itself, modeled after the old Capitol Theatre in New York City. It's the type of assembly hall that could fuel fanciful dreams, as it did for young Bobby Zimmerman.

On February 6, 1958, Bob's first performance on the grand Hibbing High stage was with his three-piece band, the Golden Chords, featuring LeRoy Hoikkala on drums, Monte Edwardson on electric guitar, and Bob on piano and vocals. The band plowed on, aggressive and loud as Bob hollered and howled "Rock and Roll Is Here to Stay" as if he were Little Richard. This was the annual Hibbing High entertainment show known as the Jacket Jamboree, and the Golden Chords were tough to tolerate. The commotion of the performance appalled Principal Kenneth

Pederson. He cut Bob's mic, and when the Golden Chords wildly carried on, the curtain was pulled. Bob was ahead of his time at Hibbing High, just like he would be at Newport '65, where legend has it, Pete Seeger and Alan Lomax where ready to slam an axe down on the power cable transmitting electrified music to a startled audience of folk enthusiasts.

Fame was Bob's fate and the train had left the station. One evening, when Bob was playing in the lobby of the National Guard Armory in Hibbing, on a makeshift platform in front of an aloof audience, the famous wrestler, Gorgeous George, who was in the main event later that night, burst through the doors with a posse of valets and women carrying roses. As Bob recalls it in *Chronicles*, the wrestler heard the music, turned his head, winked at Bob, and seemed to say, "You're making it come alive." That's all Bob needed to reinforce his burning yearning for stardom.

On January 31, 1959, a few days before the tragic plane crash that ended Buddy Holly's life, Dylan saw Holly at Duluth's National Guard Armory. When Dylan won a Grammy Award for 1997 Album of the Year with *Time Out of Mind*, his acceptance speech reflected that evening with Buddy. "I was three feet away from him and he looked at me, and I have some kind of feeling that he was—I don't know how or why—but I know he was with us all the time when we were making this record, in some kind of way." Without a wild imagination and abundant dreams and the will to see them through, there would never have been a Bob Dylan.

Jerry Garcia was an intelligent and creative soul, but his life lacked focus and purpose, which is not unusual for a carefree seventeen-year-old. What is strange, however, is that Jerry decided to join the United States Army at a recruiting office in Oakland on April 12, 1960. Ninety-nine years earlier on the same day, the Civil War began when Confederate troops opened fire on Fort Sumter in Charleston, South Carolina. Garcia didn't fire upon anybody during his six-month stint in the army. He simply had dreams of traveling to Japan or Germany and experiencing different cultures. When all he saw was discipline and San Francisco,

Garcia went AWOL on numerous occasions. Garcia was eventually convicted at a summary court-martial on October 19, 1960. The facts of what happened next are muddled, but somehow, Garcia was discharged from the army two months later.

Three years after the day Garcia signed up for army service, Bob Dylan played one of the most important concerts of his career at the Town Hall in New York City on April 12, 1963. In the short period between these two events, Dylan went from a complete unknown to a revered songwriter who penned some of the greatest anthems of his generation, and he was blazing a trail of inspiration that would change the face of popular music.

THREE

FREEWHEELIN' AMBITION

I n the 1959 Hibbing High School yearbook, there's a photo of a hand-some young man with a quaint Little Richard hairdo. Below the photo it reads that Robert Zimmerman's ambition is "to join 'Little Richard.'" Fueled by his rock and roll dreams after graduating, Bob took a bus to Fargo, North Dakota, and landed a job waiting tables at the Red Apple Café. There was a modest live music scene in the bars and cafes of Fargo. Bobby Vee and the Shadows were an up-and-coming band in the area, and Bob found a way to get a tryout with them. He told Bobby Vee that he had played piano with Conway Twitty, and using the alias of Elston Gunn, he was given an opportunity to play at a few small local gigs. Mr. Gunn didn't pass the piano audition, but he now had a real rock and roll resume, and his resolve to fulfill his ambition was unshakeable.

After his brief stay in Fargo, Dylan returned to Hibbing, and then enrolled in a liberal arts program at the University of Minnesota. His parents strongly encouraged him to graduate, hoping he'd outgrow the music and poetry phase of his life.

Two hours south of Hibbing, the Twin Cities of Minneapolis and St. Paul was the largest urban area in Minneapolis. Bob moved into a Jewish fraternity house, Sigma Alpha Mu, in Minneapolis, right on the outskirts of Dinkytown, a burgeoning Bohemian enclave. The allure of Dinkytown quickly captured Bob's imagination. Eventually the frat brothers asked him to leave the house, and after a few semesters of skipping classes and doing just enough studying to stay afloat, Bob officially dropped out of school.

Although he came up with the surname Dylan from the poet Dylan Thomas when he was in Hibbing, it wasn't until he was in Dinkytown that everybody recognized him as Bobby Dylan or Bob Dylan. After bidding farewell to the academic world, Robert Zimmerman ceased to exist. His stab at a normal college education was an ill-fated idea, doomed from the start, much like Private Garcia's stint in the military. Dylan scored himself a pocket-sized crash pad above Gray's Drugstore in the heart of Dinkytown. Armed with an acoustic guitar and free to pursue his desires, Dylan played a few gigs at the Ten O'Clock Scholar and landed a regular gig in St. Paul at the Purple Onion, a pizza restaurant, where he earned five dollars a night and some free grub.

Dylan met Dave Whitaker, a liberal intellectual with a predilection for Beat literature, poetry, politics, and social history. Whitaker and his wife, Gretel, hosted regular bashes—beer kegs flowed, and folk music and marijuana filled the air. This was Dylan's introduction to smoking pot.

Bob's appearance changed as he completely immersed himself in folk culture. He transformed the clean-cut Little Richard look into that of a scruffy traveling troubadour—ragged attire, with an indifference towards routine hygiene. He was thin and looked younger than his age, nineteen, and although he was quiet and shy, a visible energy rippled through him—hands and feet always busy. Dave Whitaker said, "He was a vessel waiting and wanting to be filled…my main role with Dylan was telling him about life on the outside, that there was an alternate life out there."

The record collection of Jon Pankake helped fill Dylan's vessel. Pankake was a student at Minnesota University, and a folk enthusiast who played banjo. Without permission, Dylan helped himself to a stack of Pankake's records. This is where Dylan probably first came across Harry Smith's *Anthology of American Folk Music*, an important six LP record collection that would also significantly influence Jerry Garcia. The music performed by bluesmen and folk musicians of the 1920s and '30s opened the door to an arcane and raw realm of America's past.

Although Pankake and Dylan played some music together, Pankake was one of Dylan's early antagonists, criticizing his style and approach to performing. Undaunted by Pankake's critiques, Dylan confidently followed his own vision. Dylan's ability to easily dispense of other's negative opinions would prove to be one of his greatest strengths. It set him on a path of fearless artistic experimentation.

Dylan's magnificent obsession with Woody Guthrie took hold during his days in Dinkytown. One day at the counter in Gray's Drugstore, Dylan's acquaintance, Flo Castner, asked him if he had heard any of Woody Guthrie's solo records. Dylan was only familiar with Woody's Stinson records with Sonny Terry and Cisco Houston. Flo's brother Lyn had a set of about a dozen double sided Woody Guthrie 78 records. Dylan was blown away by Guthrie's sound and the depth of the lyrics—the songs said something. These records were a colossal revelation. Dylan said that Guthrie's songs had "the infinite sweep of humanity in them." That's the exact description many fans would use to describe the stunning early compositions of Dylan's career.

Dave Whitaker lent Dylan a copy of Guthrie's autobiography, *Bound for Glory*, and Bob raced through the book, mesmerized by the explosive poetic flow of Woody's prose. Dylan began to perform nothing but Guthrie songs, and patterned the way he talked, and the way he sang, on Woody's Okie accent. Like his mentor, he began using a harmonica rack, which was rare in those days. Woody jumped into his soul and there was no looking back.

When Dylan found out that the Dust Bowl balladeer was hospitalized with Huntington's disease at Greystone Hospital in Morristown, New Jersey, Dylan hitchhiked to New York City for the next phase of his amazing journey. Summing up his Dinkytown days, Dylan said, "When I arrived in Minneapolis it had seemed like a big city or a big town. When I left it was like some rural outpost you see once from a passing train."

As Dylan was blazing towards the bright lights of New York City, Garcia was drifting and dreaming after his army debacle. Committed to a nonconformist lifestyle, Garcia found his Dinkytown in the burgeoning bohemian scene of Palo Alto. Kepler's Books in Menlo Park, a short walk from Stanford University, attracted an eclectic gathering of artists, poets, musicians, and social activists. Garcia enjoyed hanging around and playing guitar, but he wasn't hell-bent on chasing fame, or even a career in music. A life as a painter might have been in the cards for Garcia, but that all changed after a night of drinking with friends.

On February 20, 1961, around two in the morning, Garcia was a passenger in a car involved in a fatal crash that claimed the life of Paul Speegle Jr. The driver, Lee Adams, and Alan Trist, a friend who would become involved in Grateful Dead business ventures, were all hospitalized. Garcia went flying through the windshield and landed in a field as the rolling car toppled on Speegle. In the aftermath of the tragedy, Jerry nursed a broken collarbone, and he knew he was lucky to be alive. This is when Garcia answered his calling to be a musician with absolute certainty. In an interview, he stated the crash was "where my life began. Before then I was living at less than capacity. I was idling. That was the slingshot for the rest of my life."

Garcia soon met the man who would be his main musical collaborator, Robert Hunter. After graduating high school in Stamford, Hunter briefly attended the University of Connecticut, where he was more of a pinball wizard than a scholar. After flunking out of school, lovesick Bob Hunter traveled cross-country to California in pursuit of the lady he desired. When he realized that his quest was in vain and his love was unreciprocated, Hunter joined the National Guard. Following six months of active duty, Hunter met Garcia in Palo Alto, where they were living out of their time-battered cars in a vacant lot, and eating Hunter's supply of crushed pineapple from big tins that he received from the army. Hunter had played in a folk trio back in Connecticut, and on the fifth day of May, 1961, Hunter and Garcia played their first gig at the Arroyo Lounge. It was a five-dollar payday. In "Cumberland Blues," the Grateful Dead would sing Hunter's lyric, "Make good money, five dollars a day; if I made any more I might move away."

Making connections and bonding with like-minded individuals came easily to Jerry, and others were drawn to his relaxed charisma. It's as if he knew the people he needed in his life would show up on schedule, and time was on his side. Garcia learned a repertoire of popular songs from the leading artists of the folk revival movement—Pete Seeger, Joan Baez, the Kinston Trio, the Weavers.

At Kepler's, Garcia reacquainted himself with an old friend from middle school, Marshall Leicester, who introduced Garcia to bluegrass and old-time string bands, and taught him the basics of the fingerpicking guitar style. Garcia played a few gigs with Leicester and Hunter in the summer of '61. Wherever Garcia roamed he was armed with an acoustic guitar and a desire to jam and expand his repertoire.

Garcia started playing the banjo around this time and rapidly became an accomplished player. He was a fast learner, but the secret to his success was has obsessive commitment, his ability to play all day and night. Garcia was inspired by the brilliant banjo playing techniques of Earl Scruggs, Lester Flatt, and Bill Keith. Playing banjo requires discipline and the ability to think on your feet. Garcia's banjo foray would help him develop a unique sound when he switched back to electric guitar, and it served him well when LSD was melting his mind on stage as he was performing with the Grateful Dead in places like the Carousel Ballroom and Fillmore West.

Garcia also formed a musical partnership with David Nelson, who would achieve fame as a founding member of the New Riders of the Purple Sage. Garcia and Nelson first played together as members of the Thunder Mountain Tub Thumpers. Between 1962 and 1964, Garcia and friends formed various groups with shifting personnel. One would need a detailed scorecard to keep track of it all, but the names of the groups are catchy: Sleepy Hollow Hog Stompers, Wildwood Boys, Hart Valley Drifters, Badwater Valley Boys, Godawful Palo Alto Bluegrass Ensemble, and Black Mountain Boys. In the middle of all this, Jerry got married to Sara Ruppenthal, who gave birth to his first child, Heather. Sara would quickly discover what all the women in Garcia's life would find out; music was Jerry's only true love, and they were a distant second.

New Year's Eve is a hallowed day for Deadheads, thanks to a legacy of annual West Coast bashes featuring three-set performances from the Grateful Dead, and New Year's Eve of 1963 is when Bob Weir and Garcia first discussed forming a jug band. Wandering the backstreets of Palo Alto, Weir heard banjo music coming from Dana Morgan's music shop. Always noodling away, Garcia was waiting for a student who never showed up for his lesson on New Year's Eve. Weir, five years younger than Garcia, had his guitar with him and they jammed a few tunes. They had briefly met each other before on a few occasions. It was an unlikely pairing. Weir was a good-looking, clean-cut kid from a wealthy family, and his guitar skills were limited. His guitar idol was Jorma Kaukonen, and his charming, spacey demeanor helped him fit in with older and more talented players who referred to him as "the kid."

Garcia had already jammed a bit with Ron McKernan, affectionately known as Pigpen, the harp-playing, blues-singing organist who would be the front man of the Grateful Dead early on.

Phil Lesh had met Garcia on several occasions during these years, but Lesh was a jazz aficionado trained in classical music. The band that would soon become the Grateful Dead was an odd mix of talent and personalities. Garcia was at the nucleus, honing his skills and patiently attracting the necessary components for something he couldn't yet see, but he trusted fate and sensed he was on the right path, even though few people outside the greater San Francisco/Palo Alto area had ever heard of Jerry Garcia by 1965.

Arriving in Greenwich on January 24, 1961, Bob Dylan exploded on the scene, and the rippling effects of his artistry would expand the foundation of popular music within a modest period of time. And yet, the only tangible goal of his rendezvous to New York was to meet Woody Guthrie. Dylan accomplished that goal immediately, playing for Woody in his hospital room on several occasions. Dylan's first gigs were at Hootenanny nights at the Café Wha?, and soon after, he was opening for John Lee Hooker at Gerde's Folk City and fraternizing with Hooker after hours. He also befriended Dave Van Ronk, Ramblin' Jack Elliot, and Liam Clancy. It's as if this wannabe hobo from Hibbing had an all-access pass to the heart and soul of the folk capital of the universe in its prime.

Walking quick and talking quicker, Dylan was caught in a whirl-wind of restless ambition and tenacity as he played for greasy hamburg-ers, paltry paydays, a percentage of a tip bucket, and for free when nec-essary. Bob was on the ultimate mission from God, and New York City presented him with a series of dreams beyond his imagination. And Bob Dylan was the right person, in the right place, at the right time in history.

Most of all, Dylan got all the breaks because he created them. After Dylan's riveting performance at Gerde's Folk City, when he was on the same bill with the more experienced Greenbriar Boys, New York Times critic Robert Shelton wrote a rave review of Dylan's performance. Published on September 29, 1961, Shelton's article concludes with the famous and prophetic last words, "It matters less where he has been than where he is going, and that would seem to be straight up."

The day after the article appeared, Dylan was in a recording studio playing harmonica on three songs that would be released on Carolyn Hester's debut album. Hester was one of the first folk artists to be signed to Columbia Records by legendary producer John Hammond. Intrigued by Dylan's unique charisma, Hammond offered Dylan a record contract, which was finalized and signed on October 26. Minnesota must have seemed like another lifetime to Bob. Out of nowhere and in seemingly no time at all, Dylan had what all the talented veteran folk artists craved: a contract with a major record label. It seemed almost as fictitious as the tales Bob was spinning about his past, such as learning guitar licks from a blues musician called Wigglefoot in New Mexico.

Hammond was also intrigued that Dylan was beginning to write his own songs, which was almost unheard of amongst contemporary folk artists of the day. Dylan was slipping his own compositions into his sets. "Talking Bear Mountain Picnic Massacre Blues" was one of several early Dylan tunes that paid homage to the Woody Guthrie-style talking blues. It's a clever spoof of a massacre in which nobody dies.

On *Bob Dylan*, the eponymous debut album that was recorded in November 1961 and released four months later, two original compositions were included. "Talkin' New York" is a Guthrie-inspired romp reflecting upon Dylan's first New York winter—*New York Times said it was the coldest winter in seventeen years. It didn't feel so cold then.* "Song to Woody" is a poignant tribute from the protégée to the mentor penned on February 14 at Mills Bar on Bleeker Street. "Song to Woody" borrows the melodic structure of Guthrie's "1913 Massacre." There's an emotional texture to Dylan's vocals, a knowing that he had to move on from this stage of his development. Today he's a Guthrie devotee, tomorrow he's bound for unknown glory. No friendship or relationship could hinder or slow down Dylan's destiny.

If Dylan was sprinting to fame with Lady Luck at his side, his debut album was an anomaly. Dylan sang with conviction, and his harp and guitar playing were solid as he covered a nice selection of folk blues numbers. But the album sold poorly, and those quick to judgement called Dylan, "Hammond's Folly." All the tracks were cut in one or two takes, and Dylan didn't come into the studio with a preconceived model for making an album. The covers were songs fresh in Dylan's mind. There are three songs from these sessions that would be covered by the Grateful Dead, although their versions of "Peggy O," "See That My Grave Is Kept Clean (One Kind Favor)" and "He Was a Friend of Mine," an outtake from the sessions, were not sculpted from Dylan's versions. Jerry Garcia was tuning into, and being influenced by, the same roots music that Dylan was.

During Dylan's seminal first year in the village he met his first true love, Suze Rotolo. In *Chronicles*, Dylan recalled their initial encounter. "Right from the start I couldn't take my eyes off her. She was the most erotic thing I'd ever seen. She was fair skinned and golden haired, full-blood Italian. The air was suddenly filled with banana leaves…Cupid's arrow had whistled by my ears before, but this time it hit me in the heart and the weight of it dragged me overboard." A photo of Suze and Bob on a chilly winter's day in the village would appear on the cover of

Dylan's next album, *The Freewheelin' Bob Dylan*. It's one of the most iconic images of Greenwich Village in the early '60s.

When *Bob Dylan* was released in March of 1962 and proceeded to flop, Dylan paid it no mind because his fertile mind was in overdrive, writing songs of substance with lyrics that would tap into the psyche of his generation. Hammond introduced Dylan to Lou Levy, the head of Leeds Music Publishing Company, and Bob signed a contract giving Leeds the right to publish his songs. Dylan felt like he had a lot to say, and he sensed that writing songs would separate him from the pack of talented performers on Bleeker and McDougal Streets. Displaying his ability to tap into the times, Dylan wrote "Let Me Die in My Footsteps," a tune that expresses the fear of nuclear war and the absurdity of finding comfort in a fallout shelter. This was a precursor to the great anthems busy being born in Dylan's mind.

The songs came fast and furious, and Dylan was performing them at the Gaslight and Gerde's Folk City. "Blowin' in the Wind," one of the anthems best associated with Dylan and the civil rights movement, initially received mixed reviews from his peers, but there was an undeniable buzz surrounding Dylan's new tune. Musicians in Washington Park were singing parodies of it right away. The catchy title of the song is the answer to the questions, and the song has an eternal quality—the timeless trademark of so many future Dylan numbers. Peter, Paul and Mary's cover of "Blowin in the Wind" reached number two on the charts in 1963. Albert Grossman created the Peter, Paul and Mary trio, and by the time "Blowin' in the Wind" was on the charts, he was Dylan's manager.

In October 1962, civilization was on the brink of the ultimate disaster: a confrontation between the Soviet Union and the United States over Soviet nuclear missiles on the island of Cuba. During the Cuban Missile Crisis, Dylan wrote his apocalyptical masterpiece, "A Hard Rain's A-Gonna Fall." It's terrifying and beautiful, poetic and profound. In an interview, Dylan would later explain that every line was the start of a song he did not think he would have time to write. As soon as the song was completed, Dylan rushed down to the Gaslight to play it. The audience was spellbound, and other performers, such as Pete Seeger and Richie Havens, began playing "Hard Rain."

The first time Allen Ginsberg heard "A Hard Rain's A-Gonna Fall," the magnitude of the song moved him to tears and he commented, "The torch had been passed to a new generation." The images of the devastated landscape are startling and unforgettable: *a newborn baby with wild wolves all around it…a highway with diamonds and nobody on it.* The intense lyrics are consistent and balanced for seven minutes, and Dylan delivers the last verse magnificently—he's arrived as a performer with a unique style. One doesn't think of Woody Guthrie at all when listening to this. Recorded in Columbia Studio on December 6, 1962, this is one of those moments when Dylan unleashes a perfect track, miraculous in nature. From the driving strumming of the acoustic guitar to the crisp diction of the singer's voice, there's nothing clownish about this tune.

Pounding away at his old typewriter, Dylan came up with two of his most fabled love songs, "Girl From the North Country" and "Don't Think Twice It's Alright." Fans have debated who the girl from the North Country really was; Bob's high school girlfriend, Echo Helstrom, or his Minneapolis girl, Bonnie Beecher. As Dylan was ascending as a songwriter, he was also building a compelling mystique by never directly answering questions about his creations. By letting the songs speak for themselves, they've become entities that mean different things to different audiences, and the musicians who perform them.

Bob's passionate and rocky relationship with Suze was the inspiration for "Don't Think Twice It's Alright," which Dylan wrote while Suze was in Italy. The conflicted emotions of the narrator made it unique from other love songs of the day. The disillusioned lover expresses anger followed by compassion and forgiveness. The abundance and inventiveness of Dylan's songwriting was, and still is, hard to fathom or explain, especially if you consider these worldly songs came from the mind of someone who was only twenty-one and had spent most of his life in Hibbing, Minnesota. And Dylan's never been one to shed insight on his creative thought process. In *No Direction Home* he said, "I have a habit I picked up someplace along the way. Whatever works for me not to give that away, so easily, you know."

These four compositions would stand the test of time as some of Dylan's finest. *The Freewheelin' Bob Dylan*, released on May 27, 1963, included a fifth opus, "Masters of War." With raw language and a rebellious attitude, Dylan attacks the warmongers and the military-industrial complex. It had to be shocking for people to hear Dylan sing, "I hope that you die and your death will come soon. I will follow your casket. By the pale afternoon. And I'll watch while you're lowered down to your deathbed." It was unlike anything other artists were doing at the time. Dylan doesn't date the song by naming any masters of war. Consequently, the song has become a timeless anti-war anthem, even if that wasn't Dylan's intention.

The definitive Dylan tracks were balanced with some lighter fare, including a pair of witty talking blues numbers, making *The Freewheelin' Bob Dylan* an enormous work, even if it doesn't have the song-to-song consistency of his next album, *The Times They Are A-Changin'*. Much to Dylan's chagrin, *The Times They Are A-Changin'* would earn him the label of protest singer. The title track captured the pulse of a changing American society, and prophesied what was around the bend. Three brilliant songs on the second side, "Only a Pawn in Their Game," "When the Ship Comes In," and, "The Lonesome Death of Hattie Carroll," address issues of social and political injustice.

Dylan touched a nerve in the folk community, so much so that fans and artists wanted him to be an activist and leader. Even though Dylan was astute, and empathized with those who struggled and strived, his focus was on growing as a performing artist. However, Dylan singing with Joan Baez in front of a quarter-of-a-million protesters during the 1963 Civil Rights March on Washington may have given a few people the wrong idea about his political intentions.

Dylan began his affair with Joan Baez while he was still hanging on to Suze. Dylan had his eyes on the "Queen of Folk" while he was still an unknown, but he sensed their destinies would be linked. In *Chronicles*, Dylan wrote, "She seemed very mature, seductive, intense, magical. That she was the same age as me almost made me feel useless. However illogical it might have seemed, something told me that she was my counterpart." By 1963, Baez was smitten with Dylan, the man and the performer, and she invited him to play with her when she was the big attraction. Baez enthusiastically introduced Dylan to her audiences, and infamously, when Dylan had the chance to do the same, when he was on top of the world during his England '65 tour, he left her out in the cold. On his mad dash to fame and immortality, Dylan left a trail of broken hearts along the way. Dylan had become a huge presence and influence on the American music scene by the end of '63 . . . and then came the Beatles.

Greeted by a hysterical mob at JFK Airport on February 7, 1964, the Beatles quickly launched themselves into the American psyche and shook up the world of entertainment. Two nights after their arrival, the Beatles performed on the Ed Sullivan Show, and an esti-mated TV audience of 73 million Americans looked on in awe. In an instant rock and roll was back and bigger than ever before. The young, loveable lads from Liverpool charted four #1 hits in 1964, and their movie *A Hard Day's Night* portrayed them as hip heroes. You could be young and rebellious and still make it in this unpredictable world. After the Cuban Missile Crisis and the assassination of President John F. Kennedy, the Beatles were a fabulous diversion in the thick of trou-bled times.

Teenagers who grew up on the music of Elvis Presley, Chuck Berry, and Buddy Holly, were thrilled by the Beatles. Jerry Garcia fell into this demographic, and eventually, the Beatles won him over after he viewed *A Hard Day's Night*. He saw it as a "little model of good times," and was drawn to the fact that they could thumb their noses at authority and still be successful on a massive scale.

Garcia's passion for making it as a bluegrass performer was fad-ing for several reasons. The bluegrass scene, and the opportunities it presented, were limited in California—there wasn't any way Garcia could make a living on banjo music alone. His latest ensemble, Mother McCree's Uptown Jug Champions, included his future Grateful Dead bandmates Bob Weir and Pigpen. Their repertoire featured more blues songs, and they were playing tunes that the Dead would cover: "Viola Lee Blues," "Big Railroad Blues," and "Cold Rain and Snow."

"The Beatles were why we turned from a jug band into a rock 'n' roll band," said Weir. "What we saw them doing was impossibly attractive." The screaming girls and the orgasmic electricity was all alluring. *A Hard Day's Night* made quite an impression on Phil Lesh as well. Previously a musical elitist, Lesh was now listening to rock and roll on the radio in his post office truck. Flabbergasted by his first listen to Dylan's "Subterranean Homesick Blues," he had to pull his truck off the road and abort his route for a while. Lesh had pretty much given up on a career in music, but this unkempt, long-haired freak was being drawn back towards his calling.

When it became apparent that Mother McCree's Uptown Jug Champions were bound to plug in and go electric, they recruited the hottest young drummer in Palo Alto, Billy Kreutzmann. They didn't have to look too far to find Kreutzmann because he was teaching drum lessons at Dana Morgan's music shop. Rounding out the group on bass guitar was the owner's son, Dana Morgan Jr. The band decided to call themselves the Warlocks, and even though they rehearsed blues numbers by Jimmy Reed and other blues legends, they sounded more like a rock band than a blues ensemble. And their sound was more influenced by the Rolling Stones than the Beatles. The Stones were deeply influenced by American roots music; their songs didn't require precise group harmonies, and there was space to improvise.

The Warlocks played their first gig at Magoo's Pizza Parlor on May 5, 1965, in Menlo Park. The following week they were back at Magoo's, in front of an enthusiastic gathering playing basic R&B: "King Bee," "Walking the Dog," "Wooly Bully," and a new tune by Dylan, "It's All Over Now, Baby Blue." While going through his bluegrass stage, Garcia frowned upon most folk music, and consequently, wasn't a huge Dylan fan until he heard him play "Baby Blue" on the Les Crane show. Garcia thought it was a beautiful performance, and he was equally enamored with Dylan's mad rap during the post-performance interview. Garcia listened to *Bringing It All Back Home* repeatedly, and Dylan instantly became a significant influence for Jerry and the rest of his band.

Phil Lesh dropped some acid with friends and headed to Magoo's Pizza Parlor to see the Warlocks on May 27. Moved by Pigpen's harmonica solo during "Little Red Rooster," Lesh rose from his seat and danced, prompting management to ask him to sit down, and there was an ensuing squabble. After the set, Garcia pulled his old friend Lesh aside and insisted that he play bass for the Warlocks. Morgan Jr. wasn't cutting it on bass, and he had other obligations on the weekends. Phil was a trumpet player with a strong musical background, but he had never played bass before. Lesh joined the band, taught himself how to play bass, and developed an unconventional style that suited the sound and direction of his new group's music. Recalling his fateful first night at Magoo's, Lesh said, "I knew something great was happening, something bigger than everybody, bigger than me for sure."

Something was happening to Bob Dylan, and nobody knew what it was. As Garcia was casually allowing things to fall into place with those around him, Dylan was lobbing hand grenades and burning bridges as his creativity thundered. A couple of weeks after President Kennedy was assassinated in Dallas, the Emergency Civil Liberties Committee honored Dylan with their prestigious Tom Paine award, given to an individual who fought for social justice. To calm his nerves before the acceptance speech, Dylan may have indulged in a few too many cocktails. After insulting the committee by saying he wished he was addressing people with "hair on their head," Dylan talked about how young people should be running things. Bob's rant then turned towards the Kennedy assassination. "I got to admit that the man who shot President Kennedy, Lee Oswald, I don't know exactly where…what he thought he was doing, but I got to admit honestly that I, too…I saw some of myself in him." Bob was booed and hissed off the stage. Dylan has always had an affinity for outlaws, but that was the wrong time and place to pull the pin on that grenade.

On August 8, 1964, *Another Side of Bob Dylan* was released. Irwin Silber, the editor and co-founder of the premier folk magazine *Sing Out!*, wrote an "Open Letter to Bob Dylan," in which he criticized the new direction of Dylan's music and his perceived lust for fame. Many readers of the magazine supported Silber's view and were upset that Dylan had turned his back on the civil rights movement to write compositions of a more personal nature. Dylan never longed to be an activist, spokesperson, or politician. In many ways, he was still the rebellious North Country kid, who five years earlier was determined "to join Little Richard." He was an evolving performing artist who couldn't be stalled by ideological constraints.

Dylan sang out *for every hung-up person in the whole wide universe* in "Chimes of Freedom," the poetic tour de force of Dylan's new record. This wasn't a finger-pointing protest song but it was as liberating, compassionate, and impressive as anything he'd ever written. Recorded in Columbia Studios during a mammoth six-and-a-half-hour session, *Another Side of Bob Dylan* featured an artist on the cusp of a historic breakthrough. The beat lyrical freedom of "Spanish Harlem Incident" is riveting. And all the tracks are sandwiched between the memorable anti-love songs, "All I Really Want to Do" and "It Ain't Me Babe." This album has a complex mix of emotions, from the satire of "I Shall Be Free No. 10," to the nastiness of "Ballad in Plain D," the scene of a final falling out between Bob, Suze, and her sister Carla. Fortified with substantial songs such as "My Back Pages," "To Ramona," and "I Don't Believe You," it's hard to imagine that fans were critical of this record. Dylan's fan base was evolving, and *Another Side of Bob Dylan* was a commercial success.

All eyes were fixed on Dylan, a wiry ragamuffin, as he faced audiences that hung on to every word he sang or spoke. He was receiving extraordinary praise wherever he performed. At the 1964 Newport Folk

Festival, Ronnie Gilbert of the Weavers introduced him by saying, "This is a young man who grew out of a need. He came here because things needed saying, and he somehow had an ear on his generation. And he has set a pace for many people and is now, well he's now continuing in the same way, and there are many others that are joining him. I don't have to tell you, you know him, he's yours, Bob Dylan."

It was an introduction fit for a prophet, guru, revolutionary leader, or perhaps, the return of Christ. He wasn't about to heal the ill or reveal a new manifesto for his chosen people. He was simply coming on stage to perform a few songs. Fittingly, Dylan kicked off his set by singing, "I ain't lookin' to compete with you. Beat or cheat or mistreat you. Simplify you, classify you. Deny, defy or crucify you. All I really want to doooooooooo. Is baby, be friends with you."

Among those who wanted to be friends with Dylan were the Beatles. Although Dylan's influence had yet to creep into their songwriting, the Beatles listened to *The Freewheelin' Bob Dylan* frequently, and they had great reverence for his songwriting. Reflecting on the initial string of Beatles hits in America, Dylan said, "They were doing what nobody was doing. Their chords were just outrageous, just outrageous, and their harmonies made it all valid." When the Beatles were in New York City towards the end of the summer of '64, John Lennon asked journalist Al Aronowitz to arrange for a meeting with Dylan. Traveling from his hideout in Woodstock, Dylan and his associates were escorted into the Beatles' suite at the Hotel Delmonico. The legendary highlight of this summit came when Dylan turned the Beatles on to potent marijuana. After a few joints were smoked, the Beatles were stoned silly—seeds of their future creative experimentation sufficiently planted.

On September 20, Dylan was in attendance for the Beatles concert at the Paramount Theatre. Dylan didn't get to hear the Beatles as much as he heard a screaming wave of teenyboppers. At Dylan's shows, people were attentively transfixed upon the lyrics, and Dylan told Al Aronowitz that he was proud of that. However, Dylan must have been rekindled with the excitement of rock and roll, and the way the music made him feel when he was seeing Buddy Holly, although he never could have imagined the type of hysteria that his conversion to amplified music would stir.

Earlier in the year, on February 25, Dylan appeared on the Steve Allen show and performed "The Lonesome Death of Hattie Carroll." Dylan was bouncing his leg and twisting in his chair restlessly as he listened to Allen read critical praise. Quoting Ralph Gleason, Allen said, "Genius makes its own rules, and Dylan is a genius." The bar was set sky high. Dylan would pole vault himself into another realm of genius with *Bringing It All Back Home*.

FOUR

GENIUS MAKES ITS OWN RULES

Many labels would be pinned on Dylan, and with his fifth album, *Bringing It All Back Home*, he became the father of a new genre, folk rock. Dylan played electric guitar on one of his records for the first time, and rock musicians were hired for the sessions. Dylan had partially separated himself from the folk purists with his last album, but picking up an electric guitar was sacrilegious to the faithful. If there was an elitist myth floating about that rock and roll could never be as deep or thought-provoking as folk or other unamplified forms of music, then Dylan slayed that myth with the first side of *Bringing It All Back Home*, as he made the transition seamlessly. Dylan was on top of the world as a lyricist, and if anything, the excitement of the new format was his gateway to higher creative ground.

With a Chuck Berry-like riff, "Subterranean Homesick Blues" kicks the album off as Dylan spouts spontaneous prose in rhyme with precise timing. Drugs, revolution, chaos, and Beat poetry fill the air. *You don't need a weatherman/ To know which way the wind blows,* and *Don't follow leaders/ Watch the parkin' meters* are eternally relevant slogans from this foot-stomping tune. The alluring "She Belongs to Me" and "Love Minus Zero" could have been slipped onto one of his previous albums, although Dylan has evolved to another level as a lyricist. "Maggie's Farm" minus amplified instrumentation could have found a home on *The Times They Are A-Changin'*.

The second side of *Bringing It All Back Home* is acoustic paradise, and it begins with perfection in the form of "Mr. Tambourine Man." It's an LSD trip, it's a fairy tale, it's the perfect blend of poetry and sound—breathtaking and sublime—*my weariness amazes me*—every emotion is glorified, magnified, and dignified. It's the jingle jangle dance of life released in song. The musical arrangement and Dylan's vocals are heavenly, as beautiful a song as he ever created. In 1965, the wonderfully balanced harmonies of The Byrds rode "Mr. Tambourine Man" to the top of the charts in June, but that was the pasteurized version. "Mr. Tambourine Man" is one of the undeniable, and undefinable, masterpieces of Dylan's oeuvre.

A streaming collage of images influenced by William Blake, William Burroughs, and the Bible, flow through "Gates of Eden." Following the hypnotic second song of side two, Dylan unleashes a major work, "It's Alright Ma (I'm Only Bleeding)." The free-flowing ideas crystalize more clearly here. It's a cynical vision of modern society passionately sung over an intense guitar riff. It's one man with an acoustic guitar, but the performance explodes like rock and roll. The lines are unforgettable, and some of them have become immortal: *He who is not busy being born is busy dying...Even the president of the United States sometimes must have to stand naked...While money doesn't talk, it swears.* If Dylan was a vessel hungry for knowledge and experience during his formative years as an artist, the vessel was now overflowing into his music.

In a *60 Minutes* interview with Ed Bradley, Dylan commented on his early creative process. "I don't know how I got to write those songs. Those early songs were almost magically written." (Dylan chants the first verse of "It's Alright Ma.") "Try to sit down and write something like that. There's a magic to that, and it's not Siegfried and Roy kind of magic, you know? It's a different kind of a penetrating magic. And, you know, I did it. I did it at one time."

There's more magic on the final track, "It's All Over Now, Baby Blue." Dylan sings this one from his soul, a naked performance—they type of thing that can't be taught. The opening line, *You must leave now, take what you need, you think will last*, seemed to sum up Dylan's extraordinary artistic process. Dylan went through many phases and learned from a plethora of kindred spirits: Woody Guthrie, Dave Van Ronk, Liam Clancy, Pete Seeger, Joan Baez…etc. As he passed through their lives, there was almost a knowing that they served a purpose that would help him fulfill his destiny. Dylan was bound to move on, and what he would accomplish would be a tribute to these people. I don't believe Dylan's implying this in the context of the song, but his knack for taking what he needed, those things that he thought would last, was, and still is, crucial to his art. He does it better than anyone.

"Baby Blue" is a beloved anthem that was immediately covered by two of his peers on the rise. Van Morrison recorded a penetrating version with his group, Them, and Jerry Garcia's Warlocks were covering it at their earliest gigs. In the 1980s, "It's All Over Now, Baby Blue" became one of the most anticipated, and poignant, Grateful Dead encores.

Bringing It All Back Home reached the sixth spot on the Billboard album charts, and became his first record to sell over a million copies. Although many traditional folk fans felt betrayed by his new music, Dylan's transition from folk hero to pop star was mellifluous. He was simply following his muse. *Well, I try my best/ To be just like I am/ But everybody wants you/ To be just like them.* His LP shot to number one in the UK as Dylan played his final acoustic tour there in the spring of 1965. D. A. Pennebaker's "rockumentary," *Dont Look Back*, is a revealing glimpse into Dylan's world during that tour—we're flies on the wall and it's for the most part, unscripted. Dylan's busy typing masterpieces, performing for spellbound audiences, jamming and partying with his entourage in hotels, confronting detractors and journalists, and dodging hysterical crowds. Albert Grossman wheels and deals in a menacing manner, and Joan Baez tags along with the crew like a lovesick puppy. It would have been best if she was told not to come along ahead of time, because Dylan had moved on professionally and personally. Aside from the acoustic factor, Joan's music didn't fit in with where Dylan was headed, and the main woman in Bob's life was his future wife, Sara. Dylan's ambition trumped his compassion as he stormed towards artistic immortality.

On July 24, 1965, Dylan was back on the Newport stage for the third year in a row performing three acoustic songs. On the same day, the Paul Butterfield Blues Band drew a big crowd at a blues workshop and stunned them with a fiery performance, despite a dismissive introduction from folklorist Alan Lomax. Albert Grossman was pondering managing the band, and the snub by Lomax led to a wrestling match between him and Lomax. Dylan had already recorded "Like a Rolling Stone," which entered the charts as a single the week of the festival, with Butterfield's guitarist, Mike Bloomfield, and Al Kooper. Dylan asked the Butterfield band and Kooper to back him for a set the following night at Newport. From the time he ravaged the Hibbing High School stage with a spirited Little Richard imitation to his latest groundbreaking accomplishments, Dylan dared to advance confidently in the direction of his own dreams.

What happened the following night shouldn't have come as a surprise. But this was Newport, the spiritual retreat of folk music. On July 25, Dylan seized the stage with a brash electric band. Consequences be damned!

Dressed like a pop star in a leather jacket, polka dot shirt, tight, black pants and pointy boots, Dylan's fashion statement clashed with audience expectations based on his humble attire from past festivals. The music thundered and there were reports of the sound mix being awful, although just the shock of Dylan playing with a band was too much for the ears of Lomax and Pete Seeger to bare. Seeger threatened to cut the power cables with an axe. There are so many versions of what happened that the story has become folklore. If there was an axe or not, is not as significant as the idea of Seeger wanting to wield an axe because the music of an artist he had great admiration for disturbed him. And even though Dylan was blazing forward without regrets, he was devastated when he heard of Seeger's reaction.

Out in the audience there was turmoil and a certain amount of booing. Tales of the booing are legendary, but the tape reveals a brisk and explosive performance of "Maggie's Farm" to kick off the electric set. Bloomfield's quick-picking licks surround but don't swallow Dylan's precise singing. This was aggression unleashed, jarring even for those who enjoyed amplified music. The only person unaffected by the flood of emotions appeared to be Dylan, who, on the surface, handled his first live performance with a band as if he'd been down that road a thousand times before. The raging sound crashed to its conclusion and was met with a mixed chorus of applause, boos, and chatter. Dylan closed the set out with "Like a Rolling Stone" and "It Takes a Lot to Laugh, It Takes a Train to Cry."

The crowd was disappointed. The gripes were many. Dylan had gone electric. He was a capitalistic sell out, the sound quality was poor, and the big star of the festival played a brief set and split. Peter Yarrow brokered a peace agreement and got Dylan to come out for an acoustic encore. Dylan borrowed a guitar from Johnny Cash and threw the crowd a couple of bones; "It's All Over Now, Baby Blue" and "Mr. Tambourine Man." At a post-concert communal dinner for the musicians in a nearby mansion, Dylan was visibly shaken by the turbulent night. To try and ease his mind, Dylan's friend, folksinger Maria Muldaur, asked Bob if he'd like to dance. Dylan replied, "I'd dance with you, Maria, but my hands are on fire."

The music world was on fire with Dylan in the summer of '65. The Byrds' cover of "Mr. Tambourine Man" reached number one for a week. On September 11, "Like a Rolling Stone" was number two on the Billboard charts for the second consecutive week. "Help!" one of the Beatles' deepest compositions, was number one on the charts. Inspired by the songwriting of Dylan, the Beatles raised their game, and there's a Dylanesque tone to "Help!" In the third spot that week was another Dylan-inspired jingle, Barry McGuire's "Eve of Destruction." And with the remarkably long "Like a Rolling Stone" repeatedly taking up six minutes and thirteen seconds of airtime, Dylan's musical presence was ubiquitous.

Strike another match, go start anew. It's all over now, baby blue. The final lines of Dylan's last record make the perfect intro to his next album, *Highway 61 Revisited*. A gunshot drum beat hurls the listener into "Like a Rolling Stone." Dylan's staring anew with the fervor of a starved animal sprung from a cage to feast on a carcass of meat. Going on the offensive, Dylan howls, "Once upon a time you dressed so fine, threw the bums a dime in your prime. Didn't you?" Dylan races forth as if this is his last chance to vent and the clock is ticking. The song is a complex mix of anger, defiance, gloating, and a touch of compassion, but above all, it's liberating—a loss of innocence that yields fear and excitement. The immortal "How does it feel?" chorus borrows its riff from Richie Valens' "La Bamba." This song changed lives. The masses heard, felt, and digested Dylan's diatribe.

The holy anthem of rock and roll emanated from what Dylan described as, "This long piece of vomit, 20 pages long, and out of it I took 'Like a Rolling Stone' and made it as a single." Another unexpected twist of luck was the arrival of Al Kooper on organ. Producer Tom Wilson invited Kooper down to watch the recording session because Al was a big Dylan fan. The ambitious Kooper arrived early with an electric guitar and plugged in, hoping to look like a studio musician hired to be there. When Kooper heard the real guitar player, Mike Bloomfield, his dream of playing on the record was all but dead.

Later in the session, when Paul Griffin switched from organ to piano, Kooper occupied the bench behind the organ. Wilson realized what Kooper was up to, but he let him slide. When Dylan and company were listening to the take, Dylan asked Wilson to turn up the organ. Wilson sighed, "That cat's not an organ player."

Dylan replied, "Hey, now don't tell me who's an organ player and who's not. Just turn the organ up." Kooper hesitated a fraction of a second before each chord change to make sure he was playing the right chord. The slight hesitation and the soulfulness of Kooper's playing gave "Like a Rolling Stone" a penetrating and majestic sound.

Commenting on "Like a Rolling Stone," Paul McCartney said, "It seemed to go on and on forever. It was just beautiful...He showed all of us that it was possible to go a little further." With its free-flowing lyricism and urgent, pulsating pace, *Highway 61 Revisited* is the musical sibling of Kerouac's *On the Road*. In the fourth track of the first side, "From a Buick 6," Dylan sings, "I need a dump truck baby to unload my head." Just as he plucked the right verses from his "long piece of vomit," Dylan brilliantly unloaded the ideas in his head. His fiery breath fills up almost every second of this extraordinarily long, yet consistent album. The decision to break up the lightning pace of the album with the slow, bluesy take of "It Takes a Lot to Laugh, It Takes a Train to Cry" was sublime, since there were so many frenzied electric versions of that song. Who was Dylan's Mr. Jones? Fans would delight in pondering that "Ballad of a Thin Man" mystery. "Tombstone Blues," "Queen Jane Approximately," "Just Like Tom Thumb;" the titles were almost as exquisite as the songs. The record ends with the majestically sprawling "Desolation Row." Dylan links fictional, biblical, and historical characters in this alley of desolation: Cinderella, Romeo, Cain, Abel, the hunchback of Notre Dame, Ophelia, Einstein (disguised as Robin Hood), Casanova, Ezra Pound, T. S. Elliot. It's impossible for an artist to cram more quality music onto a vinyl disc than Dylan did during this hour-long epic.

Dylan successfully fused folk and rock, but he detested the simplicity of the folk-rock label. He hoped that *Highway 61 Revisited* crushed the notion of him being a folk-rocker. In one of his combative 1965 press conferences, he said, "I don't play folk rock…I prefer to think of it more in terms of visionary music—it's mathematical music."

Highway 61 Revisited was visionary music for the Grateful Dead, who went on to cover five of the album's nine songs in concert: "It Takes a Lot to Laugh, It Takes a Train to Cry," "Ballad of a Thin Man," "Queen Jane Approximately," "Just Like Tom Thumb's Blues," "Desolation Row." And they played the title track, "Highway 61 Revisited" with Dylan in 1987 during their joint tour. In the summer of '65, Jerry Garcia and the Warlocks were soaking in the mind-blowing music from Dylan and the Beatles. That was a special summer for pop music. The Rolling Stones had a number one hit with "Satisfaction (I Can't Get No)," and the Beach Boys personified the California sound with "Help Me

Rhonda" and "California Girls." Anything was possible after "Like a Rolling Stone," and the Warlocks were poised to ride the wave, but they wouldn't do it with that name.

Someone in the band thought they saw a 45 in a record store by a group called the Warlocks. Since the band was heading to Golden State Studios to record a few songs, they came up with a temporary name, calling themselves the Emergency Crew. The record label was Autumn Records, and Sylvester Stone was the house producer. Later in the decade, Sly & the Family Stone dazzled half-a-million hippies at Woodstock, and then brought funk music to the mainstream with a string of hits and innovative albums.

Of the six tracks recorded by the Emergency Crew on November 3, 1965, the most compelling is "Can't Come Down," a Dylan-influenced number featuring lyrics by Jerry Garcia. The rhyming delivery of the song is reminiscent of "Subterranean Homesick Blues," and musically it has a Rolling Stones flow and feel to it. It was a decent original, considering it was hurriedly composed.

Not long after the recording session, the band was hanging around with friends in Phil's apartment on High Street, smoking DMT. Seeking a better name than Emergency Crew was on the agenda. Garcia began flipping through a Funk and Wagnalls dictionary, and the group's new name appeared. Describing the revelatory moment, Garcia said, "There was 'grateful dead,' those words juxtaposed. It was one of those moments, y'know, like everything else on the page went blank, diffused, just sort of oozed away, and there was *grateful dead*. Big black letters edged all around in gold, man, blasting out at me, such a stunning combination. So I said, 'How about Grateful Dead?' and that was it."

Garcia and mates weren't convinced that the name would stick, but when they asked friends for their opinions, they all enthusiastically embraced the name. Calling themselves the Grateful Dead was an enormous and serendipitous move. The name looked appealing, had a nice rhythmic bounce, and it had mysterious and contradictory qualities—dangerous, thankful, magical, elusive. It made you want to find out who was in the band and what kind of music they played. And when skulls, skeletons, and psychedelic art became attached to the name via posters and album covers, an iconic image of the band emerged and flourished. These free-spirited goofballs with no business sense came up with the ideal name to market and brand their music to the audience they wanted to reach.

The term *grateful dead* derives from a European folk tale, and involves a person who was in debt when he died and could not afford a proper burial. Along comes a friend or traveler who provides this corpse with a proper burial, and the spirit of the deceased returns the favor through another traveler, who performs a heroic deed for the person who provided the burial. There are many variations to this tale, and the weirdness of the folklore befits the band that adopted the moniker.

Over the next year or two, the Grateful Dead created little tangible music history, but they were in the thick of a revolution in human consciousness. They would intertwine with people who were mythological figures, or who were on their way to cosmic immortality. After coming up with their new identity, Garcia, Weir, and Lesh attended the first Acid Test at Ken Babb's place in Santa Cruz. The band didn't play at this test, but they were invited to plug in and join the freak show at future tests. Allen Ginsberg, Ken Kesey, Neal Cassady, and all the Merry Pranksters were on hand. Kesey, revered for his novel *One Flew Over the Cuckoo's Nest*, had just published *Sometimes a Great Notion* the year before. In Kerouac's *On the Road*, the Dean Moriarty character was based on Neal Cassady. Kesey, Cassady, and their fellow Pranksters had recently returned from a drug-fueled adventure across America in a bus covered in bright-colored psychedelic art. The bus was dubbed *Furthur*. Upon his return to his residence in La Honda, Kesey hosted outrageous LSD parties, and these gatherings expanded into the Acid Tests. As he politely declined taking LSD, Tom Wolfe documented much of this odyssey in his book *The Electric Kool-Aid Acid Test*.

At the December 18, 1965, Acid Test in Muir Beach, the band played and met Owsley "Bear" Stanley for the first time. Owsley already had a reputation for making the finest high-grade LSD in town. This was also Stanley's initial interaction with Kesey's acid scene. There are few accurate reports of what the Grateful Dead played on this occasion, but Owsley was captivated, and a bit frightened by Garcia's "cosmic electric intensity." Another strange notion crossed his tripping mind that night. He thought that the Grateful Dead would be bigger than the Beatles. Freaked out by the weirdness of the evening, Owsley jumped into his car and drove straight into a tree.

The totality of the Acid Test experience minimalized the musical results. Sometimes the band would play for ten minutes and shut it down because they were too high, and some nights the jam took off and people danced wildly. The Dead had to coexist with the Pranksters' sound and light show. Cassady and Kesey often narrated the scene with mad raps on their sound equipment. The audience was the communal entertainment, and there were no schedules, expectations, or limitations. "We weren't famous. Nobody came to the Acid Test to see us," Garcia said. "We had an opportunity to visit highly experimental places under the influence of highly experimental chemicals before a highly experimental audience." The seeds of the Grateful Dead show, and the relationship between Deadheads and the band, evolved out of the Acid Tests. Everybody was in it together, seeking a euphoric journey through the band's music; and mind-expanding supplements were encouraged.

Owsley was infatuated with the Grateful Dead and inquired about working for them. When Lesh told Owsley they didn't have a sound man, the Bear jumped on the opportunity. He had never worked sound before, but like Lesh, he was a quick learner with a sharp mind. In February of 1966, the Acid Tests moved into Los Angeles and the Grateful Dead went along for the ride. They rented a big pink stucco house on the outskirts of Watts, located next to a whorehouse. Owsley became their patron, paying all the bills. Since the band was broke and just playing occasional paying gigs, Bear controlled everything, and he believed in an all-meat diet. The fridge was filled with nothing but giant slabs of red meat and milk. Vegetables were prohibited.

During this period of *captivity* in Los Angeles, the band lived on a non-Kosher diet of fried steak, milk, and potent LSD. They practiced loud and often, and they were appreciative of Owsley for this opportunity to have a blast while stretching musically. Their most infamous test while they were in town was the Watts Acid Test, held in an old warehouse on Lincoln's Birthday. A couple of 30-gallon garbage pails were filled with laced Kool-Aid. Six cups of Kool-Aid was the recommended dose to get high. After numerous people were sufficiently dosed, the math was recalculated, and it turned out that the suggested dose was ten times too high. Things got extremely weird and wild, and thankfully there were no casualties. In a traditional sense, the Grateful Dead were not in the music business, and what they accomplished could not be measured in a quantifiable way, but they had gone where no other band had gone, and expanded their music into a realm that they could call their own.

Of all the mythical characters that Garcia encountered, the one who left a lasting influence on him, and his band mates, was Neal Cassady. In a 1994 interview, Garcia said, "It's hard to even know what to say about Cassady. He had an incredible mind. You might not see him for months and he would pick up exactly where he left off the last time he saw you; like in the middle of a sentence…It was so mind-boggling you couldn't believe he was doing it." Neal Cassady was an artist, and the man himself was the living, breathing canvas. Cassady's fearless driving exploits, his garrulous verbal barrages, and his athletic dexterity amazed all the writers and musicians that crossed paths with him. Cassady embodied a distinctive way of living. That was the way the Grateful Dead wanted to play music.

Being in the right place at the right time in history was essential to launching the careers of both Garcia (San Francisco 1965-1966) and Dylan (New York 1961-1962). After Dylan created two of the most influential albums in the history of music, he took his visionary music on the road. Following Newport, Dylan put together a talented electric band consisting of Robbie Robertson (guitar), Levon Helm (drums),

Al Kooper (organ), and Harvey Brooks (bass), to back him for a gig at Forest Hills Tennis Stadium in Queens on August 28, 1965. Dylan opened the show with an acoustic set that was enthusiastically received. For the second set, Dylan and his talented band confronted the audience with loud electric music. The audience was prepared to boo, and they did so lustily. The audience sang along with Dylan's hit "Like a Rolling Stone," and when the song was over, they remembered to boo. Following their next gig at the Hollywood Bowl on September 3, Dylan reunited Robertson and Helm with their bandmates, the Hawks, Rick Danko, Richard Manuel, and Levon Helm.

Dylan forged ahead with the same format; an acoustic set followed by a set of unrelenting rock and roll. Undaunted by the audiences that jeered his visionary music, Dylan crisscrossed America playing forty shows before the tour ended in Santa Monica in the middle of December. On November 6, the tour made a stop in Barton Hall, on the campus of Cornell University in Ithaca, New York. Barton Hall became a shrine to fans of the Grateful Dead after they performed there on a snowy night in May of 1977. Certain venues have an electric vibe that entices memorable moments and performances.

In between songs in Dylan's electric set, one of the detractors close to the stage hollered, "We want the real Dylan!"

Dylan replied, "OK, you got him." Two days after the show, the *Cornell Daily Sun* printed a review of the show by Charlie Nash, who was impressed with what he heard.

"It must have taken a great deal of discipline to sit there coldly and watch him (Dylan) perform. His harp makes us want to dance. Sharp, shrill, searing, soaring—like Coltrane. While there's always someone to bring you down (the audience). While the great beautiful sound rolls over you, wrapping you in its fold. So strong you can touch it. LEVON & the HAWKS: strong, staccato bass; organ and piano blurring into one complete whole, shrill harp and guitar rising above. WOW."

For those who came to protest that Dylan wasn't a protest singer any more, this kind of muscular sound was easy to hiss at—Dylan was fulfilling his role as the antagonist. When Robbie Robertson and Dylan listened to tapes of the shows in hotel rooms after they played, they were satisfied with the results and committed to carry on. The gifted drummer/singer from Turkey Scratch, Arkansas, Levon Helm, enjoyed and respected Dylan's music, but he couldn't handle the barrage of negative feedback. Levon abandoned the tour at the end of November to work on oil rigs in the Gulf of Mexico.

In October, Dylan's single "Positively 4th Street" ascended to the seventh spot on the US charts and hit number one in Canada. Four days after the chaos of the '65 Newport Festival, Dylan went into Colombia Studios and unleashed a screed against those who had the nerve to say they were his friends. This can easily be interpreted as a rant against old friends from the village, but Dylan touched a nerve as he struck universal sentiments that anyone could relate to, although nothing like this had been heard before in a hit song. *Yes, I wish that for just one time/ You could stand inside my shoes/ You'd know what a drag it is/ To see you.*

Jerry Garcia covered "Positively 4th Street" with Merl Saunders in the '70s and with the Jerry Garcia Band in the '80s. "It was the beautiful sound of 'Positively 4th Street' that got to me more than the bitterness of the lyric," said Garcia. "The combination of the beauty and the bitterness, to me, is wonderful. It's like a combination of something being funny and horrible—it's a great combination of two odd ingredients in the human experience." The catchiness of the melody softens the tirade and makes it easier to digest. By the end of the song we can empathize with the singer's disillusionment, and what a drag it is for him to have to see his tormentor again.

In a secret ceremony, Dylan married Sara Lownds in late November, and did his best to keep the news from everyone, even longtime friends. With fresh inspiration in his life, Dylan wrote some of his most compelling and poetic lyrics, and began recording a new album with the Hawks. Unsatisfied with early results, Dylan sought different studio musicians. Producer Bob Johnston, who replaced Tom Wilson early on during the making of *Highway 61 Revisited*, suggested some Nashville musicians. Albert Grossman was vehemently opposed to the idea, but Dylan figured this was the kick his new record needed, so the *Blonde on Blonde* sessions moved to Nashville. Only Robbie Robertson would join the Nashville crew.

Recording with an esteemed cast of Nashville studio musicians steeped in country and R & B, this album would come as close as Dylan ever came to capturing "That thin, that wild mercury sound" that he heard inside his head. For "Rainy Day Women # 12 & 35," Dylan got the musicians stoned and intoxicated for a rehearsal of a song they thought was called "Everybody Must Get Stoned." After they laughed their way through a take, they were surprised to learn that was the keeper, the track that would appear on the album. Dylan had a hit song and stoners had an eternal anthem.

The Nashville cats were amazed when they rehearsed "Sad Eyed Lady of the Lowlands" for the first time. The song never ended, as Dylan sang verse after verse. A striking poetic tribute to his wife, the song ended up being eleven minutes and twenty-three seconds long, an unheard of length for a song in popular music. "Sad Eyed Lady of the Lowlands" takes up the entire fourth side of *Blonde on Blonde*.

"Visions of Johana" and "Stuck Inside of Mobile with the Memphis Blues Again" are lyrical extravaganzas. The harmonica intro to "Visions" is silky smooth and the acoustic arrangement is sublime—*Ain't it just like the night to play tricks when you're trying to be so quiet.* Somehow this subtle arrangement plays tricks on the listener's mind—when the song plays everything else but Dylan's lyrics and the arrangement fades away, and you're left wondering how the magician pulled off the aural sensation. In a 1985 interview, Dylan said, "Songs are supposed to be heroic enough to give the illusion of stopping time." Mission accomplished. The lyrical magnificence of "Visions" and "Stuck Inside of Mobile" transcend time. The Grateful Dead covered both songs decades after *Blonde on Blonde* was released, another testament to the lasting power of Dylan's music.

The diversity of *Blonde on Blonde* is stunning—the sexual swagger of "I Want You," the emotional tenderness of "Just Like a Woman," the driving desire of "Absolutely Sweet Marie," and the bluesy heartbreak of "Temporarily Like Achilles." Dylan also displays his predilection for using adverbs in song titles. *Blonde on Blonde* completed Dylan's trilogy of albums that remain in the pantheon of the most influential and revered works in popular music. Dylan was only twenty-four, and he recorded these albums in little more than one year.

The Nashville *Blonde on Blonde* sessions began in February as Dylan's world tour touched down in Memphis. The sessions were resumed and concluded in early March. In April, Dylan played a show in Hawaii before playing seven shows in Australia. Dylan raged on with his acoustic/electric format. The European leg of the tour began in Stockholm, Sweden, on April 29, 1966. Last time through Europe, Dylan stood in front of his spellbound audiences with an acoustic guitar and absorbed the stinging criticism of those who disapproved of his move towards commercial electric music. This time around, with the Hawks and drummer Mickey Jones backing him, Dylan was kicking ass and taking names on his electric crusade, and the audiences were ready to rumble.

Appearing wafer thin with a pale complexion and bird's nest hairdo, Dylan popped, smoked, and chugged whatever he needed to get him through the tour. Bob experimented with psychedelics, but he wasn't on the same wavelength as Garcia, Kesey, and Owsley. Hashish and amphetamines helped fuel his frantic pace. Dylan outraged folkies at Newport '65, but the tables were turned on him in the Free Trade Hall in Manchester, England, on May 17. For decades, bootleg tapes and records of this show were improperly labeled as being from the Royal Albert Hall. This is a peak performance from Dylan and The Band.

They opened with a whimsical composition, "Tell Me Mama," the type of jingle that would have fit snuggly on the upcoming Basement Tape sessions. "I Don't Believe You" roared as if its only possible destiny was as an electric number. The clapping crowd tried to interrupt

Dylan between songs, but Dylan pranked them by talking gibberish until they stopped to listen, when Dylan said, "If only just wouldn't clap so hard." Garth Hudson's organ swamped the hall as Dylan informed Mr. Jones and all his supporters that something was happening. Dylan readied himself for the eighth and last song of the set, when an angry voice hollered,

"JUDAS!"

"I don't believe you," countered Dylan. Strumming the opening chords of "Like a Rolling Stone," the welterweight performer bellowed, "You're a liar!" Bob turned towards the band and implored them to "play fuckin' loud!" The anger and defiance of the performance surpassed the emotion of anything he had previously performed. It's a jarring rendition, almost too raw to love. One day they proclaim him a genius, and the next, they call him Judas. A week later, on his twenty-fifth birthday, Dylan performed in Paris with a giant American flag unfurled behind him on stage as America's escalating involvement in the Vietnam War was receiving worldwide condemnation. A weary and exhausted Dylan wrapped up the tour two days later at London's majestic Royal Albert Hall.

Mentally and physically shot, Dylan still had a mountain of commitments when he returned to Woodstock. He was directing a film project on his '66 tour, *Eat the Document*, and Macmillan Press was ready to publish Dylan's book, *Tarantula*. Both projects were suffering, and well below the high quality standard of the Dylan trademark. Albert Grossman had sixty-four more tour dates lined up for Bob, and Grossman was negotiating a new contract with Columbia Records that would require a new record. Temporarily, Dylan's creative well was running dry.

In a stunning development, the world learned that Bob Dylan was hurt in a motorcycle accident on the morning of July 29, 1966. To this day, nobody knows what really happened except Bob and Sara. After leaving the Grossmans' house in Bearsville, Bob fell off his motorcycle somewhere nearby. By most accounts, the accident wasn't as serious as reported. Dylan rehabbed in privacy, recovering from the strains and rigors of his insane climb to fame, as well as the injuries from the accident. A month after the motorcycle mishap, the Beatles played their final concert in front of screaming fanatics in San Francisco's Candlestick Park. The Beatles, heavily under the influence of Dylan, set out to create their legacy via visionary studio work. Attempting to retreat into a peaceful family existence, Dylan wouldn't tour again until 1974.

FIVE

AMERICAN BEAUTY

I f Dylan's motorcycle mishap had been fatal, he would have undoubtedly been hailed as the greatest songwriter ever. He amassed an
astounding oeuvre in just five years. As Dylan rejuvenated his soul and
spirit in Woodstock, the Grateful Dead legend took flight. During the
years Dylan was off the road, 1967-1973, the Grateful Dead played 792
concerts, and Garcia, with different configurations, played an additional
241 shows. With the exception of Pigpen, the boys in the band continued to indulge in LSD, although the Acid Test days were winding down.
The utter anarchy of the scene, and an impending state law that made
the possession and manufacture of LSD illegal, laid the Acid Tests to
rest. However, San Francisco buzzed with hippie optimism. There were
dance parties in clubs and auditoriums featuring cutting edge music
from Jefferson Airplane, the Grateful Dead, and Quicksilver Messenger
Service. Psychedelic substances fueled an upbeat, free-spirited vibe.

After the Acid Tests, the band moved into a complex of buildings
known as Rancho Olompali, located in Norther Marin County. There
was a swimming pool, and lots of Owsley acid floating about. The band
jammed for gatherings of friends and fans regularly, and many unin-
hibited souls pranced around Olompali naked. It was a final vacation
of pure hedonism until the band returned to San Francisco to get on
with their calling. Towards the end of 1966, the Dead moved into 710
Ashbury Street where their managers, Rock Scully and Danny Rifkin,
resided. By this time, Jerry and Sara had amiably ended their marriage.

A diverse amalgamation of musicians influenced the Grateful Dead
sound. Garcia loved the old-school blues guys, Freddy King and B.B.

King, and there was a new blues band making a huge impression. The Paul Butterfield Blues Band, featuring Mike Bloomfield and Elvin Bishop on guitar, was the envy of local musicians. Bloomfield's talents awed Garcia. Of all the influences, the Dead seemed to agree that John Coltrane's improvisation showed them the light. It wasn't the type of thing they sought to emulate, but Coltrane's smooth, post-bebop style showed them it was possible to get way out there and still make the music balance out like a mathematical equation. Garcia said, "I've been influenced a lot by Coltrane...I've been impressed with that thing of flow, and of making statements that to my ears sound like paragraphs... Perceptually an idea that's been very important to me in playing has been the whole 'odyssey' idea—journeys, voyages and adventures along the way."

The Grateful Dead was attracting interest from record companies. Warner Brothers Records, looking to cash in on the burgeoning San Francisco music scene, signed the Dead to make their debut record. Prior to those sessions, Garcia supported Jefferson Airplane by playing acoustic guitar on four tracks on their second album, *Surrealistic Pillow*. Released in February 1967, the album peaked at number three on the Billboard charts. A revered musician in the Bay Area, Garcia had yet to make a splash elsewhere.

The debut album, simply titled *Grateful Dead*, had two original compositions, and the rest of the record was filled with an assortment of traditional songs. Even though the band never worked "The Golden Road (To Unlimited Devotion)" into their live repertoire, the opening track is an exuberant shuffle through Haight Ashbury before the "Summer of Love." It's a quick number with adequate songwriting, yet Garcia's perky vocal delivery and crisp guitar shredding have made this a favorite amongst Deadheads. The other original, "Cream Puff War," is one the band wished they never wrote, although there's some fuel-injected outro leads courtesy of Garcia.

The legacy of this album is the core group of songs that remained in the group's rotation for the duration of their playing days: "Cold

Rain & Snow," "Beat It Down the Line," "Morning Dew," and "New New Minglewood Blues." "Morning Dew" became the Holy Grail for fans seeing the band through the years, although the album version is neutered compared to what the song was live. Penned by Canadian folksinger Bonnie Dobson, "Morning Dew" is a melancholy vision of the world after a nuclear war. Lyrically it doesn't compare to "A Hard Rain's A-Gonna Fall," but thanks to Garcia's poignant vocal and climactic guitar solos, a live "Morning Dew" can come off like a transcendent religious experience. *Grateful Dead* concludes with "Viola Lee Blues," a traditional number that rages for more than ten minutes— rolling crescendo after rolling crescendo—the undeniable gem of their debut effort. The album sold well locally, but it received little national recognition or radio time.

Disenchanted young people poured into San Francisco during the summer of 1967, and most of them converged on the Haight Ashbury district. Timothy Leary's motto was, "Turn on, tune in, drop out," and the message resonated. They were drawn by cheap rents, the utopian ideal of communal sharing, a vibrant music and art scene, and an abundance of psychedelic treats; Haight Ashbury became the hippie promised land. Long-haired freaks wore tie-dyes, bell bottoms, ripped jeans, colorful dresses, peace signs, and flowers. Face painting was normal. It was a haven for all sorts of artists; poets, dancers, poster designers, lithographers, film makers. In Golden Gate Park there was free food, drugs, love, and a free clinic. This was an anti-Vietnam War and anti-establishment crowd, but peace and love, and being in the moment, ruled the day. Boundless enthusiasm and excitement filled the air. It was all a crazy dream, and somehow it worked for a summer.

The Grateful Dead found themselves in the thick of it all at 710 Ashbury Street. The national media was intrigued with this story; news cameras and reporters were everywhere. As much as the band enjoyed being part of it all, they downplayed the attention they received, and they didn't want to be viewed as gurus. Garcia said, "We don't want to change anybody. We want people to have the chance to feel a little better.

That's the absolute most we want to do with our music. The music we make is an act of love, an act of joy…We're not telling people to go get stoned, or drop out. We're just playing and they can take that any way they want."

Whether it was a live performance on TV or an anticipated performance at the Newport Folk Festival, Dylan thrived, or at least created controversy, in important situations early in his career. He embodied theatre. The Grateful Dead had their first crack in a big spot at the Monterey Pop Festival on June 18, 1967. Band management foolishly decided not to let film makers use footage of their set for what would become the iconic documentary of Monterey. They also had the misfortune of being sandwiched between The Who and Jimi Hendrix on the final day of the festival. Their performance was good, but between The Who destroying their equipment and Hendrix setting his guitar on fire, the Dead set wasn't historic, although they performed an extreme version of "Viola Lee Blues" that received a rapturous ovation.

Robert Hunter returned from his adventures in New Mexico and Colorado shortly after Monterey. While he was in New Mexico, he mailed the lyrics of three songs to Garcia; one of them was "Alligator," which the band had set music to by the time Hunter returned. Inspired by Dylan's latest works, Hunter let his lyrical inspiration flow. "I first started waking up to the possibilities of rock lyrics being serious with *Blonde on Blonde*," said Hunter. "It opened up everything; it said it was okay to be as serious as you wanted in rock." The Grateful Dead had themselves a lyricist.

The world's premier lyricist was recording demos in the basement of a pink house in West Saugerties, New York, during the Summer of Love, a year after the Grateful Dead were in their pink stucco house in Los Angeles, jamming on acid and eating meat. The Hawks, who were soon to be forever known as The Band, rented this West Saugerties house primarily to use it as a recording studio. Four or five times a week, Dylan made the twenty-minute drive from the bucolic artist's colony of Woodstock to record with his former mates. The informal sessions produced 138 songs, and a significant batch of Dylan originals were recorded to fulfill contractual songwriting commitments. Out of the coziness of the Big Pink basement came quirky jingles like, "Yeah Heavy and a Bottle of Bread!" and "Clothes Line Saga." And then there was the heavy ammunition: "Quinn the Eskimo," "Too Much of Nothing," and "You Ain't Going Nowhere," which soon became hits for other artists.

These West Saugerties sessions became legendary. A bootleg album called *The Great White Wonder* surfaced in 1969. It was a mixture of Dylan sessions that included several basement demos. On July 1, 1968, The Band released *Music from Big Pink,* a landmark album that influenced everybody from Eric Clapton to the Grateful Dead. The record featured three Dylan tunes from the sessions, "Tears of Rage," "This Wheel's on Fire," and "I Shall Be Released." In 1975, Columbia Records finally released *The Basement Tapes*, a double album compilation of the tracks that Dylan and The Band had recorded years earlier. This music inspired rock historian Greil Marcus to write *Old Weird America, The World of Bob Dylan's Basement Tapes*. Even though Dylan was just laying low and recording demos with peers, this piece of his life became folklore.

Before 1967 was over, Dylan released *John Wesley Harding*. It had been a shade under two years since *Blonde on Blonde* came out. Fans were salivating to hear where Dylan would take them next. Dylan sounded like a man who had nothing to prove as his new album cut right to the bone and was loaded with biblical references. There was little finger-pointing or protest, but the concise songs were intense. "All Along the Watchtower" sounded like a simple arrangement on the surface, but Jimi Hendrix found the beast within. "The Ballad of Frankie Lee and Judas Priest," the longest track on the album, was a dialogue between "the best of friends." It's the evil and the good living side by side, a fable of temptation and illusion. *John Wesley Harding* went against the current music trend. Dylan had changed the course of songwriting and album making. Now he was stripping it naked. Dylan's lyrics and diction were sincere without putting on any airs. He had taken his visionary music beyond anyone's expectation, and now he was a calm observer preaching wisdom as he continued to question authority. The album takes a sharp turn on the last two country-tinged tracks, "Down Along the Cove" and "I'll Be Your Baby Tonight," pointing to Dylan's next destination, *Nashville Skyline*.

Anthem of the Sun, the Grateful Dead's second album, fit in with the pioneering attitude of the day; the recording studio as an essential part of the album making process. Inspired by the Beach Boys' *Pet Sounds* and the Beatles' *Sgt. Pepper's Lonely Hearts Club Band*, many groups eagerly experimented with studio technology. Lesh, Garcia, and the band's new soundman, Dan Healy, spliced an ambitious mix of layered studio jamming with live performances. *Anthem of the Sun* is a wildly adventurous affair with no breaks between songs; three on the first side, and a pair of tracks on side two.

The Grateful Dead added two new members for the making of this album. Drummer Mickey Hart had joined the band, giving the Dead a distinctive and pulsating beat for dancers. Tom Constanten was recruited by Phil Lesh to play piano and provide electronic tape effects. Brazen psychedelic artwork on the album cover completed the package. The only song that lasted in the band's live rotation through the years was "The Other One," part of a larger suite of songs that opened the album. Released on July 18, 1968, *Anthem of the Sun* was an adventurous artistic effort, but the mainstream music media ignored it, and the album did little to build the band's fan base.

Anthem of the Sun accurately portrays the innovative Grateful Dead signature style of segueing songs. During their live shows, the jams were bigger than the songs, as if the songs were logs being tossed into a bonfire. Certain combinations worked better than others, but any song in their repertoire could suddenly arise out of a jam. The ability to pull this off required a sophisticated level of listening, cooperation, and trust between band members. The vehicle that launched many of these jams was the Hunter/ Garcia collaboration, "Dark Star," which was debuted live in December '67.

While the Dead were rehearsing some of their new *Anthem of the Sun* numbers at a friend's ranch in Rio Nido, Robert Hunter was listening in a cabin nearby when the lyrics of "Dark Star" came to him. "I heard the music and just started writing 'Dark Star' lying on my bed," said Hunter. "I wrote the first half of it and I went in and I think I handed what I'd written to Jerry. He said, 'Oh, this will fit just fine,' and he started singing it. That's true collaboration."

Aoxomoxoa, the band's palindrome titled third album, was released in June of 1969. The super-psychedelic cover is a wondrous vision featuring an orange sun shining down on a smiling skull and crossbones. The branding of the mysterious Grateful Dead image was taking hold. And the songs within were as wonderfully arcane as the cover. The opening track, "St. Stephen," was written by Garcia, Lesh, and Hunter, and the other eight tunes are Garcia/Hunter compositions. "St. Stephen" captures the distinctive raw energy of the band's early days in sound, style, and lyric. It's a surreal blast with shifting cadences and tempos, and it became an instant Deadhead favorite thanks to memorable lines like *One man gathers what another man spills*. "St. Stephen" would have fit in well with the non-stop jamming of *Anthem of the Sun*, although it's at home as part of the cryptic tapestry of *Aoxomoxoa*.

Drawing upon an old folk tale, Hunter and Garcia composed "Dupree's Diamond Blues," the second track of the album. Garcia's growth as a singer is palpable as he spins this cautionary tale of bringing your gun to town. The carnival-like organ playing behind the acoustic guitars of Garcia and Weir takes this out of the traditional folk realm. For good or ill, there's a dose of Grateful Dead weirdness originality in everything on *Aoxomoxoa*.

"Mountains of the Moon" and "Rosemary" are lovely acoustic jingles with odd poetic lyrics. During "Rosemary," it sounds like Garcia's singing from a submerged submarine. On this album, he emerges as a singer with a great deal of emotional depth, and it's a friendly voice directly from the soul. "China Cat Sunflower" kicks off side two.

Already a regular in the live rotation, "China Cat" would keep getting hotter year after year, and emerge as one of the most anticipated songs at shows. The album version doesn't capture that magic, and "What's Become of the Baby?" is a visionary flop, like the Beatles' "Revolution #9." More unique chord sequencing and odd shifts in tempo occur at the end of side one with "Doin' That Rag," a jug band-like tune with a trippy twist. "Comic Charlie" closes *Aoxomoxoa* by goofing on a wannabe hippie—*Go on home your mama's calling you.* Or as Dylan might ask, *Something is happening and you don't know what it is/ Do you, Mr. Jones?*

There were no Pigpen numbers on this album. Pigpen was still laying down lengthy raps during barnburners such as "Turn on Your Love Light," "Good Morning Little Schoolgirl," and "King Bee," but this was Garcia's band. Jerry didn't care about the accolades; his passions burned with the music he was generating with Hunter. These old army buddies who used to share government pineapple from a tin can were on the verge of creating an on the road scene that Kerouac couldn't have dreamed of. "Cosmic Charlie" needed some traveling partners, so Hunter created the likes of "Ramble on Rose," "Tennessee Jed," "Mr. Charlie," and "Jack Straw."

In the middle of August 1969, Woodstock, the mother of all music festivals, went down on Yasgur's Farm in Bethel, New York. Half-a-million beautiful hippies descended on the three-day festival of peace and music. The Grateful Dead had a prime billing on the second night between Mountain and Creedence Clearwater Revival. Their appearance was a disaster. There were announcements about the bad brown acid. Heavy winds, rain, and the muddy grounds made the stage unsafe—the band feared it might collapse. And there were electrical ground issues. "Every time I touched my instrument, I got a shock," said Weir. "The stage was wet and the electricity was coming through me. I was conducting! Touching my guitar was nearly fatal. There was a great blue spark about the size of a baseball. And I got lifted off my feet and sent back about eight or ten feet to my amplifier."

There were many excuses for the band's subpar performance, and once again, band management decided to keep the Dead's performance out of the documentary. I'm sure the filmmakers could have salvaged something from their set and the Grateful Dead would have been part of the most iconic rock and roll documentary, *Woodstock*. However, there were no short cuts for the Grateful Dead, who seemed destined to inch their way to fame a half-step at a time.

Dylan avoided the Woodstock Festival as if it were a ship of contagious fools. Bethel, home of the Woodstock Festival, was an hour and a half southwest of the real Woodstock, where the festival was originally scheduled to take place. If any hippies decided to take a pilgrimage to visit Woodstock in search of Bob Dylan, he had split town. Dylan was over in England, playing his second concert since grounding his road show after the mysterious motorcycle mishap. Two weekends after the freak show in Bethel, Dylan played the Isle of Wight Festival. Backed by The Band, Dylan appeared on stage in a cream-colored suit with short hair and neat beard. He mixed songs from his latest albums, *Nashville Skyline* and *John Wesley Harding*, with some old favorites. The performance was clean, but it lacked the spark and thunder of his last electric tour. The Beatles and 150,000 English music fans were at the festival to witness a historic Dylan moment. This performance couldn't be classified as a failure, but it was unremarkable.

Dylan once again surprised critics and fans with *Nashville Skyline*, released on April 9, 1969. Dylan was an enigma more than ever after *John Wesley Harding*, and expectations were high that he would create something topical. With anti-war protests raging, and the assassinations of Martin Luther King Jr. and Bobby Kennedy, fans hoped Dylan would write a song that expressed their feelings. After all, Dylan had championed outlaws and underdogs on *John Wesley Harding*. Dylan completely detached himself from the turbulent times and brought his listeners into the cozy confines of marital bliss in Woodstock. His state of the union report was delivered during the bridge of "I Threw It All Away." *Love is all there is/ It makes the world go round/ Love and only love, it can't be denied.*

Nashville Skyline is a joyful skip across a dewy meadow. At just under thirty minutes in length, it's Dylan's shortest album, and it left some thinking that the tank of inspiration had run dry. You can hear the Hank Williams influence and some Elvis in there as Dylan croons country all the way through. Dylan quit smoking cigarettes, and his voice changed noticeably. There was a polished emotional tone to his crooning. "Lay Lady Lay" reached number five on the charts, and the album peaked at the third spot on US Billboard charts. *Nashville Skyline* was a commercial success, but it was a bitter pill for those who championed civil rights and social justice to swallow, because country music was associated with conservatism and racism. Dylan didn't mean no harm, he was just following his heart.

On his next record, *Self Portrait*, which came out in the summer of 1970, one has to question Dylan's motives. In his famous review of the record for *Rolling Stone*, Greil Marcus asked, "What is this shit?" In *Chronicles*, Dylan's answer was, "I released one album (a double one) where I just threw everything I could think of at the wall and whatever stuck, released it, and then went back and scooped everything that didn't stick and released that, too." The very fame that Dylan had chased and conquered was now a cancer he was trying to eradicate. But even in his self-sabotage phase, Dylan continued to make himself the most compelling musician in the universe.

Repelled by popular trends in music, the Grateful Dead launched their own realm of art with different rules and regulations. But thanks to the influence of *John Wesley Harding* and The Band's, *Music from Big Pink*, the Dead shifted their approach to songwriting and album making. Eric Clapton, Al Kooper, and several other respected musicians raved about *Music from Big Pink*. After the studio excesses spurred by *Pet Sounds* and *Sgt. Pepper's Lonely Hearts Club Band*, The Band's first album was a return to simplicity with a unique fusion of folk rock, country, R & B, soul, and classical. The whole was bigger than the parts, and the collective sounds and harmonies of the musicians ruled the aural landscape.

Hunter was intrigued with the mythical stories and characters brought to life by the lyrics of Robbie Robertson and his mates. Hunter said, "I was very much impressed with the area Robertson was working in. I took it and moved it west, which is the area I'm familiar with, and thought, 'Okay, how about modern ethic?' Regional, but not South, because everyone was going back to the South for inspiration at the time."

Garcia, Hunter, and their girlfriends moved into a house in Madrone Canyon in early 1969. Hunter stayed up at nights, chain-smoking and typing lyrics. These songwriting sessions produced immediate results: "High Time," Casey Jones," and "Dire Wolf," tunes that landed on their next studio album, *Workingman's Dead*. These numbers warned of the perils of gambling, whiskey, operating trains on cocaine—*Nothing's for certain/ It can always go wrong*. This was the beginning of a Grateful Dead milieu—underdogs and outlaws trying to survive through any means or vices available to them. Garcia's poignant voice conveyed Hunter's imagery as if they were one mind, and the band's harmonies improved. These were songs built to stand on their own without elongated jams.

"New Speedway Boogie," the darkest track of *Workingman's Dead*, was Hunter and Garcia's response to the tragedy that was the mega-concert with the Rolling Stones, Jefferson Airplane, and others at Altamont Speedway on December 6, 1969. There's still disagreement over the security details for the show, but Hell's Angels bikers were hired to run security in exchange for all the beer they could guzzle. Intoxicated bikers, high on acid, speed, and downers, doled out violent justice. Marty Balin, lead singer for Jefferson Airplane, was knocked unconscious when he tried to restrain an Angel from beating on somebody. When they learned of the chaos, the Grateful Dead bailed on playing their set before the Rolling Stones.

During the Stones' performance, the Angels continued to beat people with pool cues, and they stabbed a man to death. This was the end of festival innocence. A lot of people with good intentions tried to please the masses with a spectacular entertainment event, and things got ugly. Garcia admitted that "New Speedway Boogie" was a bit of an overreaction to the events. The band stopped performing the song in 1970, but brought it back twenty years later. A great song remains a great song, even if the original message no longer resonates.

"Uncle John's Band," another Garcia/Hunter masterpiece, was magnificent as an acoustic arrangement on *Workingman's Dead*, and a majestic electric staple in the band's live rotation through the years. It was a fully developed song with an alluring melody and rich harmonies, and a flexible structure ideal for improvisation. Hunter's lyrics contained slogans and mantras that would fill bumper stickers and t-shirts for decades to come: *Wo, oh, what I want to know, is are you kind? ...?.Ain't no time to hate/ Barely time to wait... Anybody's choice, I can hear your voice. Wo, oh, what I want to know, how does the song go?* The mystical muse of music—Garcia and Hunter chased after it, and "Uncle John's Band" celebrates that inspiration.

"Cumberland Blues," "Easy Wind," and "Black Peter" rounded out an album that would introduce the Grateful Dead to radio audiences across America. Recorded at Pacific High Studio in February 1970, the record features Garcia on pedal steel guitar for the first time. Crosby, Stills, Nash & Young invited Garcia to play his new pedal steel on "Teach Your Children," for their record *Déjà vu*. The Dead finished off their recording sessions in three weeks, and *Workingman's Dead* was released on June 14. It rose to number twenty-seven on the charts. "Uncle John's Band" and "Casey Jones," along with several numbers from their next album, *American Beauty*, became FM radio classics that would define who the Grateful Dead were to generations of classic rock fans. There's no flamboyant soloing from Garcia on these tunes, and that probably explains why Garcia is an underrated guitarist in the classic rock demographic.

Less than six months after the release of *Workingman's Dead*, *American Beauty* was available to the record-buying public on November 1, 1970. They used the same bare-bones approach to make this record, and *American Beauty* turned out to be a potent sequel with more diversity than its predecessor. On a professional and personal level, the band was experiencing tough times during the making of this album. Earlier in the year, Mickey Hart's father, Lenny, who was the band's money manager, disappeared with approximately $150,000 of the band's profits. This obviously became an uncomfortable situation for Mickey, who left the band.

On January 31, 1970, the Grateful Dead were busted for possession of marijuana after playing shows at the Warehouse in New Orleans. The absurdity of the bust was infamously captured on "Truckin'." *Busted down on Bourbon Street/ Set up like a bowling pin/ Knocked down it gets to wearing thin/ They just won't let you be.* This road tale gave birth to the band's most famous tagline: *What a long, strange trip it's been*, and the *living on reds, Vitamin C and cocaine* line anchored the group's image as a hedonistic party band in the minds of radio listeners. Taking the lead vocals on two numbers, "Truckin'" and "Sugar Magnolia," Weir established a rock star persona. He was more than the aloof, spacey kid along for the ride. Except for "Easy Wind," Garcia was the dominant singer on *Workingman's Dead*. The new LP had another Pigpen number, "Operator," and the record kicks off with a song that became Phil Lesh's eternal anthem.

Lesh wanted a song he could sing for his dying father, and the words materialized. "If ever a lyric 'wrote itself,' this did—as fast as the pen would pull," said Hunter. "Box of Rain" is a touching journey through life, and when the song was being recorded, Garcia found out that his mother, Ruth, was critically injured in an automobile accident. Jerry's mom passed away three weeks later. Phil digs deep for his best vocal on "Box of Rain," and when Jerry and Bob join in, the harmonies become a flood of emotion.

One afternoon during the Grateful Dead's first trip to England, to play at the Hollywood Festival in Newcastle, Robert Hunter had the greatest two-hour writing session that any lyricist has ever had. He penned two anthems for *American Beauty*, and "To Lay Me Down," which would be on Garcia's first solo album. "I wrote 'Ripple,' 'Brokedown Palace,' and 'To Lay Me Down' all in about a two-hour period the first day I ever went to England," Hunter said. "I sat there with a case of retsina and I opened up a bottle of that stuff, and the sun was shining. I was in England, which I'd always wanted to visit, and for some reason this creative energy started racing through me and I could do no wrong—write, write, write, write!"

"Ripple" is the sacred song of *American Beauty*. Garcia's singing and Hunter's lyrics form a heavenly union that start with the opening line. *If my words did glow with the gold of sunshine*. And in the second verse Garcia sings, "Let it be known there is a fountain. That was not made by the hands of men." Garcia sings it as if this song is the fountain that was not made by man. Divine spirit ripples through this tune, which culminates in a seductive singalong: *If I knew the way, I would take you home. La da da da, La da dad da da...*

Another timeless gem that must be praised in any discussion of *American Beauty* is "Friend of the Devil." A quick-strumming acoustic country/bluegrass beat sets the stage for an adventurous saga of heartache, an outlaw on the run borrowing from his only remaining friend, the devil. Garcia croons, "Got two reasons why I cry away each lonely night." *Why I cry away*—irresistible rhythm and rhyme. The narrator can't settle down with his heart's delight, sweet Ann Marie, because the sheriff is on his trail. *There must be some way out of here, said the joker to the thief.* "Friend of the Devil" is the type of song Dylan would have loved to write, but these days, the Gods of inspiration were shining on Garcia and Hunter.

SIX

EUROPE '72 AND THE EPIC TOURS OF '74

In the early '70s, the parade of iconic albums continued unabated. *Abraxas*, Santana; *Bitches Brew*, Miles Davis; *Live at the Fillmore East*, Allman Brothers; *Tapestry*, Carole King; *Blue*, Joni Mitchell; *Who's Next*, The Who; *What's Going On*, Marvin Gaye; *Sticky Fingers*, Rolling Stones; *Moondance*, Van Morrison. The individual who kicked off the golden age of album making, Bob Dylan, was no longer a force, or so it seemed. He wasn't writing or recording anything monumental, and he wasn't touring. Separating himself from his past accomplishments seemed to be his professional priority, but Dylan Nation held out hope that their hero still had something to say. On Sunday August 1, 1971, in Madison Square Garden, Dylan put on two brilliant performances, and proved that the old inspiration still burned within.

Spurred on by Indian musician and renowned sitar player Ravi Shanker, George Harrison arranged a benefit concert for the newly formed nation of Bangladesh, which was suffering a humanitarian crisis brought on by natural disasters and a brutal civil war. Enjoying life as an ex-Beatle with a chart-topping album and the number one hit "My Sweet Lord," Harrison arranged for a star-studded benefit show at Madison Square Garden. He recruited Ringo Starr, Eric Clapton, Billy Preston, Leon Russel, Badfinger, and possibly Dylan. Bob showed up for the practice sessions, but he was still indecisive about stepping out and performing on the Madison Square Garden stage. The benefit concert quickly sold out and a second show was added to the bill. To raise further proceeds for the people in need, this show would be made into a movie and a double album titled *Concert for Bangladesh*.

The afternoon show commenced with Ravi Shanker's Indian music, followed by performances from the all-star troupe. After Harrison played "Here Comes the Sun" live for the first time, he looked to the side of the stage, where he saw Dylan pacing around nervously. The decisive moment had arrived, and Harrison was still not sure what Dylan was going to do. Wearing a denim jacket, shades, a harmonica rack, and carrying an acoustic guitar, Dylan swiftly moved towards the microphone at center stage as a rapturous roar filled Madison Square Garden. Dylan opened with "A Hard Rain's A-Gonna-Fall," and followed that with "Blowin' in the Wind," "It Takes a lot to Laugh, It Takes a Train to Cry," "Love Minus Zero," and "Just Like a Woman." Dylan, Harrison, and Madison Square Garden were ecstatic. Dylan's evening set, which was used on the album, was even better.

"Like to bring on a friend of us all, Mr. Bob Dylan." With that intro from George, Dylan kicked off the evening show with "A Hard Rain's A-Gonna-Fall." Dylan's voice is smooth, with the same tonality displayed on *Nashville Skyline*. There's some tentativeness early, but by the second verse Dylan's cadence is perfect, and the tension builds precisely throughout. Backed by George Harrison, Ringo Starr, and Leon Russel, there's great excitement because Dylan's playing "Hard Rain" with two ex-Beatles. As Dylan brings "Hard Rain" to a perfectly pitched climax, the audience explodes. Already, this is a historic Madison Square Garden moment.

Dylan switches up the order of the set by playing "It Takes a lot to Laugh, It Takes a Train to Cry" before "Blowin' in the Wind." The fact that he's played two of his *Freewheelin'* anthems sends waves of optimism through Madison Square Garden. Dylan's growth as a performer is obvious—his voice is seductively smooth, yet still emotional. It sounds as if he's been playing these tunes on a regular basis. For the late show, Dylan replaces "Love Minus Zero" with a stunning "Mr. Tambourine Man." The enthused crowd claps along hastily, and Dylan coolly delivers a harp solo for the third consecutive tune.

Making his debut in the "World's most famous arena," in the city that gave birth to his legend, with two Beatles by his side and 20,000 fans feeling the love, Dylan closes the set with "Just Like a Woman." This is one of those extraordinary performances that stops time in its tracks. Dylan teases the sublime melody as he blows into his harmonica and tunes his guitar. He creates a vacuum of anticipation for those in the Garden, and those listening decades into the future. Dylan's sincere voice unveils one of the great opening lines of modern song, "Nobody feels any pain." Those four words never sounded better. As the song shifts into the chorus, Harrison and Russel sing the title with Dylan, "Just like a woman." The wonderful harmonies are filled with tenderness that makes the song sound fresh. Dylan adlibs, "and she bakes, just like a woman." As was the case with every song in this set, the momentum rises as the music rolls forth.

Dylan finished to one of the great crowd eruptions in Madison Square Garden history. It would have been louder if it were not for the silence of those choked up by tears of joy. It was the type of triumph the Beatles never got to experience due to screaming fans rendering their performances meaningless. The lights came on and it appeared every person in the arena was clapping and howling as one. Dylan won an unharmonious decision and pumped his arms above his head in victory. In addition to adding a legendary performance to his resume, Dylan, Harrison, and friends raised $12 million for Bangladesh. *The Concert for Bangladesh* was the model for future benefits like Live Aid and Farm Aid. In the aftermath of his majestic showing, Dylan returned to hibernation.

Jerry Garcia celebrated his twenty-ninth birthday as Dylan thrilled Madison Square Garden with George Harrison. Garcia wasn't there, but he was an hour away the night before, gigging with the Grateful Dead at the Yale Bowl in New Haven, Connecticut. Four nights later, they were playing in Terminal Island Correctional Facility in San Pedro, California. Their old comrade and soundman, who provided them with acid, milk, and meat, Owsley Stanley, was serving time there for possession of 350,000 doses of LSD from a 1967 bust. The Grateful Dead barnstormed across America in 1971 after the success of *Workingman's*

Dead and *American Beauty*. Despite their surging national fame, they were a band in debt, building a legacy on the road.

Live Dead, released in 1969, the year it was performed, captures the band's energetic and groundbreaking psychedelic explorations. The double album consisted of seven songs. Dark Star > St. Stephen > The Eleven filled up the first two sides, an accurate portrayal of an hour-long cosmic thunderstorm erasing the lines between jazz, rock and roll, and time. If one composition best captures the highs and pitfalls of this era, it's "The Eleven." The lyrics and the structure of the song were bizarre, but the jam was something to behold. The title is a reference to the 11/8 time signature of the song. Once Garcia and company dip into the beast, massive energy is unleashed. If you take the jam away, what's left is an extremely fragile song.

The explosive energy of the music and the friendly/euphoric surroundings created fans for life, and many were taping the shows. Members of the Dead empathized with the tapers because a few years earlier, they were in their shoes. Weir taped Jorma Kaukonen shows before he joined forces with Jerry, and Garcia took a cross-country trip with Sandy Rothman and David Nelson to record Bill Monroe and his talented band at bluegrass festivals. The Grateful Dead provided their admirers with tape-worthy performances.

From 1968 to 1969, the band doubled the size of their repertoire thanks in large part to the influx of Hunter tunes. At the end of the year they began playing acoustic sets, adding songs like "Monkey and the Engineer," "Little Sadie," "Dark Hollow," and "Deep Elem Blues," to go with some of the new numbers from *Workingman's Dead*.

Bill Graham's Fillmore East became a breeding ground for New York City Deadheads. The band played there seventeen times in 1970, including a pair of fabled three-set shows on February 13 and 14. The performances featured two electric sets with an acoustic set in between. Long, improvisational jams raged during the final sets on both nights. These shows were always amongst the most popular bootleg tapes. In 1973, the band officially released *The History of the Grateful Dead*

(Bear's Choice). The album opens with an acoustic side. Side two features two Pigpen numbers, Howlin' Wolf's "Smokestack Lightning" and Otis Redding's "Hard to Handle." The band's archivist, Dick Latvala, immortalized the remainder of these shows on *Dick's Pick's Volume 4* in 1996. This three-CD release should be an essential part of any Grateful Dead collection.

As if these long shows were not enough of a workout for Garcia, he was playing pedal steel with the New Riders of the Purple Sage as the opening act. Formed in 1969, the original NRPS lineup consisted of Garcia, Lesh, Hart, David Nelson, and John Dawson. Lesh and Hart were eventually replaced, but Garcia continued to jam with the New Riders through the end of 1971.

The body of work Garcia amassed and took part in in the early '70s is no less astonishing than what Dylan did in the early '60s, even though it's largely unheralded. In October of 1970, Garcia began gigging with keyboardist Merl Saunders, bassist John Kahn, and drummer Bill Vitt at small local clubs like The Matrix and Keystone Korner. The configurations of the group shifted. Some nights Tom Fogerty joined them on guitar, and after playing 47 shows by the end of the following year, the jams flowed like lava. The group, billed as Jerry Garcia and Merl Saunders, played a mix of soul, R & B, jazz, and Dylan tunes. John Kahn and Garcia developed a tight personal and professional partnership for the rest of Garcia's life. When the Grateful Dead rested, Garcia and Kahn continued their musical crusade and dazzled Deadheads in intimate venues along the West Coast and East Coast.

On February 6, 1972, Garcia and Saunders played at Pacific High Studio, where the Grateful Dead recorded *Aoxomoxoa* and *Workingman's Dead*. The show was broadcast on KSAN, San Francisco. With Billy Kreutzmann on drums, the band locks into a tight groove on a pair of Motown instrumentals, "Expressway (To Your Heart)," and "I Was Made to Love Her." Garcia's ideas stream freely—Coltrane-like—brilliant, beautiful, and balanced. Garcia's singing and guitar virtuosity stand out on Ray Charles's, "Lonely Avenue," one of the finest blues performances of Jerry's career. The show, performed in front of a live audience of around fifty fans, kicks off with "It Takes a lot to Laugh, It Takes a Train to Cry." The band lays down a seductive, hypnotic groove. Garcia eventually gets around to singing a couple of verses, but this celebrates, and pays homage to, the easy blues beat that Dylan created for the *Highway 61 Revisited* version of the song.

Later in the show, Garcia breaks out "When I Paint my Masterpiece," which had just come out on *Dylan's Greatest Hits Volume 2* and The Band's *Cahoots*. The awe Garcia has for this song comes through as he croons the opening line, "Oh, the streets of Rome are filled with rubble, ancient footprints are everywhere." In Garcia's world, Dylan's visions are glorified: *Inside the Coliseum, dodging lions and wasting time...I landed in Brussels, on a plane ride so bumpy that I almost cried...Train wheels running through the back of my memory...Young men in uniform and young girls pulling mussels...Newspaper man eating candy, had to be held back by big police.* Garcia skips the "land of Coca-Cola" bridge, but three searing guitar solos help the lyrics resonate, giving the listener a chance to soak in the sights and sounds of Dylan's wondrous journey. The Pacific High show is probably the most revered Garcia show that hasn't been officially released as of the publication of this book.

Grateful Dead (also known as *Skulls and Roses*) ended up being the title of the band's second live album, which was available in record stores in late 1971. The group wanted to call the album *Skull Fuck*. Predictably, record executives nixed that notion. It's an album that mixes new originals; "Bertha," "Playin' in the Band," and "Wharf Rat," with an assortment of covers. Recorded at shows earlier in the year, the album's crowning glory is a Not Fade Away > Goin' Down the Road Feelin' Bad > Not Fade Away combo. Although it didn't get much radio play, the combination was crisp, by Grateful Dead standards, and easier for the average music fan to digest than a run of songs from *Anthem of the Sun*. *Skulls and Roses* also includes an acknowledgement of the growing legion of fans addicted to the music and the good times associated with a Grateful Dead concert. Imprinted on the inside of the double album there's a call for brotherhood. The message reads:

DEAD FREAKS UNITE
Where are You? Who are You?
How are you?
send us your name and address
and we'll keep you informed
Dead Heads
P.O. Box 1065
San Rafael, California
94901

A week after the release of *Skull and Roses*, the Grateful Dead put on a savage rock and roll exhibition on Halloween in Columbus, Ohio. With Pigpen ailing from years of hardcore boozing, the Grateful Dead added Keith Godchaux to their lineup. He was the inevitable replacement for Pigpen, although Pig continued to play when he could. Keith's wife, Donna, would join the band as a background vocalist soon after. Keith was a talented player, and his addition sparked the band's explosive playing in late '71. Part of the second set of the Halloween Columbus show was released decades later as *Volume 2* (a single CD) in the Dick's Picks Series. Thank you, Dick! Kicking off with a "Dark Star" that bounces around the galaxies but never loses focus, this disc is tour de force Dead. A romping "Sugar Magnolia" set the stage for "St. Stephen," a tune that was being played less frequently, and soon it would be dropped from the rotation. The band roars under the guidance of one drummer, Billy Kreutzmann.

"Can you answer? Yes I can. But what would be the answer to the answer man?" A fraction of silence gives way to Billy the drummer as Garcia and Weir channel a beat more primitive than anything Buddy Holly could have imagined. Everything clicks as Garcia and friends blast "Not Fade Away" beyond any previous threshold—improvisational, psychedelic rock without a misstep or dull second. The jam flows into "Goin Down the Road Feelin' Bad." Only sorcerers like the Grateful Dead could conceive of taking a Buddy Holly song and slicing it into a traditional folk tune. This combo exemplifies the Dead's unbridled brilliance for taking existing songs and molding them into a distinctive creation. Following a spunky "Goin' Down the Road Feelin' Bad," a wondrous segue jam emerges. The band is conflicted, yet united. Half of the band steps towards NFA, while the other half tinkers with GDRFB. Garcia's in full tease mood, alternating soft, controlled playing with rebellious rock outbursts, and somehow the rest of the band is riding the wave. The return explosion into NFA disrupts the physics of gravity in Columbus, Ohio. Garcia's voice bubbles with glee as he chants the reprise with Weir. As Weir shrieks falsetto screams, Garcia unleashes frenzied riffs. The climactic crescendo is worthy of The Who and an equipment-bashing tantrum. This is the definitive Grateful Dead rock and roll extravaganza.

In April 1972, the band set off for their first major tour of Europe, and it became one of the most fabled tours in rock history, although nobody had any inkling at the time. Legend of the tour began with the release of the triple album *Europe '72* later in the year. The Dead hoped that the tour would ignite passion for the band's music overseas, but the Deadhead phenomena never materialized in any significant way in Europe. However, these twenty-two European shows revealed the artistic maturity of the Dead as they expanded their repertoire and broke barriers within existing songs. The versions of "Dark Star" from this tour are stunning rhapsodies that could come off as sophisticated, articulate, radiant, and jubilant, and then the mood might shift as the playing creeped into a dark vortex of elaborate improvisation. You could ditto that description and apply it to live versions of "The Other One" from this tour. Tapes from these shows have stood the test of time and remain extremely popular. Almost forty years after the tour, a seventy-three CD box set of the twenty-two concerts were made available. In all, 7,200 box sets were produced, and they sold out in a four-day pre-order. Each set cost $450. That brought a cool $3.24 million dollars into the Grateful Dead coffers forty years later.

The original album featured a rich batch of new Hunter tunes that on its own would have made a fine studio album to stand alongside *Workingman's Dead* and *American Beauty* as part of a trilogy. "Ramble on Rose," "Tennessee Jed," and "Brown-Eyed Woman" were Garcia songs that became lifers in the band's rotation. Weir got plenty of mileage out of "Jack Straw" and "One More Saturday Night." "Jack Straw" was a crowd favorite, and it became an ideal opener that gave the band a chance to warm up by unleashing an explosive jam within a contained song structure.

Europe '72 is an ironic title for an album that portrays a distinctive American musical odyssey. Garcia sings a Hank Williams number, "You Win Again," and Pigpen belts out Elmore James's "It Hurts Me Too." There's a tight connection between these old-timey tunes and the Hunter/Garcia compositions, as if "Jack Straw," "Tennessee Jed," "Mr. Charlie," and "Ramble on Rose" were peers of Williams and James, or characters that Hank, or Elmore, might have invented. What makes this unique from what Dylan and The Band did in the pink house is the expansive sonic landscape. Everything's fused and sealed with the Grateful Dead's secret psychedelic sauce. In "Cumberland Blues" the band pecks away, straddling the borders of blues, bluegrass, and rock. Keith Godchaux's piano playing imbues "Ramble on Rose" with a ragtime feel. There's the slow, spiritual dirges, "He's Gone" and "Morning Dew," set against the energy of "One More Saturday Night" and "Sugar Magnolia." It's all there—blues, jazz, country, and folk.

Commenting on Hunter's lyrics, Garcia said, "I don't very often relate to the characters in the songs. I don't feel like 'Okay, now this is me singing this song'...Actually, I relate better to Dylan songs more often than not. Sometimes I feel like I'm right in those songs; that is to say, that it's me speaking...That rarely happens to me with Hunter songs, but something else happens to me with Hunter songs that I think is more special. And that's the thing of coming from a world—some kind of mythos or alternate universe that's got a lot of interesting stuff in it."

Europe '72 is visionary music steeped in American tradition—music that would catch the ear of Dylan, especially on the heels of *American Beauty*. Dylan saw his first Grateful Dead show April 27, 1971, at the Fillmore East, and was also spotted with David Bromberg at a Dead concert on July 18, 1972, at Roosevelt Stadium, a Minor League ballpark in Jersey City. Dylan made a guest appearance at The Band's 1971 New Year's Eve Concert, joining them on four songs at the Academy of Music in Manhattan. After the show, Levon Helm asked Dylan when they would go on the road together again. Dylan replied, "I'm thinking of touring with the Dead." Details on interactions between Garcia and Dylan around this time are unclear, but according to Garcia's future wife, Dylan visited Jerry and Mountain Girl at their home in Stinson Beach, California, in 1973.

The desire to write and perform wasn't burning within Dylan from 1970 to 1973. Fans were happy to have a new album of original compositions with the release of *New Morning*, a few months after *Self Portrait*. Along the lines of *Nashville Skyline*, there were three quality love songs, "If Not for You" "Time Passes Slowly," and "The Man in Me." "Day of the Locusts" captures the absurdity of the afternoon when Dylan, against his best instincts, went to receive an honorary doctorate at Princeton University. *New Morning* was an unusual hodgepodge of short songs. Reflecting on *New Morning*, Dylan said, "The album itself had no specific resonance to the shackles and bolts that were strapping the country down, nothing to threaten the status quo."

In addition to their vast musical tastes, Dylan and Garcia shared a passion for movies, as connoisseurs, and both would embrace huge cinematic projects down the line. Dylan accepted a supporting acting role to appear in *Pat Garrett & Billy the Kid*, a Western directed by Sam Peckinpah. Filming began in Durango, Mexico, in late 1972. The weather was awful, and much of the cast and crew became sick with the flu. Dylan played a character called Alias in a limited role, but his mere stage presence helped a subpar film. Dylan's hit song for the film, "Knockin' on Heaven's Door," has become an immortal rock anthem played by everybody from Guns & Roses to the Grateful Dead. In addition to the songs already mentioned, in this period of relative inactivity, Dylan wrote "I'd Have You Anytime," "Watching the River Flow," "When I Paint My Masterpiece," "Wallflower," and "George Jackson." Even though he was not actively pursuing his muse, Dylan still remained one of the top songwriters of the early '70s.

The Hunter and Garcia express couldn't be slowed down. Pigpen (Ron McKernan), died on March 8, 1973. It was tragic and shocking because he was only twenty-seven; yet the band wasn't adversely affected from a professional perspective. Keith had stepped in brilliantly on piano as Pigpen's illness inevitably faded him out of the picture. A month prior to Pigpen's passing, the Grateful Dead debuted seven new Hunter/Garcia numbers live at Roscoe Maples Pavilion, Stanford University. Four of those songs were included on their next album, *Wake of the Flood*. These new tunes were high-quality compositions unlike anything Garcia and Hunter had previously attempted. The Grateful Dead were moving away from Old Weird America and creating their own genre of dance/jam music.

The standout song of the batch debuted in Stanford on 2-9-73 was "Eyes of the World." Garcia described it as "kind of a Brazilian thing." The infectious samba-like flow of the song accentuates the uplifting lyrics—*Wake up to find out that you are the eyes of the world/ The heart has its beaches, its homeland and thoughts of its own...Sometimes we ride on your horses, sometimes we walk alone/ Sometimes the songs that we hear are just songs of our own.* This song provided the band four opportunities to solo, and the last solo was an extended jazzy jam with sophisticated nuances and tempo shifts. "Eyes of the World" drained thousands of gallons of hippie sweat every time it was performed.

Their new record didn't have the mojo of their previous two studio albums; *Wake of the Flood* did not capture the essence of the songs.

On two of the album's great numbers, "Mississippi Half Step Uptown Toodeloo," and "Eyes of the World," the truncated versions are fortified with violins and horns. In its own vacuum, the songs are entertaining, but they sound phony and flat in comparison to what they were live. And the band had no record executives to blame because they had just formed their own record label. The Dead were wet fish on dry land in the studio. As strong as *Workingman's Dead* and *American Beauty* were, they really didn't reflect the true sound of the band either.

Prior to *Wake of the Flood*, Weir found his songwriting partner, John Perry Barlow. With contributions from Eric Anderson, they composed "Weather Report Suite," an intricate arrangement combining a lovely acoustic prelude with "Let it Grow," which would go on to be an electrifying first set closer and showpiece for Garcia's virtuosity. The continued emergence of Weir as a songwriter, singer, and front man fortified the popularity of the band. The band was still breaking off mind-bending jams, mostly in the second set, but now they had a robust repertoire to show off, and their shorter songs were still seven to eleven minutes long. Describing a band beyond description, Bill Graham said, "They're not the best at what they do, they're the only ones who do what they do."

What they did next was tour with a colossal sound system that was as ambitious as it was cumbersome. The Grateful Dead proudly presented the Wall of Sound—distortion-free concert gear, which allowed the musicians to individually monitor their sound. This was Owsley Stanley's baby. After his release from jail in 1972, Owsley, with help from Dan Healy and Mark Raizene, put together the largest concert sound system of its time. Transporting, erecting, and dismantling the wall was a minor engineering miracle that required a dedicated army of employees. Throughout 1974, the Wall of Sound provided Deadheads with the ultimate listening experience—it was a smashing success artistically. However, moving this sound monstrosity from city to city made the venture unprofitable. Grateful Dead record sales were impressive, and the band was selling out larger and larger venues, but the band was in debt.

Towards the end of 1973, the fire within Dylan began to burn, and a massive tour was planned with The Band. In November, Dylan and The Band swiftly recorded *Planet Waves*. Released on January 17, 1974, the album ascended to number one on the charts. All was not well in paradise. "I hate myself for loving you," sings Dylan at the start of "The Dirge." The edgy attitude of Dylan's voice was back. The cover artwork by Dylan also provided a description of what was inside: "Cast-iron songs & torch ballads." At times, *Planet Waves* burns with overt sexual passion. "Tough Mama" is a prenominal performance. The plush, sweeping sound of Garth Hudson's organ cushions the truculent vocals of the singer. "You Angel You," "On a Night Like This," and "Never Say Goodbye" are some of Dylan's richest love songs. *Planet Waves*, Dylan's best record since *Blonde on Blonde*, included two takes of Dylan's sentimental hymn "Forever Young." Typical of a Dylan classic, there's cohesive flow to the album—the songs feed off each other and take the listener on an emotional journey. This album is underrated because it lives in the shadows of Dylan's next record, *Blood on the Tracks*. Garcia was fond of *Planet Waves*. The Jerry Garcia Band performed expanded versions of "Tough Mama," "Going, Going Gone," and "Forever Young."

The Wall of Sound was the grandest sound experiment in rock and roll, but Dylan and The Band's tour of '74 was the epic event—forty concerts over a six-week period in the largest theatres and indoor sports complexes. There was a great deal of hype and anticipation associated with this tour, which generated a gross of $5 million.

They kicked off the tour in Chicago Stadium on January 3, 1974. Swift, bone-crunching rock accompanied Dylan's strong and emphatic vocals. The music didn't have the innovative edginess of his last tour with The Band, but the performances washed over the audience like a tidal wave. If there was nervousness about performing before these large audiences, Dylan channeled it into the tempo of his playing. Even the acoustic sets had a rushed feel. And with the Watergate hearings dominating news coverage, the timeless line, "Even the president of the

United States sometimes must have to stand naked," was acknowledged with an enormous roar. Dylan's fine comeback tour was captured on the double album *Before the Flood*, released later in the year.

While Dylan was on the road to the next remarkable stage of his career as a performing artist, the Grateful Dead mojo was evaporating. Burnt out from the road, years of hedonism, and the struggle to financially keep themselves afloat, the Grateful Dead decided to take a long break, and possibly retire. The band and their traveling employees were also reeling from the cocaine craze. The old acid scene was inexpensive and communal. Cocaine was draining bank accounts, and the *yayo* was horded, as much as it was shared. The mood of the Grateful Dead seemed to mirror the psyche of a weary nation. American troops were fleeing Vietnam, and on August 9, Nixon resigned from the presidency in disgrace. When the Grateful Dead played a five-night stand at Bill Graham's Winterland in October, the tickets were stamped THE LAST ONE. Leon Gast, director of *When We Were Kings*, the documentary of the Ali/Foreman fight in Zaire, brought in a camera crew to film these potentially historic shows. Dylan's mad dash to fame eventually led to a prolonged period out of the public eye. Now Deadheads were left to wonder when, or if, they'd ever see the Grateful Dead again.

SEVEN

INSPIRATION AND SALVATION

Dylan habitually exceeded expectations as a phenom on the rise. Following *Blonde on Blonde*, Dylan's albums featured fabulous original compositions, and they all failed to come close to matching the majesty of his mid-'60s trilogy, or stirring up passions for social causes. Fans craved the old Dylan, but they began to believe that guy no longer existed. They were right. With the release of *Blood on the Tracks* on January 20, 1975, the music world was reintroduced to Dylan. He was back in the business of setting new standards for songwriting and artistic creativity. *Blood on the Tracks* caused mass euphoria among Dylanologists, satisfying both those who longed for his acoustic material and those who desired his visionary music.

As he was going through a separation with Sara, Dylan began recording *Blood on the Tracks* in September, at Colombia's New York studio. The songs contained deeply personal lyrics performed by a singer with a heavy heart. The album was cut and ready to be released, but Dylan slammed on the brakes and decided to re-record some of the tracks in Minnesota with a new group of musicians. Bob's brother, David, assisted in putting the band together and making studio arrangements. The new versions featured plush acoustical arrangements that helped give *Blood on the Tracks* its exquisite sound. Some of the lyrics were altered so it wouldn't appear that Dylan was singing about his marital difficulties. *Blood on the Tracks* went to number one on the album charts, critics and peers swamped Dylan with praise, and the album is generally regarded as a groundbreaking masterpiece.

One of Dylan's influences for *Blood on the Tracks* was Norman Raeben, a seventy-three-year-old painter. Bob had taken one of Raeben's classes in an art studio in Carnegie Hall, and it changed the way he thought about constructing his own songs. A painting can depict several times and places. On the album's opening number, "Tangled Up in Blue," Dylan succeeds in evoking the past, present, and future, simultaneously. It's a personal song, yet not autobiographical. Each verse is a new scene in a loosely connected tale of lovers on the road. Dylan's exotic language sticks like glue: *revolution in the air…She lit a burner on the stove and offered me a pipe…I'm still on the road/ Headin' for another joint…Written by an Italian poet from the thirteenth century… keep on keepin' on like a bird that flew…* It's like a movie, painting, and poem, all rolled into song.

The following tune tells a similar tale of missed romance and regret, except the mood has shifted. After a rollicking road adventure, "Simple Twist of Fate" evolves like a mysterious dream. The imagery is unforgettable: *She dropped a coin into the cup of a blind man at the gate…he felt a spark tingle to his bones…stopped into a strange hotel with a neon burnin' bright.* Dylan's evoking all the senses as his voice stretches out rhyming syllables. His harp solo is delicately placed like an artist dabbing paint onto a canvas. "You're a Big Girl Now" balances intimacy, compassion, and anger. Dylan sings of a conversation that's short, sweet, and it nearly swept him off his feet. And he sings of a pain that stops and starts like a corkscrew to the heart. The first three songs explode into the epic "Idiot Wind." The song titles themselves are immense and unforgettable.

This is a glimpse into Dylan's world. In response to the euphoric praise for *Blood on the Tracks*, Dylan couldn't understand how people could enjoy such pain. Just as Dylan had channeled the fears and hopes of a generation, he universalized the timeless and bittersweet human experience of falling in and out of love with a group of songs that was more direct and expressive than anything heard before. These songs were darker and deeper than "Don't Think Twice It's Alright" and "It

Ain't Me Babe." Dylan seemingly has the ability to experience events personally and transform them universally.

"Tangled Up in Blue" and "Simple Twist of Fate" became regulars in the live Jerry Garcia Band rotation. Garcia was loving the latest Dylan albums, and he was still on a massive songwriting roll with Hunter. A few months after their "farewell" Winterland concert of October '74, the Grateful Dead were creating a new album in Bob Weir's home studio. There was no preparation or preconceived ideas coming into this project, except all the music would evolve organically out of these sessions and everybody in the group would contribute. The last two studio albums for their own record label, *Wake of the Flood* and *Mars Motel*, produced models of grooving jam tunes that would work well live— songs like "Eyes of the World," "Let it Grow," and "Scarlet Begonias." Most of the material on these records was already fully formed when the band recorded. The new album, *Blues for Allah*, was their first album truly created in the studio.

Masterfully fused together at the start of *Blues for Allah*, the combo of Help on the Way > Slipknot! > Franklin's Tower is the record's glorious artistic statement. There's an optimistic bounce to the riff of "Help on the Way." Jerry's soulful singing breathes bliss into Hunter's lyrics. The uplifting final lines, *Without love in the dream/ It will never come true,* effortlessly leads the excursion into "Slipknot!" a jazzy instrumental that climaxes with an intricate series of chord changes that explode into the repetitive dancing rhythms of "Franklin's Tower." Help on the Way > Slipknot! would go in and out of the band's live cycle through the years. "Franklin's Tower," a simpler song that automatically triggered frenzied dancing outbursts, remained in the rotation. "The Music Never Stopped" and "Crazy Fingers" were the other splendid *Blues for Allah* tunes one might see at a Dead gig.

Mickey Hart was back in the band for good during the creation of *Blues for Allah*, which peaked at the twelfth spot on the charts, although it didn't receive much radio play. The album has a pair of brief instrumentals with thick grooves teetering between rhythm and blues, and jazz. The title track is an arcane creature that overstays its welcome. The album was a worthy achievement, yet the Grateful Dead still failed to capture or display their true essence in the studio. Part of the problem was the album format. Fully developed live renditions of Help on the Way > Slipknot! > Franklin's Tower can last thirty minutes. "The Music Never Stopped" is a quality track that clocks in at a shade under five minutes. In concert, the band unleashes a thunderous rock and roll jam at the end, extending the song to eight riveting minutes. The studio track teases a jam, but ultimately sputters into a fade-out. It would be hard for a rock critic to listen to an album like this and deduce that Jerry Garcia was one of the elite guitarists, up there with Hendrix, Clapton, Beck, or Santana. His virtuosity was obvious on record, and there was some impressive playing on live releases, but the record-buying public had yet to experience the X factor of Grateful Dead concerts and the extended soloing that had Deadheads proclaiming that Garcia was God.

There was no touring for the band in 1975, but the Dead played a benefit show and three other gigs in San Francisco, where they exercised songs from their new album. Garcia remained busy working on solo studio projects with other band members, and he toured with Saunders, Kahn, drummer Ron Tutt, and horn player Martin Fierro in a group named Legion of Mary. Later in '75, Jerry would tour with Kahn, Tutt, and pianist extraordinaire Nicky Hopkins in the first incarnation of the Jerry Garcia Band. These gigs didn't pay nearly as well as Dead shows, and everyone in the Dead's extended musical family was hungry for cash. It was inevitable that the Grateful Dead would soon return to their calling.

While the Dead's live improvisation was always evolving with a growing repertoire, and no two shows were ever the same, there were few jarring changes in what they did—no wardrobe coordination or schematic themes to the show. The musical journey was everything.

After Dylan's thunderous comeback tour with The Band in large arenas, he hit the road again with a barnstorming troupe of performers looking to create an intimate aural experience with a theatrical component. This stealth tour kicked off in the War Memorial Auditorium in Plymouth, Massachusetts, on October 30, 1975, and it was called the Rolling Thunder Revue.

The notion of this tour caught fire when Dylan began hanging out in various Greenwich Village establishments again as a vibrant music scene blossomed. During the summer, Dylan joined Ramblin' Jack Elliot on stage for three songs and debuted a new composition, "Abandoned Love," an excellent tune that would later be released as an outtake on Dylan's *Biograph* box set. Bob rounded up a core group for his tour that consisted of T-Bone Burnett, Steven Soles, Rob Stoner, Mick Ronson, Dave Mansfield, Roger McGuinn, Howie Wyeth, Luther Rix, Bob Neuwirth, Ronee Blakely, and a complete unknown, Scarlet Rivera.

Dylan was cruising down 13th Street when he saw a tall, long-haired woman bouncing down the street with a violin case. Bob pulled up alongside Scarlet and asked, "Can you play that thing?" Rivera, a fiddle player from the Midwest, was playing with a local salsa band at the time. After displaying her talents for Dylan in a Colombia studio the following day, she was recruited for the tour, and to be part of Dylan's next album. Scarlet's violin is a key ingredient to the idiosyncratic sound of *Desire*.

With almost no warning or promotion, and fueled by Colombian *yayo*, the Rolling Thunder Revue blitzed across America. There was no way Dylan could keep this thing under the radar, but the buzz was special while it lasted. The concept was to have different musicians and artists join the hedonistic caravan for as long as they wanted, and then those artists would be replaced by other top-shelf performers, and the tour would roll on and on. Why would any troubadour want to leave a party like this? This illustrates a stark difference between Dylan and Garcia and the musicians that surrounded them. An unknown like Rivera could never find a way into what had become the Grateful Dead. With a few minor personnel changes in the Jerry Garcia Band, those around Garcia were permanent—made members. Throughout his journey, Dylan thrived on working with undiscovered talent and journeymen. He trusted his instincts and it usually served him well.

On most nights of the Rolling Thunder Revue, Dylan appeared on stage wearing a white shirt tucked into faded jeans with a black vest. His fedora was decorated with flowers or a red feather, and sometimes his face was painted white. With his eyes locked straight ahead, Dylan ripped into his songs as if he was in a deep trance. Different artists would kick off the show before Dylan joined them. Bob would start off with an electric set. He turned "A Hard Rain's A-Gonna Fall" into a piercing rocker, and displayed other classics alongside the newbies, "Isis" and "Romance in Durango." He sang intensely during his acoustic sets and thrilled the crowd with shrill harp solos, which were absent from his previous tour. Joan Baez was an integral performer in the show. She would appear on stage and sing "I Shall Be Released" with Bob on the same mic, and then do a set of her own songs, featuring her new tune about her affair with Dylan, "Diamonds and Rust." Later in the show, Bob would sing "Sara" for his wife, who was traveling with the revue. Dylan was trying to reconcile his relationship with Sara, and it seemed to work briefly. This tour is thoroughly documented in Larry "Ratso" Sloman's book, *On the Road with Bob Dylan.*

Joni Mitchell joined the traveling show on November 13, 1975. Allen Ginsberg and Ramblin' Jack Elliot were already along for the ride. The tour ended up in some larger venues because it was impossible to sneak across America with a troupe of iconic celebrities. Theatre director and songwriter Jacques Levy was on board for Rolling Thunder. Levy was Dylan's songwriting collaborator for *Desire*, which was released after the first leg of the tour on January 5, 1976.

Levy's theatrical influence is evident from the opening line of "Hurricane." *Pistol shots ring out in the barroom night. Enter Patty Valentine from the upper hall. She sees a bartender and a pool of blood. Cries out, "My God, they killed them all!"* This was a protest song and a call for justice to free Rubin "Hurricane" Carter, a middleweight boxer who was convicted of a 1966 triple murder in Patterson, New Jersey. Dylan drives a gripping narrative as Scarlet's violin wails in anguish between verses. There's nothing vague or mysterious about Dylan's presentation of the events. Carter was eventually freed from jail, and decades later, Denzel Washington played Carter in the major motion picture *Hurricane*. Nobody knows for sure if Carter was innocent. The crime has never been solved.

Desire doesn't share the timeless qualities of other elite Dylan albums; many of the songs are linked to specific people, places, and events. "Isis," a mythical song of marriage, is followed by a romantic jaunt to "Mozambique." "One More Cup of Coffee" returns a mystical vibe. "Your breath is sweet/ Your eyes are like two jewels in the sky," Dylan sings with a cantorial ring. As the album advances, there's a song about a gangster, Joey Gallo, a flashback to Dylan's experience while filming *Pat Garret & Billy the Kid* in Durango, Mexico, and a ballad paying homage to Sara. On the surface, it seems like a mixed bag, but the mood set by Scarlet's violin, and the steady acoustic strumming and righteousness of Dylan's voice, makes *Desire* work like episodes in a TV series. There's a wonderful flow to the music—one song leaves the listener salivating for the next one—a related collection of timepieces that shine in unity. Individually, these tunes were rarely performed after Dylan's 1978 tour.

Desire completed Dylan's third two-year period of genius, each era featuring three brilliant albums: '63–'64 *The Freewheelin' Bob Dylan*, *The Times They Are A-Changin'*, *Another Side of Bob Dylan*; '65–'66 *Bringing It All Back Home*, *Highway 61 Revisited*, *Blonde on Blonde*; '74–'75 *Planet Waves*, *Blood on the Tracks*, *Desire*. Each album fed off the one before it. And within these trilogies, Dylan pushes his art in new directions without sacrificing the high quality of his compositions and performances.

The Grateful Dead had one long run of creative brilliance from 1969–1977 that could be broken down into two periods. It's tougher to quantify what they did because their best efforts were always recorded outside of a studio. The first of these runs of brilliance was from 1969–1972, beginning with *Live Dead* and *Skulls and Roses*, combined with the studio gems *Workingman's Dead* and *American Beauty*. *Europe '72* topped off that era with a batch of new originals and fine live performances. From 1973–1977, the band began a new period of creativity with *Wake of Flood*, creating the sound that would define them in concert. *Mars Hotel*, *Blues for Allah*, and *Terrapin Station* (1977) stocked their repertoire with songs they would jam on for the next twenty years. The Grateful Dead's best live run was during these eight years. Each show was a unique creation, and at least two hundred of those concerts would make worthwhile albums.

Kicking off a new era of touring after their eighteen-month hiatus, the Grateful Dead performed at the Paramount Theatre on June 3, 1976. After playing two shows in Oregon, the band headed east to play intimate theatres; Boston Music Hall, Capitol Theatre, Passaic, NJ, Beacon Theatre, NY, and the Tower Theatre, Upper Darby, PA. There was an extraordinary demand for tickets. Deadheads were thrilled their heroes were touring again, but things had changed. Gone was the Wall of Sound, and the endless jamming in songs like "Dark Star" and "Playin' in the Band." The Dead still jammed longer than anybody else, but with all the new tunes at their command, they became more song-orientated. The band also had to adapt to Mickey Hart's return. Regardless of how talented the drummers are, it's easier for a band to play behind one great drummer like Billy Kreutzmann than it is to coordinate with two percussionists. By the end of the year, the band's execution was precise, setting the stage for the Dead's most historic year.

Let my inspiration flow/ in token lines suggesting rhythm/ that will not forsake me/ until my tale is told and done. Those were the first words sung at the first show of 1977 at the Swing Auditorium in San Bernardino, California, on February 26. Without trepidation, the Dead set sail into Robert Hunter's tour de force, "Terrapin Station." The band opened the show with a number they'd never played before, and it was lyrically the longest song they'd ever attempted. Symbolic of things to come, the Grateful Dead attacked this task with swagger. On March 18, in the Winterland arena, the band segued from "Scarlet Begonias" into "Fire on the Mountain," a song from their impending record, *Terrapin*

Station. With its danceable groove, upbeat vibe, and its flexibility for multiple rounds of improvisation, Scarlet > Fire became a treasured live segment that ignited many second sets.

Scarlet > Fire set the stage for the most ballyhooed performances in Dead history, at Barton Hall, Cornell University, Ithaca, NY, on 5-8-77. You're not a Deadhead unless you've heard this show and have a definitive opinion of it. Excellent soundboard and audience recordings of this performance circulated quickly after the show. *Deadbase*, the statistical bible for Deadheads, polled fans to find out their favorites shows and favorite versions of different songs. The '77 Cornell show was ranked the greatest, and several versions of songs from that show achieved the same ranking. The rush of Cornell sycophants led to a backlash that created a legion of Cornell detractors who called the show overrated, and claimed that the performances the nights before and after were better. If anything becomes too popular in Deadhead circles, it sparks cynicism.

Both sides of the Cornell debate have credibility, but a myth like this could never have been born if the tape wasn't worthy of iconic status. It's not like there was a committee of Cornellians and Ivy League professors promoting the tape. The stunning performance of Scarlet > Fire, and the way the band simultaneously leaves "Scarlet Begonias" as it enters "Fire on the Mountain," is a hypnotic mindbender—segue paradise. For several minutes, the borders between the songs are erased and the listener can experience the past, present, and future all at once. And Garcia's last "Fire on the Mountain" solo is stupendous. The second set ends with the only Not Fade Away > St. Stephen > Not Fade Away > St. Stephen > Morning Dew combo in history. The sanctified anthems never sounded better than they did on that snowy May night in Ithaca.

The Dead tapes of 1977 became the bait that would lure Deadheads into a lifestyle of following the band around. There were several radio broadcasts of shows that year, the most famous being the one from Raceway Park in Englishtown, New Jersey, on Labor Day weekend, when 150,000 fans crammed onto the racetrack for a concert that also featured the Marshall Tucker Band and the New Riders of the Purple

Sage. The Grateful Dead may have bombed at Woodstock and played a subpar show in front of 600,000 fans in Watkins Glens in 1973, but in Englishtown, on a scorching and sticky summer's day, the band played two brilliant sets, and Deadheads around the country taped this radio broadcast. There wasn't much weirdness or confusion on the Englishtown or Cornell tapes. This was a possessed band that could rock as hard as Led Zeppelin and still improvise lengthy jams. These shows couldn't be obtained at local record shops, but the Grateful Dead developed an intense cult following that would continue to mutate and pay dividends down the line.

June 1, 1977, was another enormous day in a fateful year for the Dead. Garcia's pet project, *The Grateful Dead* movie, premiered at the Ziegfeld Theatre in New York. After the '74 Winterland shows, Garcia took 125 hours of raw footage to his house in Mill Valley and became obsessed with this movie project. The estimated budget of $125,000 swelled to $600,000 by the movie's completion. There was no way the film would generate box office receipts to recoup the cost. Fans loved the movie and rock critics generally praised it.

The movie was a microcosm of Grateful Dead business practices. Initially, the results were painful. The long-term benefits from this movie were priceless. *The Grateful Dead* movie became a midnight matinee classic. The film shows the band jamming in their prime, and there's an equal focus on the scene. Garcia, as the main editor of the documentary, is infatuated with the behavior of his devotees. Garcia captures the strange dancing, rituals, hedonism, and freedom of Deadheads as they groove to the music. It wasn't his intention, but Garcia created the ultimate recruiting and propaganda piece for Deadheads. Generations of fans learned everything they needed to know about the Dead scene from this movie before they attended their first show.

Dylan's film project, *Renaldo and Clara*, which featured footage from the Rolling Thunder Revue, starred Dylan, Joan Baez, and Sara Dylan. The movie premiered on January 25, 1978, in theatres in Los Angeles and New York City. Outside of the impressive snippets of concert footage, the film is a four-hour travesty trampled upon by critics. It was tough to follow, comprehend, or endure. Even Dylan's most enthusiastic supporters had trouble stomaching *Renaldo and Clara*. Perhaps Dylan tried to do too much with this endeavor, which cost him $1.25 million. Dylan was coming off a publicized divorce with Sara that was financially and emotionally draining. At times like this, the road can be a legend's only friend.

Dylan changed masks again, embarking on an ambitious world tour throughout 1978. Commencing in Tokyo and heading to Australia in March, Dylan traveled with fourteen band members, including Steven Douglas on sax, and four female backup singers. The big band show was styled after tours by Neil Diamond and Elvis Presley. Some saw Dylan's show as a tribute to Elvis, who passed away on August 16, 1977.

Reviews of these shows were mixed, and Colombia released *Bob Dylan at Budokan* in 1979. The standouts from this album are a reggae version of "Don't Think Twice It's Alright," a "Maggie's Farm" bursting with hot lead guitar from Billy Cross, "One More Cup of Coffee," and a soulful "I Shall Be Released." There were a lot of greatest hit type selections during this tour, but Dylan rearranged most of the compositions. The tour peaked as Dylan rolled through Europe in June and July.

Coinciding with his first European concert at Earl's Court was the release of Dylan's latest record, *Street Legal*. Using his touring band with the female backup singers in the studio, this album sounded like no other Dylan album. Most critics hammered *Street Legal*. The sound quality was muddy and the overall production was lacking. There was the dark shadow of a relationship gone bad influencing lyrics that some found to be sexist. However, there is a lot to admire on *Street Legal*, especially the last four songs from the mysterious and moody, "Senor (Tales of Yankee Power)," to the powerfully haunting "Where Are You Tonight?" *Street Legal* was remastered on CD in 2004, and it was a constructive facelift for an underrated album. "Senor" is the only tune that had any staying power in Dylan's live rotation, and that was only on an occasional basis. The Jerry Garcia Band began playing a stunning and hypnotic rendition of "Senor" in 1990.

Touring wasn't enough to replenish Dylan's soul. He'd soon find salvation through Jesus. To stave off the growing pressures of being the spiritual and musical leader of the Grateful Dead, Jerry Garcia found salvation in Persian, a refined heroin that was often smoked in tinfoil pipes. Garcia had abundantly binged on a smorgasbord of drugs since he was a young man, but Persian was his Achilles heel. He would battle this demon in vain for the rest of his life.

As good as 1977 had been for the Dead on the road, the chemistry in the band changed. Garcia was drifting away from spending time with other band members, and Keith Godchaux was nodding out at gigs while he was playing piano. Keith's heroin addiction took a noticeable toll on his playing. Halfway through the year his contributions went from inventive and inspired, to simply just keeping pace with the band.

The Grateful Dead machine rolled on in 1978. They were too talented not to have played several excellent shows, but there was a noticeable lull on certain nights—shorter sets with predictable patterns. They played their best shows of the year at the sanctified Red Rocks Amphitheatre in August. Two months later, the band lived out a fantasy by playing three nights in front of the Great Pyramids in Egypt. An unbelievable spiritual conquest and experience for the Dead didn't lead to any monumental music. From this subpar three-night run, the new Garcia/Hunter composition, "Shakedown Street," was the star from the 9-16-78 gig.

The second live performance of this song culminates with a long, weird jam that grooves, dissolves, and then rockets around the moon. The ensuing *Shakedown Street* album missed the mark, as did its predecessor, *Terrapin Station*, which was produced by Keith Olsen. Little Feat's Lowell George produced their new album. Even with the help of two of the better producers around, the Grateful Dead sound remained elusive in the studio. People chastised the single version of "Shakedown Street" as Disco Dead. The albums made money, gave the band additional material for their shows, and some limited radio play, but they did little to build any kind of legacy.

Life with the Dead ceased for Keith and Donna Godchaux on February 17, 1979, their last show with band at the Oakland Coliseum. Keith's drug problems made him a shell of the performer he used to be, and Donna's singing was often off-key and out of place. Her improvised vocal screams during jams were often counterproductive for the direction of the music and distracting for listeners. A talented singer with a pleasant stage presence, Donna never really found her niche in the musical scheme, and her bandmates didn't find a way to properly utilize her talents. Her two-year tenure with the Jerry Garcia Band through 1978 flowed easier because her role as a backup singer was clearly defined. The musical scheme was less complicated than the Dead's constantly shifting tempos and styles.

Brent Mydland, a keyboardist and vocalist for Bob Weir's band, took over for Keith, who died in an automobile accident a year after leaving the band. Brent didn't have the virtuosic touch of Keith in his prime, but his electric keyboard playing energized the sound of the band. His backing vocals blended effortlessly on both Garcia and Weir songs. Keith and Donna for Brent Mydland was a beneficial trade for the Grateful Dead, but serious problems loomed.

In early '78, Jerry had a case of laryngitis that made Bob Weir the band's only lead singer for a couple of shows. In November, Garcia was hospitalized with bronchitis, exasperated by chain-smoking cigarettes, freebasing cocaine, smoking Persian, and the strains of singing night after night. Jerry frequently wore shades on stage, and his long, frizzy hair accented his unkempt appearance and carefree attire—blue jeans and black shirt. As he played he still had a smile that could bring instant joy to his kingdom. Although his appearance was beastly to the sober world, his stoned look was uniquely rock and roll cool. The fact that Garcia sailed through the '60s and '70s without suffering any major health scares or overdosing was miraculous. The next decade wouldn't be so kind.

What Dylan had gone through between his comeback tour with The Band and his 1978 World Tour was probably more grueling than his meteoric rise to immortal icon at the age of twenty-five. The baggage of being Bob Dylan irreparably damaged his personal life, and critics took pleasure in pouncing on his perceived failures. Dylan had always been a spiritual and religious person who had used biblical references in many of his works, and he was intrigued with other beliefs besides Judaism. Dylan became close with, and had affairs with, the African-American female singers on his world tour. Dylan enjoyed their company and respected their opinions and beliefs. These women were filled with the spirit of Jesus. In San Diego, Dylan picked up a cross that a fan threw on stage and began wearing it. On December 2, 1978, during a sound check before a gig in Nashville, Dylan played a religious number from his upcoming album, "Slow Train Coming." The ladies most instrumental in his conversion to born-again Christianity were Carolyn Dennis and Mary Alice Artes.

Sometime in January 1979, Bob accepted Jesus Christ as the Messiah, and spent the next three months attending Bible class with Artes at the Vineyard Fellowship's School of Discipleship. Inspired by his new faith, Dylan poured his passion into songs. Dylan went down to Muscle Shoals Sound Studios in Alabama to record his new album. Dylan disciple and lead guitarist and singer for Dire Straits, Mark Knopfler, was invited to play on the record by producer Jerry Wexler. Despite the preachy lyrics, *Slow Train Coming* was a huge success, propelled by the single "Gotta Serve Somebody," which earned Dylan his first Grammy Award for Best Male Rock Vocal Performance. Even though Dylan's audience may not have enjoyed hearing Dylan preach lines such as, "Ya either got faith or ya got unbelief and there ain't no neutral ground," and, "It may be the devil or it may be the Lord. But you're gonna have to serve somebody," the stunning music and vocal performances transcended the message. *Slow Train Coming* wasn't on the same mountain as *Desire* or *Blood on the Tracks*, but it was an album Dylan could be proud of.

Controversy over Dylan's religiosity exploded with the commencement of his first tour of 1979 at San Francisco's Fox Warfield theatre in November. The shows started out as gospel revivals with his backup singers belting out six or seven songs, and then Dylan would appear on stage in a black leather jacket armed with an electric guitar to turn up the heat. Including encores, Dylan would play around seventeen songs, and they were all songs preaching his new faith. A lot of these tunes would appear on his next album, *Saved*. People were protesting outside the theatre and yelling at him inside. His Jewish fans were upset with his conversion, and Christians were questioning the authenticity of his born-again status.

In 1966, some fans rallied around his rock performances with The Band. This time, he seemed to piss everybody off, despite the success of *Slow Train Coming*. Dylan and his band delivered crisp performances at the Warfield, but that was secondary to the circus surrounding his religious conversion and his unflinching will to serenade his fans with songs preaching the teachings of Jesus.

Admonishing a crowd that was hollering for rock and roll in Tempe, Arizona, Dylan said, "Well. What a rude bunch tonight, huh? You all know how to be real rude. You know about the spirit of the anti-Christ? Does anybody here know about that? Well, it's clear the anti-Christ is loose right now… You wanna rock-n-roll you can go down and rock-n-roll. You can go see Kiss and you rock-n-roll all your way down to the pit."

Fifteen years earlier, Dylan ambushed folk purists in Newport with thunderous rock and roll, and now he was condemning concert-goers for wanting to hear that music. The times were a-changing. How long would Dylan stay on this path of righteousness? If ever this kind of evangelical message were to resonate with Dylan fans in America, the time was right. As American hostages were being humiliated in Iran, the Soviet Union invaded Afghanistan. Motorists waited hours in lines to fill up their tanks at gas stations. The economy was reeling—stagnation, inflation, recession. As Dylan and the Grateful Dead drifted into the next decade, their futures were as uncertain as America's.

EIGHT

AFTERMATH OF AN UNSPEAKABLE TRAGEDY

Remember, this is just a football game, no matter who wins or loses. An unspeakable tragedy confirmed to us by ABC News in New York City. John Lennon, outside of his apartment building on the West Side of New York City. The most famous of perhaps all the Beatles, was shot twice in the back and rushed to Roosevelt Hospital. Dead on arrival. Hard to go back to the game after that news flash.

Howard Cosell, Monday Night Football, December 8, 1980

Millions of Americans found out about the murder of a beloved Beatle as they watched a Monday Night Football contest between the Miami Dolphins and the New England Patriots. Violence in America had no limits. Four months after Lennon was murdered in the city he loved, President Ronald Reagan was shot and nearly killed in the nation's capital. Car and motorcycle accidents, plane crashes, and drug overdoses have tragically claimed the lives of talented rock stars, but the random act of a lunatic targeting a legend sent shock waves through the world of music.

A year earlier in Cincinnati, eleven fans were trampled to death by a surging crowd trying to get into a general admission concert to see The Who. Neil Young was singing, "Hey hey, my my, rock and roll will never die." While this axiom was true, rock and roll had seen better days.

In 2012, *Rolling Stone* published a list of the Top 500 albums of all time. These lists are overblown. How can you calculate what the 343rd best album is, and who cares? Ranking more than one hundred albums is superfluous. The golden age of great albums began with *Bringing It All Back Home* in 1965, and ended in 1980 with *London Calling* by The Clash. Excluding compilations, if you break down the top fifty albums on the list and group them in five-year spans, 1965 to 1970 produced nineteen of the top fifty, 1971 to 1975 accounted for thirteen of the elite albums, and 1976 to 1980 had four selections on the list. Over the next six years, starting in 1981, only Michael Jackson's *Thriller* made the top fifty. There are lots of reasons for this decline, including MTV, which debuted on August 1, 1981 (Jerry Garcia's 39th birthday). Making a fetching music video became an easier road to popularity than creating an entire album. Madonna, Michael Jackson, and several one-hit wonders thrived in this video format, as new wave and musical simplicity became the craze of the day. Dylan was with Jesus, and The Who, Rolling Stones, Pink Floyd, and Led Zeppelin were fading after their domination of the '70s. And with the assassination of Lennon, George Harrison and other icons decided to take a break from the music business.

In these culturally depraved times, the Grateful Dead road show became an irresistible option for those craving an authentic music adventure—a traveling caravan of hedonistic freaks pulling together as a community—a throwback to the Haight-Ashbury days. During the '80s, I saw 150 Grateful Dead shows and 50 Jerry Garcia Band shows, and towards the end of the decade, I found my way to 50 Dylan concerts. As a witness to what transpired between Dylan and the Dead later in the decade, and as a case study on how an obsessive rock fan finds himself on tour with the Grateful Dead, here's my story.

When John Lennon was gunned down on the outskirts of Central Park, I was a rebellious seventeen-year-old teenager watching Monday

Night Football. Howard Cosell broke news of the unspeakable tragedy. Cosell and Lennon, the heroes and voices of my childhood, would be forever tangled in a historical nightmare.

When I was in third grade, I had to do a presentation in front of my peers. I chose to imitate a Howard Cosell Talking Sports newsflash, which he used to broadcast on 77 WABC radio in New York. More than any other announcer, Cosell's honking Brooklyn accent and his fancy vocabulary became part of the big event. It's hard to think of Muhammed Ali in his prime without Cosell being part of the soundtrack. And prior to the night of December 8, 1980, his most famous call was "Down goes Frazier! Down goes Frazier! Down goes Frazier!" as George Foreman pummeled Joe Frazier in a shocking upset to win the Heavyweight Championship of the World. I also felt an affinity for Cosell because we shared the same name. There weren't many famous Howards scoring touchdowns or singing hit songs on the radio.

My older cousins turned me on to the Beatles when I was six. Until that time, my three favorite albums from my father's collection were *West Side Story*, *Fiddler on the Roof*, and *Herb Alpert & the Tijuana Brass Greatest Hits*. My father bought *Let It Be* for me, and I disappeared into my room and listened to nothing but that album and some AM radio for at least a year. My cousins were Beatles fanatics, and above all, they preached the virtues of Lennon.

On the night John was murdered, I was sitting on a sofa in the basement of my parents' house in the suburban town of Nanuet, New York. Hearing Cosell broadcast those words was a deathblow to any remaining youthful innocence inside me. I was a chronic class-cutting, pot-smoking kid, and then I decided to go all the way and drop out of high school. I went to a community college to get my GED, but I didn't believe in academic or religious institutions. The only thing I believed in was the world of song, and soon that would lead me to Jerry Garcia.

My friend Doug was the only cat I knew who had a passion for music that was equal to mine. We devoured every classic and progressive rock album out there. We knew every lyric, lick, and subtle nuance of every album by bands such as The Who, Rolling Stones, Doors, Beatles, Yes, ELO, ELP, Jethro Tull, Santana, Pink Floyd, etc....We knew Dylan's greatest hits, but there wasn't enough jamming on the surface for us to explore any further. As for the Grateful Dead, we admired their *Skeletons in the Closet* compilation and *American Beauty*, but lack of overwhelming lead guitar kept us from going further down that road.

After spending the summer of 1980 at a Jewish sleepaway camp, Doug returned home a devout Deadhead, and Jerry Garcia was the Messiah. The idea of putting Garcia in the same class as Clapton, Hendrix, or the emerging guitar god Eddie Van Halen seemed ludicrous. Doug tried to steer me into his camp, but I didn't initially get it. Listening to the Grateful Dead is like trying to learn a new language—some pick it up quickly and run with it; for others, there's a learning curve before it overtakes them, and some folks slam the door shut on the Dead. I held out hope. If Garcia could overwhelm a music lover like my charismatic friend, there had to be merit in the music, somewhere, and that intrigued me.

My Grateful Dead revelation occurred seven weeks after Lennon's death, on January 24, 1981. I remember the date because on that night, I witnessed hockey history at the Nassau Coliseum. Mike Bossy, the young French Canadian star of my favorite hockey team, the New York Islanders, scored two goals in the last five minutes of the game to become the second player in NHL history to score fifty goals in the first fifty games of a season. The thrilling event paled in comparison to the ride home. The driver, Seymour, my friend Scott's brother, popped *Europe '72* into his tape deck and turned the volume up full blast. I don't know if it was the dopamine high of the thrilling sports spectacle or the potent bone we smoked on the way home, but I salivated in stunned silence as I experienced the true majestic sweep of the Grateful Dead for the first time.

"Cumberland Blues" blasted away—electrified, psychedelic hillbilly music. An arcane world emerged. "Jack Straw" from Wichita was on the run from sea to shining sea. The hypnotic, jazzy jamming of "China Cat Sunflower" was surreal and seductive, unlike any music I'd ever heard. "The news is out all over town," crooned Garcia in a sad, smooth tone that paid tribute to Hank Williams but was pure Jerry in style. Pigpen hammered the blues with "It Hurst Me Too." I don't think I'd ever heard Hank Williams or Elmore James before. A door to another world opened. Instantly, I felt linked to an alternate musical reality.

Hearing "Ramble on Rose" put me over the edge—fascinating lyrics and alliteration placed upon a plush melody and delivered with deliberate ragtime flavor. Garcia's pitch-perfect-voice connected characters, real and imagined, from different times and places: Jack the Ripper, Billy Sunday, Mary Shelly, Mojo Hand, Crazy Otto, Frankenstein, New York City, Jericho. It was a beautifully crafted song with a searing guitar solo. The following day I rode my bicycle to Tapesville USA, a record shop located in front of the Nanuet Mall, and purchased *Europe '72*. Within a few weeks, I'd purchased every Dead record in the bin.

I still had to overcome the Jerry Garcia is the greatest guitarist hurdle. I saw my first show at Madison Square Garden on March 9, 1981. The band endeared themselves to me by playing "Ramble on Rose" as the fourth song of the night. The Garden roared in unison when Garcia sang, "Just like New York City," and Jerry's guitar roared out a scathing, yet lyrically beautiful, guitar solo. I recognized most of the songs, but I lost my focus during the long, spacey jams, like the one connecting "Estimated Prophet" to "Uncle John's Band." Grateful Dead appreciation is an acquired taste that takes patience and the willingness to approach listening to music differently. A few months after my Dead debut, I scored a copy of the MSG show and realized it was a spectacular show. I was there, but not really.

My first bootleg tape was a ninety-minute BASF cassette of highlights from a show at Raceway Park, Englishtown, New Jersey, on September 3, 1977. My Garcia is god epiphany arrived when I heard "Mississippi Half Step Uptown Toodeloo." The dynamic energy of the performance was superior to the truncated studio track. The between-verse guitar solos sparkled, but there was a long, masterful musical segment prior to the band singing the "Across the Rio Grande" bridge. Phil's bass rumbled as the band paved the way for a two-tiered climax from Garcia. And then the Dead created something that had never existed before. Godchaux tinkled his keyboards in a manner that pleased Garcia. Jerry tweeted back like a singing robin. Everybody in the band was listening and slowly contributing. Things got heated, and before there was another soaring crescendo, the band wisely eased into the "Rio Grande" chorus—no need to be redundant. This was a distinctive masterpiece that could never be duplicated.

A few weeks later, Doug turned me on to the Cornell tape, the legendary show from 5-8-77. An extraordinary half-hour Scarlet > Fire kicks off the second set. Everything is sublime: inviting rhythm and tempo, expressive singing by Garcia, intricate improvisation by all involved. The music played the band. The segue between "Scarlet Begonias" and "Fire on the Mountain" separated the Dead from any other band I'd heard. They channeled strange alchemy and seemingly suspended time by dabbling in both songs—coming and going in the present moment. And few instrumentals in the band's history match the burning intensity of the last solo in "Fire," or the colossal jam in "Morning Dew."

Bootleg tapes like Englishtown and Cornell, as well as many other shows from 1969-1977, represent the Grateful Dead's finest music. Bob Dylan is an outstanding live performer; however, you don't have to listen to bootlegged performances to understand and measure his greatness. Although, sampling his unreleased live material is highly recommended because Dylan's songs tend to evolve and change form as he plays them through the years. To truly understand the Grateful Dead—what they do, and what they are capable of—listening to their shows is essential.

Years after Garcia's death, Englishtown was released as Volume 13 in the Dick's Picks series. On the 40th anniversary of the Cornell show, the revered concert was officially released. But in 1981, either you were in the know and had connections to trade bootleg tapes with other Deadheads, or you listened to the albums. Most Dead aficionados only listened to boots because there were so many high-quality tapes. Once drawn into the intoxicating realm of Dead boots, I quit listening to their albums.

I was a music-first Deadhead, but the on the road caravan that traveled from city to city turned out to be irresistibly appealing—one of the last great American road adventures. On April 6, 1982, I made my first road trip to Philadelphia to see the Dead. The night before, a blizzard dumped eighteen inches of snow on my hometown of Nanuet. Calling off our rendezvous with destiny was not an option. Heading towards Philly with Scott and Seymour in that tiny white Honda (same car, cast, and crew from the night I discovered *Europe '72* after a hockey game), we encountered hazardous conditions until we reached the New Jersey Turnpike—all roads to Philly were clear from that point. We passed the Oranges (East and West), the Amboys (Perth and South), crossed the Benjamin Franklin Bridge, and arrived in the Philadelphia Spectrum in plenty of time to enjoy the parking lot pageantry. An army of tie-dyed hippies pranced around as an intoxicating cloud of marijuana and hash smoke mixed with the aroma of burnt pretzels. As the blue-collar grind of another Tuesday in South Philly faded into twilight, the Deadhead invasion of Broad Street was complete.

"Cold Rain and Snow," a beloved tune, especially on this night, opened the show. The flexibility of the band's repertoire allowed them to communicate with their audiences, if they pleased, based on where they were, how they were feeling, and even the weather conditions. The spirited first set consisted of twelve songs; tunes of outlaws on the run gambling, rambling, carousing, and bootlegging whiskey—a vivid depiction of Old Weird America. I sensed the band was strategically saving their best jams for the second set. If I could have slipped the band a wish list between sets it would have looked like this: "Shakedown Street," "Terrapin Station," "Morning Dew," "Sugar Magnolia."

A thunderous bass bomb set Deadheads in motion to the funky groove of "Shakedown Street" to open set two. Garcia mimicked Mydland's keyboard leads, a prelude to a rousing jam. The fourth song of the set, "Terrapin Station," whipped the crowd into a state of euphoria. Emotions soared as the crowd swayed and sang Hunter's epic anthem with Garcia as if this were Holy Scripture. The instrumental refrain hammered home the magnificence of the moment. As the drummers took over for their nightly duet, I knew they'd play "Morning Dew" when it was time for Jerry's next selection. It was rarely played over the last four years, but this had turned into a special night that demanded an exclamation point.

While enjoying a briskly paced and fiery Truckin' > The Other One, I stood on a chair in row fifteen and sent waves of mental telepathy toward Garcia, pleading for the Holy Grail, "Morning Dew." As "The Other One" ended, there was a fractioned second of silence before Garcia hit the magical "Dew" chord. I wasn't the only one pining for "The Dew." Deadheads screamed, yodeled, hugged, and cried. The transcendent performance had the sweep of a religious revival—indicative of the elusive powers of heroic music. A rollicking "Sugar Magnolia" closed the set and the encore was "It's All Over Now, Baby Blue." This was the only time in Grateful Dead history that "Shakedown Street," "Terrapin Station," "Morning Dew," and "Sugar Magnolia" appeared together in the same show. Just once in 2,318 shows.

I'm sure I wasn't the only fan in Philadelphia who felt that their presence inspired the band, and there definitely was a communal pull to the proceedings, unlike any relationship between fans and musicians at rock concerts. Every night the Dead played a completely different set list than the night before, except for occasions when they would break in a new composition by playing it a few nights in a row. The Dead respected the intelligence of the diehard fans that followed them around, and conversely, the fans understood the unofficial pact, and the consequences of it. Those seeing the following show in Syracuse on April 8 had no chance of seeing "Shakedown," "Terrapin," "Dew," or "Sugar Mag." This approach to constructing shows led to an occasional subpar show. However, the positives far outweighed the negatives. The arrangement created passionate customer loyalty and made the concerts feel more like a live sporting event than a preconceived presentation.

The experience of following the Grateful Dead became a real-life soap opera. On the way home from the Philly show, Seymour hit an ice patch on the Palisades Parkway, and suddenly we were spinning like socks in a dryer. When the spinning ceased, the pillbox Honda was lodged in a snowbank, a few feet short of pine trees on the side of the road. It was the most exciting day of my life. I felt compelled to follow the band. I collected tapes and relived the great shows of the past and I was now a witness to musical history, in hot pursuit of the next great jam. I spent the next five years listening to nothing but the Grateful Dead and Jerry Garcia Band . . . until I stumbled onto *Blood on the Tracks*.

NINE

SURVIVING IN A RUTHLESS WORLD

John Lennon was still among the living when Jerry Garcia joined Bob Dylan on stage for the first time on November 16, 1980, during Dylan's twelve-night residency at San Francisco's Fox-Warfield. Bob was still singing songs of faith, but he mixed in some old classics and cut back on the number of gospel songs for his backup singers. Prior to Garcia's appearance, Carlos Santana played with Dylan on 11-13, and Mike Bloomfield joined him on stage two nights later. It was the last time they'd see each other. Bloomfield died three months later from a drug overdose.

After a slippery start, Dylan rallied to give Garcia a flattering introduction: "Well, I don't know exactly what to say here. Different peoples been coming down to the theater every night so far. And this night is no exception I guess. Anyway this is, keep . . . here's a young man I know you know who he is. I've played with him a few times before. I'm a great admirer and fan of his and support his group all the way, Jerry Garcia. He's gonna play with us, in the key of C."

The song was "To Ramona," and Garcia unleashed an A+ jam in the key of C. It was a long solo by Dylan standards. Garcia remained on stage for eleven songs, including a song covered by the Jerry Garcia Band, "Simple Twist of Fate," and a tune that would later be covered by the JGB, "Senor." After his spirited outburst in "To Ramona," Garcia dutifully fit in as just another guy in Dylan's band. Everything from Dylan's performance to the sound of the band was spot on during this Fox-Warfield residency.

Prior to Dylan's stay in the Warfield, Deadheads invaded this theatre from September 25 through October 14 for fifteen unique Grateful

Dead shows. Next on the Dead's itinerary was two nights at Saenger Performing Arts Center in New Orleans, before Deadhead Nation convened in Manhattan's Radio City Music Hall for eight concerts. All twenty-five of these concerts featured the Grateful Dead playing an opening acoustic set followed by two electric sets. It was the first time they'd done something like this since 1970. This batch of shows yielded a pay-per-view performance on Halloween in Radio City, a video, *Dead Ahead*, and two albums, *Reckoning* and *Dead Set*.

Released on April 1, 1981, *Reckoning* is a masterful double album meshing Dead originals with traditional songs. It rolls together organically. "Deep Elem Blues" and "Oh Babe It Ain't No Lie" are siblings to the Garcia/Hunter compositions "Dire Wolf" and "To Lay Me Down." The desperation of "Dark Hollow" matches that of "China Doll." The album ends with "Birdsong" and "Ripple" back to back. For all their psychedelic rock and jazzy explorations, this album proved that the Grateful Dead could strip down to the roots with anybody. *Reckoning* sold reasonably well, reaching forty-three on the album charts, and "Dire Wolf" had a nice run on FM radio.

Unfortunately, in August, the band released *Dead Set*. If I could steer Dead newbies away from one album, this is it. These are live electric selections from the Warfield/Radio City run. The singing's solid, and the recording is pristine, but the band played cautiously, as if they were in a studio and they were aware that they were using these cuts on an album. The electric sets during these runs were weak in comparison to the 1980 summer tour, when the Grateful Dead celebrated their fifteenth anniversary. Anyway, this acoustic/electric endeavor paid off just like *The Grateful Dead* movie. The spinoff albums and videos continued to propagate the band's brand, which was becoming extremely attractive to a generation of new fans turned off by '80s culture.

Bob Dylan's relevance in America was sliding south. In the summer of 1980, Dylan's album *Saved* didn't sell as well as *Slow Train Coming*. The novelty of Dylan's conversion was old news, and the album didn't have the musical pop of its predecessor, although, there were three strong performances: "In the Garden," "Solid Rock," and "Covenant Woman." The following summer, Dylan moved away from full preaching mode and delivered *Shot of Love*, a curious mix of compositions. It included one of his best songs of the decade, "Every Grain of Sand." It's a compassionate take on his religious conversion, with the deepest lyrics of his Christian trilogy, sung from the heart, and a poignant harmonica solo completes the package. "Every Grain of Sand" is the last song of the album, and the road to get to there is rocky.

"Property of Jesus" and "Dead Man, Dead Man," come off as preachy and humorless. Parts of this album suffer from dull arrangements, mediocre performances from Dylan and the assembled musicians, and poor production. "Heart of Mine" and "In the Summertime" are fine tunes with catchy hooks, but they'll never be mistaken as Dylan classics. In "Lenny Bruce," Dylan empathizes with the plight of the controversial comedian. *They stamped him and they labeled him like they do with pants and shirts. He fought a war on a battlefield where every victory hurts.* This song, and the entire album, had potential that wasn't realized.

When Dylan's in the thick of cutting-edge music like *Blood on the Tracks* he has a vision, and everybody in the studio from the musicians to the producers are infected with the passion. Even in the simplicity of *Nashville Skyline* Dylan is on purpose with his muse. With *Shot of Love*, and some of Dylan's upcoming '80s albums, the world's greatest songwriter was still doing his thing, but his vision, judgement, and unflinching confidence weren't what they used to be.

The Grateful Dead avoided making another studio album for seven years after *Go to Heaven* (1980). The album produced some worthwhile material for their live shows. The Hunter/Garcia tunes "Alabama Getaway" and "Althea" became popular first-set additions, and the Weir/Barlow combo Lost Sailor > Saint of Circumstance fit nicely in the second set behind "Shakedown Street" or Scarlet > Fire. Brent Mydland added his compositions "Far from Me" and "Easy to Love

You," co-written by Barlow. After the album was released, Garcia said, "I think of recording as sort of a necessary evil in a way."

Grateful Dead albums consistently produced appealing cover art. That streak ended with the lame cover of *Go to Heaven*, which featured the band members in white suits, supposedly in heaven.

Unlike Dylan fans, who obsessed over his album releases, Deadheads didn't expect much out of studio releases. There was an active community of fans trading and exchanging tapes at shows and through the mail. Every show was recorded, usually by a small army of tapers. All the while fans were hunting down the old classics: 2-13-70 Fillmore East; 8-6-71 Hollywood Palladium; 8-27-72 Venita, Oregon; 11-17-73 UCLA; 6-18-74 Louisville; 8-4-76 Roosevelt Stadium. There was an endless amount of music to analyze and enjoy, and the band fed the archives with each new performance. Crazed Deadheads could never get enough Jerry.

Whether there would be enough Jerry to go around became a concern. Garcia had a few illnesses in '78 and '79, and a cigarette smoking heroin addict with a healthy appetite for all kinds of recreational drugs always faces the risk of sudden tragedy. In 1983, Garcia's appearance became beastly as he put on weight at a scary rate. "The fat man rocks" bumper stickers decorated many of the dilapidated vehicles of Deadville. The immobile guitar guru also had a passion for Haagen-Dazs ice cream. Outside of performing and practicing by himself, Garcia exerted minimal energy.

The year 1983 was a sensational year for Garcia as a guitarist. The best guitar performances I witnessed from Garcia occurred during an eight-day stretch from late May into early June with the Jerry Garcia Band, and later in the year during the Grateful Dead's East Coast fall '83 tour. For those looking to explore some of this music further, my JGB recommendations are 5-28-83 Cape Cod; 5-31 + 6-1-83 Roseland Ballroom; and my Dead suggestions are 10-11 + 10-12-83 Madison Square Garden; 10-17-83 Lake Placid; and 10-14-83 Hartford Civic Center, which is available as *Dick's Picks Volume 6*. The second set of the Hartford show has the best Scarlet > Fire you'll ever hear, and ditto for the Help > Slipknot! > Franklin's Tower at Madison Square Garden. The caveat here is that Garcia's voice is a little cranky, but the guitar expeditions are generous and mellifluous, without a wrong turn or wasted note. Garcia's unkempt and bloated appearance in black t-shirts and blue jeans gave him a grandfatherly Buddha-like presence. To play guitar like that in his physical condition was astounding. But inevitably Garcia, the rest of the band, and his kingdom of admirers would have to face reality.

According to manager Rock Scully's book *Living with the Dead*, concerned band members and the Dead business family set up an intervention. Scully wasn't thrilled with this because he was hooked on Persian as well, and he was one of Jerry's enablers, often getting high with him. Billy Kreutzmann delivered the ultimatum to Jerry, "Either you gotta quit this Persian shit or you're fired."

Garcia countered, "Promises, promises! Okay, after careful consideration, I'm afraid I have to go with the Persian…Anyway, who you gonna hire? It's a lot easier to find a drummer than it is a lead guitar player." Jerry could do as he pleased; nobody had the leverage to fire or force him to do anything. As sincere as the desire to help Jerry was, there was no escaping that Garcia was their meal ticket, and that was one of the triggers that drove Jerry to Persian. Like Dylan, he was worshipped by a massive fanatical following. Jerry was the leader of an extended musical family, which on one hand he loved, but on the other hand, the responsibility had trapped and suffocated him. Jerry did his Persian, but he never crossed the family. Dylan easily divorced himself from scenes, and relationships with peers and fans. He seemingly thrived on it.

Dylan spent time contemplating his faith in 1982. While he didn't renounce his Christian conversion, he distanced himself from the Vineyard Fellowship, and in 1983 was photographed wearing a yarmulke at the Wailing Wall in Jerusalem. Just as he was influenced by multiple genres of music, Dylan was pressing on, adding his born-again experience to his larger and ever expanding vision of religion. The year

1982 was one of those mysterious disappearing periods where Dylan was on the lam, but his mind was fertile as he advanced towards his next dance with genius.

With the invention of the compact disc and the growing popularity of MTV, Dylan sought the production and guitar skills of Mark Knopfler for his new album. The final product, released on October 27, 1983, had a crisp sound and an iconic shot of a scruffy-faced Dylan behind shades on the cover. *Infidels*, Dylan's twenty-second studio album, was a return to secular music. Although critics greeted *Infidels* with mixed reviews and skepticism, it was a cohesive grouping of songs that achieved a sound similar to *Slow Train Coming*. Dylan initially wanted to call this album *Surviving in a Ruthless World*. *Infidels* went on to be a modest commercial success, and it was undervalued by critics and fans who were soured by Dylan's Christian trilogy—anything less than the next *Blood on the Tracks* wouldn't suffice. The disappointing legacy of these sessions is that Dylan had a masterpiece at his disposal, but he decided not to release it.

An acoustic version of "Blind Willie McTell," recorded during the *Infidels* sessions and later released on the *Bob Dylan Bootleg Series Volume 1-3*, is widely revered by Dylan aficionados, and regarded as one of his great works. Like "Lenny Bruce," it's not autobiographical in nature. The unraveling narrative is a chilling vision of African-American history in the South, and Dylan sings it as if he were a contemporary of the great blues singer Blind Willie McTell. It comes off like a painting that is haunting, yet beautiful: *Smell that sweet magnolia blooming/ See the ghosts of slavery ships*. Dylan gets outside of himself and sings with virtuous sincerity. He's doesn't try to sound like a blues singer; the lyrics seemingly sing the song and Dylan is just the vehicle. Dylan's piano playing sets an ominous tone, and the acoustic guitar licks are the emotional brushstrokes.

When asked why he left "Blind Willie McTell" off *Infidels*, Dylan said, "It was never developed fully, I never got around to completing it." Dylan initially looked at that piano/guitar version as a demo, and then attempted a few electric versions of the song. These renditions are gripping, but sloppy. The acoustic version wouldn't have fit into the symmetrical flow and sound of *Infidels*. But there was enough extra material from these sessions and the *Shot of Love* sessions to turn this into a double album. Side three could have opened with "Blind Willie McTell" and been followed by "Angelina" and "Caribbean Wind," outstanding *Shot of Love* outtakes. Throw those songs in with the best left off *Infidels*: "Foot of Pride," "Someone's Got a Hold of My Heart," "Tell Me," "Julius and Ethel, and "Lord Protect My Child," and there's more than enough material for a powerful double album. For the time being, Dylan was content storing these compositions in the attic.

With Dire Straits on tour in Europe, Dylan felt he couldn't wait for Knopfler's return, so he went into the studio and remixed the songs with his own engineer. The sound of the album seemed targeted for a new generation of fans, and Dylan's performing style is powerful enough to lift lyrics that, on paper, are not among his best. "Jokerman" is a difficult song to dissect. Who is the Jokerman, if he's anyone at all? There are biblical references, flashy language, and compassionate sentiments, yet the story doesn't really come together. Coherence aside, "Jokerman" is a listening pleasure thanks to a spirited Dylan performance as he unwinds strings of intriguing language.

Some found Dylan's lyrics sexist in "Sweetheart Like You." To overanalyze takes the joy out of the listening experience. The narrator of the song is a character who states, "A woman like you should be at home, that's where you belong. Taking care of somebody nice who don't know how to do you wrong." Within the context of the music, it's easy to enjoy this as an old-fashioned love sentiment.

Dylan's singing, timing, and ability to draw exactly what he needs from his assembled musicians is uncanny. "Sweetheart" fades out with an impressive guitar solo with thick notes. The much maligned "Neighborhood Bully," which is a pro-Israeli timepiece, plods forward repetitively. It's not the type of song I would listen to unless it were part of *Infidels*, but within the album, I would never consider skipping past "Neighborhood Bully." It's part of the album's chemistry.

The dueling guitar solos of Knopfler and Mick Taylor escalate the tension of "Man of Peace." "I and I" has an intriguing opening: *Been so long since a strange woman has slept in my bed/ Look how sweet she sleeps, how free must be her dreams.* On *Desire*, "One More Cup of Coffee" shares a similarly exotic start: *Your breath is sweet/ Your eyes are like two jewels in the sky/ Your back is straight your hair is smooth/ On the pillow where you lie.* "Don't Fall Apart on Me Tonight" ends the album with a touching romantic ballad. Dylan's short harp solo after the bridge is dropped in perfectly. Three videos were produced for MTV. "Jokerman" was a major production with questionable results, and "Sweetheart Like You" was weak. The gem of the videos was the outtake of "Don't Fall Apart on Me Tonight." Dylan's performance is deliciously sloppy and inventive. Knopfler and the band were loose and having a blast as they basked in Dylan's offbeat annunciations. In the first verse, Dylan's timing and pitch are all over the place, and then he settles into a nice groove for verse two before reliving the herky-jerky delivery he created during the first verse. This is a raw performance that lacks authentic emotion but Dylan's just letting it rip, and that's desirable.

Dylan launched a summer tour of Europe in 1984 that featured Santana and Joan Baez. Dylan embraced his old songs with a slight tip of the hat to his latest records. Baez expected that she would receive equal billing with Bob and perform with him. Playing to partially filled stadiums as the opening act, Baez split the tour, disillusioned with her role in Dylan's shows. She received better treatment during the Rolling Thunder Revue, but this was like England 1965 all over again. Dylan seemed to have aged during his two-year layoff from touring. A single album, *Real Live,* was released from this tour, and the re-written rendition of "Tangled Up in Blue" is phenomenal.

The Grateful Dead and Jerry Garcia Band adhered to the adage, "Keep on keepin' on like a bird that flew." By 1984, this long, strange trip was becoming Orwellian in nature. Garcia was Big Brother, and his tie-dye-wearing followers dutifully clapped along to the "Not Fade Away" reprise, chanting, "You know our love will not fade away." Some veterans who lived for the music were starting to question why they were following Garcia around. The sets were getting shorter and the playing was sloppier. And then, out of nowhere, Garcia would slay his jaded followers with a "Morning Dew" in Maine, or the hottest "Jack Straw" on record in the Syracuse Carrier Dome, making it impossible to quit touring. In another brilliant public relations move, the Grateful Dead sanctioned a taping section at their shows. Now tapers could buy tickets and stroll through security, tape equipment in hand. As Nancy Reagan rolled out her "Just Say No to Drugs" campaign, joining the Grateful Dead caravan was tantalizing. Fans of Dylan and the Dead needed them now more than ever, and these two American institutions would soon cross paths in an improbable twist of cosmic fate.

TEN

WE ARE THE WORLD

"Some artists' work speaks for itself. Some artists' work speaks for its generation. It's my deep personal pleasure to present to you one of America's great voices of freedom. It can only be one man, the transcendent Bob Dylan!"

The Transcendent One appeared center stage to a thunderous ovation in Philadelphia's JFK Stadium after the rousing introduction from Jack Nicholson. Looking sharp with dangling gold earrings, a harmonica rack, and wearing a white suit, Dylan introduced Keith Richards and Ron Wood, and then wondered aloud, "I don't know where they are." Based on the quality of their performance, Ron and Keith didn't seem to know where they were either. It was July 13, 1985, and Dylan was the headline act in the grandest benefit concert ever, Live Aid.

A worldwide audience of one billion were about to witness three legends bumble and stumble through a three-song, fifteen-minute acoustic set. If Dylan was still interested in diminishing his fame, these next fifteen minutes were bound to render him a relic. This was worse self-sabotage than *Self Portrait*.

Instead of warming up with a popular crowd pleaser, Dylan launched into "The Ballad of Hollis Brown," a tale of starvation and desperation that fit in with the theme of raising money to feed people who were starving to death in Ethiopia. If the benefit concert were in an intimate theatre with crisp sound, Dylan might have had a chance. On the JFK stage, Dylan had to contend with feedback from an awful audio setup. And the Rolling Stones guitar heroes bashed at their acoustic guitars as if they had never heard "Hollis Brown" before. Dylan and his friends had been loosening up with a few too many libations in their trailer on this steamy summer's day. Sweat dripped down from Dylan's brow throughout the entire performance.

Before continuing with the musical segment, Dylan said, "Thank you. I thought that was a fitting song for this important occasion. You know while I'm here, I just hope that some of the money that's raised for the people in Africa, maybe they could just take just a little bit of it, 1 or 2 million maybe, and use it to, maybe use it to pay the mortgages on some of the farms, that the farmers here owe to the banks." Helping American farmers was a noble idea, but the focus of this event was saving the lives from a famine that had already starved a million victims. Dylan's suggestion stunned organizers of the event. But if Dylan had not made that statement, would Farm Aid, the charity concert for American farmers that took place a few months later, have materialized as quickly as it did? Probably not.

As if the sound setup wasn't bad enough, Dylan had to deal with the backstage noise of a trial run of the grand finale, "We are the World" as he charged into "When the Ship Comes In." With his peers doing a better job smoking cigarettes with no hands than providing acoustic accompaniment, Dylan's singing veered off course as if he were doing a whiny parody of himself. Before the final number, Dylan asked over the mic, "How much time we got?" There wasn't enough to make amends, yet he couldn't flee from the stage quick enough. Dylan continued to chase the ghost of his past by concluding with "Blowin' in the Wind." Two lines in, Bob began to cough, and later on a string on his guitar broke. Ron Wood gave Bob his guitar, and Dylan rallied to salvage a good rendition of his earliest anthem. However, Dylan came off as a whiny-sounding legend, and this performance was fodder for comedians who impersonated Dylan for laughs.

While Dylan was struggling, and sweating to his oldies in JFK, Jerry was *en fuego* with the Grateful Dead at the Ventura County Fairgrounds on July 13, 1985. As the rest of the planet had their eyes on mega superstars performing at stadiums in Philadelphia and London,

Deadheads swayed and danced in the bliss of their own reality. Three weeks earlier, the Grateful Dead celebrated their twentieth anniversary with three shows at the Greek Theatre in Berkeley. The celebration continued for the rest of the year. In Ventura, there was a giant banner behind the band showing a skeleton with a guitar, dressed and posing like a Minuteman in front of an American flag. The banner read, "Grateful Dead Twenty Years So Far." And after all the shows through the years, they still managed to surprise the crowd with a combo they had never played before.

A decent video of this gig can be found on YouTube. The bootlegger did a nice job focusing on the band with a handheld camera about thirty yards from the stage. At times the video is hazy and the camera strays, but it gives you an authentic feel for what it was like to be in the crowd. Being that it was a Saturday, it was inevitable that the band would play "One More Saturday Night." Instead of playing it as an encore or set ender, the Dead opened the show with it for the first time. Garcia looked much better than he had the year before. In a red shirt and black pants, his trimmed gray mane blew in the Ventura winds, and it was obvious that he'd lost a little weight. Rocking in a light-colored polo shirt and jeans, saliva spritzed through the air as Weir excitedly sang "One More Saturday Night." Feeling adventurous, the band segued into "Fire on the Mountain," as a wildfire burned on a mountain nearby.

Garcia ignited his own blaze with three unique "Fire" solos, balancing creative expression with mathematical precision. Each solo was hotter than the one that preceded it. Garcia's voice was breaking up here and there, but his soulful singing was full of hope. Garcia was locked in—gold-rimmed glasses hanging down at the tip of his nose as he manhandled his Tiger guitar with grace. The final "Fire" solo was a three-tiered gem. Garcia developed an idea, brought it to a logical climax, and then latched onto a different idea and resolved it with a slightly more dramatic climax, and then did it again—three lovely musical paragraphs in an essay. As Live Aid played out worldwide, Deadheads basked in the awe and wonder of their own little universe.

Dylan tunes were regularly featured at Jerry Garcia Band shows, and by the end of 1985, the Grateful Dead had "It's All Over Now, Baby Blue," "Just Like Tom Thumb's Blues," "She Belongs to Me," and "Quinn the Eskimo" in their live rotation, and there would be many more in their near future. A batch of new Grateful Dead songs entered the rotation between 1982 and 1983, yet they were in no rush to return to a recording studio. The growing legion of Dead fans only hungered for more live Jerry, and everybody was content to let the good times roll. The band was expanding their legacy as they easily packed major venues on successive nights. Even though they were performing old songs, everything seemed fresh and exciting to Deadheads. On the other hand, Dylan had a vast, immobilized, and skeptical fan base. Many clamored for the Old Dylan, and their hero was starting to feel like a relic.

Inspired by Dylan's comments at Live Aid, Willie Nelson, Neil Young, and John Melencamp organized Farm Aid to benefit American farmers. Held at Memorial Stadium in Champaign, Illinois, on September 22, 1985, the concert featured performances from the organizers, Billy Joel, B.B. King, Roy Orbison, and Bob Dylan backed by Tom Petty & the Heartbreakers. Dylan, Petty, and Orbison, the three American members of the group that would become the Traveling Wilburys, were performing on the same bill for the first time. Heavily influenced by Dylan, Petty's talented and versatile band featuring guitarist Mike Campbell, keyboardist Benmont Tench, and Stan Lynch on drums, performed admirably during Dylan's six-song set. Three of the tunes were from Dylan's latest studio effort, *Empire Burlesque*.

Although Dylan's showing at Farm Aid was superior to his effort at Live Aid, the public remembered his flop with Wood and Richards, and his nasally/whiny contribution to the number one hit "We Are the World." In the thick of all the iconic voices on that track, Dylan's voice stood out the most, for good or ill.

Empire Burlesque, released a month before Live Aid, was met with critical indifference and mediocre sales. The lyrics included famous lines from classic black-and-white movies. The love songs were a touch sappy, and the female singers were back. There was a laughable MTV video for "Tight Connection to my Heart," a re-write of "Someone's Got a Hold of My Heart," an *Infidels* outtake. The best tracks from this collection were "Seeing the Real You at Last," "I'll Remember You," and "Dark Eyes." In the '60s and '70s, Dylan had uncanny studio mojo. *Empire Burlesque* is a fine collection of songs that lacked an element of passion and purpose, and the production was '80s dull. It was the type of record that wouldn't attract new fans, and it wasn't the antidote those who loved the old Dylan were looking for.

Towards the end of 1985, Columbia Records released a three-CD box set called *Biograph*, a retrospective of Dylan's career including unreleased outtakes and live recordings, with an extensive booklet of liner notes. This was the first box set of its kind from a living artist, and its success set off a box set craze as other major artists scrambled to cash in on the willingness of music lovers to buy retrospective collections with bonus tracks. The liner notes included a revealing interview with Cameron Crow, during which Dylan revealed his weary mind-set: "Sometimes you feel like a club fighter who gets off the bus in the middle of nowhere, punches his way through ten rounds, vomits up the pain in the back room...Sometimes like a troubadour out of the dark ages, singing for your supper and rambling the land."

Biograph gave Dylan fans who weren't privy to his bootlegged material their initial taste of unreleased outtakes, including "Caribbean Wind" and "Groom's Still Waiting at the Altar" from the *Shot of Love* Sessions; "Abandoned Love," a *Desire* outtake; "Up to Me," left off *Blood on the Tracks*; and various outtakes from Dylan's early days. The sequencing and selection of songs on *Biograph* is exquisite. There's a logical pull to the music that makes this a distinctive listening experience. Even though these tracks are chronologically scattered, one song leads to the next, and as a unified work of art it's a thrilling presentation.

Dylan and Garcia were both trapped by their past accomplishments and the baggage of their fame. Jerry was somewhat content doing what he was doing, but he could never free himself from the Grateful Dead family that revolved around him. A hiatus from touring to pursue other musical paths meant unemployment for everyone connected to him through the years. His only other musical outlet was the Jerry Garcia Band.

With the Live Aid debacle, and a retrospective hailing twenty-five years as one of the most important recording artists of his time, Dylan began to believe that he was washed up. Reflecting on this part of his career in *Chronicles*, Dylan wrote, "I'm a '60s troubadour, a folk-rock relic, a wordsmith from bygone days, a fictitious head of state from a place nobody knows." Dylan and the Grateful Dead were about to cross paths and open new and unexpected chapters in their legacies.

Jerry Garcia performing with the JGB. Cheney, Washington, 10-27-78
© Ben Upham www.magicalmomentphotos.com

The Grateful Dead celebrating their twentieth anniversary in the Greek
Theater 6-14-85
© Robbi Cohn www.deadimages.com

Jerry in red with the Dead. Ventura County Fairgrounds, 7-14-85
© Robbi Cohn

Dylan & the Dead in Autzen Stadium, Eugene, Oregon, 7-19-87
© Jay Blakesberg www.blakesberg.com

Dylan and Garcia jamming. Autzen Stadium, Eugene, Oregon, 7-19-87
© Jay Blakesberg

Dylan playing harp in South Hampton, New York, 8-19-02
© Scott Gibson

Dylan crooning at the Indio Polo Club, California, 10-7-16,
© Chad Anderson

Breaking it wide open like the early Roman kings. Indio Polo Club, 10-7-16
© Chad Anderson

ELEVEN

TOO MUCH OF NOTHING

Periods of intense activity for Bob Dylan usually equals outbursts of creative genius. In 1986, Dylan toured with Tom Petty & the Heartbreakers on the same bill with the Grateful Dead, and performed with Stevie Wonder and Dire Straits. He recorded a new album, *Knocked Out Loaded*, released a concert video, *Hard to Handle*, starred in a motion picture, *Hearts of Fire*, and wrote and recorded the title track for the movie *Band of the Hand*. Dylan won an award from the American Society of Composers, and made speeches at events honoring Willie Nelson and Gordon Lightfoot, and gave many revealing interviews to several journalists. For Dylan, and his fans, it was one of the most disappointing years of his career.

After their smooth collaboration at Farm Aid, Dylan asked Petty to tour with him. It was an advantageous proposition for both artists. Petty's career had plateaued by 1985, and the experience of working with Dylan, and introducing his music to an older fan base, was appealing. Conversely, Dylan benefitted from playing with some younger musicians who attracted a younger crowd. Their debut tour kicked off with two shows in New Zealand, followed by thirteen dates in Australia, and concluded with four performances in Japan. The shows featured around twenty-five to twenty-eight songs from Dylan, and usually four songs from Petty & the Heartbreakers without Dylan on stage. Bob mixed new tunes with the expected classics and a compelling batch of covers, such as, "I'll Forget More Than You'll Ever Now," "I'm moving On," "Across the Borderline," and "Uranium Rock." Petty's band easily handled the eclectic mix of songs with skilled professionalism.

The selections for the *Hard to Handle* video were taken from the February 24 and 25 shows at the Entertainment Centre in Sydney, Australia. Dylan looked fit in a black vest and a sleeveless shirt, and his bouffant hairdo was perfect. The footage starts with a rap from Dylan: "Here's a song about my hero. Everybody's got their own hero. I don't know who your hero is. Maybe Mel Gibson. All right! Let's hear it for Mel Gibson. Maybe your hero will be…Michael Jackson. Bruce Springsteen. Oh. Anyway. Now I don't care nothing about none of those people. I got my own hero. I'm gonna sing it…about my hero now." Dylan's hero is Jesus, and he performs a crisp version of "In the Garden." Of the ten songs on this video, four are from Dylan's recent albums, and these versions are clearly better than the studio tracks. Dylan maneuvers confidently with Petty's band. He may have lost some passion for touring as the year moved forward, but there's some excellent performances here. Even the classics "Just Like a Woman," "Like a Rolling Stone," and "Ballad of a Thin Man" are performed well, even though they seem stuck in autopilot mode.

The newer songs, "Lenny Bruce" and "When the Night Come Falling from the Sky," burn with relaxed confidence from the band and the singer, and capture the spark missing from the album versions. "I'll Remember You," a sentimental ballad from *Empire Burlesque*, dazzles in the ninth spot. As Dylan moves to the song's bridge he asks, "Didn't I, Didn't I try to love you?" And adlibs, "Ah, you know I did!" When Dylan has the mojo rolling, he'll occasionally answer the question he poses. Campbell unleashes a concise solo after the final verse, and Dylan leads the continuing charge as the band repeats the triumphant chord progression a few times before sticking a perfect ending. The *Hard to Handle* soundtrack gives off the illusion that "I'll Remember You" segues into "Knockin' on Heaven's Door." There are about twenty songs played between them, but the sequencing is excellent. A vibrant live performance of a new composition shakes hands with a best-ever rendition of an iconic Dylan anthem.

"Knockin' on Heaven's Door" reached No. 12 on the Billboard charts in 1973. The mood, tone, and texture of the two-verse tune was a perfect fit in *Pat Garret & Billy the Kid*. If ever a great Dylan song felt like a demo that was begging to be covered and extended, this was it. The lyrics and emotional ascension towards heaven's door make this an ideal encore, as it was both nights in Sydney. Throughout 1986, Dylan and Petty performed consistently excellent versions of "Knockin' on Heaven's Door," but the one on the video from February 25 is sublime. As Petty and Campbell strum the opening chord progression, Dylan produces a harmonica, assumes a wide stance, wraps his hands around the microphone with the harmonica, and tapping into a spiritual sanctuary, he begins to blow. All the sadness and glory of making the transition to heaven, feelings that can't be captured in prose, pour from Dylan as he bares his soul with eyes closed. Leaning into the solo, Dylan gently rocks the mic stand. He's absorbed in his muse, and his stance is graceful—Rod Carew digging in at the plate with the game on the line.

As Stan Lynch kicks in an authoritative drumbeat, the Maestro takes his right hand off the mic and signals for the band to take it down a notch as he doubles down on the sorrowful feeling—chilling and beautiful. Dylan attentively finishes the solo—every breath perfect and measured, like every grain of sand.

You can hear the brilliance of this harmonica solo without the video, but seeing Dylan in this moment is mesmerizing. After the solo, he strums his acoustic once, and then tries to slip the harmonica in his back pocket. This doesn't work, so he peeks over his left shoulder and nonchalantly tosses his harmonica backstage, to the delight of Campbell. Mike smiles as if he just witnessed Jesus performing a miracle. Dylan has that irresistible allure, an aura of coolness that makes other celebrities awestruck to be in his presence.

Hovered over the same mic, Dylan and Petty sing the entire song together. Dylan's voice dominates, Petty is merely backing him. Bob must have liked the effect of having Petty by his side for the grand finale. This version, which unfolds over eight minutes, has an extra verse, and concise solos from Tench and Campbell. The addition of the "Just like so many times before" line to the chorus after three "knock,

knock, knockin' on heaven's door" chants is a masterful stroke. The song is now complete and its promise unleashed.

In a gracious nod to his backup singers, the Queens of Rhythm, Dylan howls, "Ah tell me about it!" as they chime in with a round of knock-knock-knockin'. As he did during the harp solo, the Maestro slows it down and builds tension by repeating, "Just like so many times before," as the crowd sways prior to the band picking up the pace for the rousing fanfare. Dylan, by his own admission, lost touch with his muse around this time, but on this night in Sydney, he was the Transcendent One.

On March 19, 1986, the Grateful Dead conducted business as usual by kicking off their annual East Coast tour in the Hampton Roads Coliseum, Hampton, Virginia. In the first set, Garcia debuted a deliberate "Visions of Johanna." It was a poignant attempt, but this didn't resonate as well as his last two Dylan breakouts, "She Belongs to Me" and "Quinn the Eskimo." Six nights later, the Dead played their first "Desolation Row." Weir did a fine job tackling Dylan's epic work in the sold-out Philadelphia Spectrum.

After Garcia was busted in his BMW with several bindles of heroin on the north side of Golden Gate Park in January of 1985, he began a plan to slowly ween himself off Persian. By the spring of 1986, he was temporarily free of his addiction. Acquaintances spoke of an attentive Jerry, the guy they knew from years gone by, but it all looked familiar to fans like myself. Jerry may have been a few pounds lighter, but a revitalized Garcia wasn't evident in the performances.

Much of 1985 was a topsy-turvy affair for the band. Just when the Dead would falter with a pair of flat and predictable shows, making me wonder why I was following them, Garcia would turn it around and settle all scores with a scorching performance, as good as anything I'd seen. In the spring of 1986 there were still inconsistencies, and unfortunately, the highs didn't equal those of the year before.

I attended my 100th Grateful Dead show at the Philadelphia Spectrum on March 23, 1986. A one-time-only Gimme Some Lovin' > Deal opened the show, and when Garcia crooned "Candyman" and

"Comes a Time," there wasn't a dry eye in the house. The following two nights at the Spectrum weren't as powerful. The sets from this tour were generally short, and the jams weren't as adventurous as the year before. More than one man's drug habits affect the outcome of a Grateful Dead show, and perhaps the band was stuck in a bit of a rut after the 20th Anniversary Tour.

If the Grateful Dead needed a boost, they were about to play on the same bill with Dylan and Tom Petty & the Heartbreakers at five stadium dates in June and July. Despite not having put out a studio album in six years, the Grateful Dead were a bigger concert attraction than Dylan. When Dylan played with Petty at the Greek Theatre in June, Garcia and Dylan enjoyed each other's company after the show for several hours. Although they'd spent time together before, on this night, they bonded as friends. Ten days prior to the Greek shows, in a secret ceremony, Dylan married Carolyn Dennis, one of his backup singers and mother of his daughter, Desiree. The press and most of Dylan's friends knew nothing of this marriage, which lasted four years.

At the second concert of the tour, in the Rubber Bowl in Akron, Ohio, on July 2, Dylan joined the Grateful Dead on stage for three songs during the first set. Dylan played along on "Little Red Rooster" before the Dead played their only version of "Don't Think Twice It's Alright." It was a rocky adventure because the Dead had a slow, methodical style that didn't naturally match with Dylan's unpredictable cadences and rhythms. Garcia adjusted to Dylan's style nicely, but more practice was needed if Dylan and the Dead were to play together. "It's All Over Now, Baby Blue" was in the Dead's rotation as an encore, but with Dylan on stage, they gave it a go. Garcia took lead vocal and made space for Dylan to join him, but Bob's voice was rough, and didn't mesh with Garcia's polished, high-pitched interpretation. Deadheads roared lustily as Weir thanked Dylan for joining them on stage. "Don't Think Twice It's Alright" showcased that Dylan and Garcia could easily adapt to each other, however, the three-song preview hinted that a possible Dylan/Dead affair wouldn't be as smooth as Dylan's transition to playing with Petty.

On July 4, 1986, the second Farm Aid concert was held in Austin, Texas, as the Grateful Dead and Dylan and Petty performed in Buffalo's Rich Stadium. Both bands contributed short sets to the Farm Aid simulcast. I made the journey out to Buffalo to celebrate American independence with the Grateful Dead, and it would be my first time seeing Dylan live. The Dead opened for Dylan on this occasion. The first set was a six-song flop, brief and insipid. Unbeknownst to most of those in the Dead's inner circle, Garcia began to dabble with coke and heroin again during this summer tour.

Maybe Garcia found himself a nice score between sets because he played like a demon early in set two. The skies turned charcoal gray as howling winds were briefly accompanied by thick raindrops. Tapping into the moment with "Cold Rain & Snow," the band segued into "Fire on the Mountain." Ninety-nine percent of the time, "Fire" was preceded by "Scarlet Begonias." Against a rambunctious beat, Garcia worked the fretboard with blazing precision, as if he could make amends for all the missteps of his recent past. Like a mythical figure, Garcia's guitar playing onslaught continued during a biblical serving of "Samson and Delilah."

Bob Weir welcomed the national TV audience tuned in to Farm Aid. Sufficiently warmed up from the first three songs of set two, the Grateful Dead segued three of their finest compositions: The Wheel > I Need a Miracle > Uncle John's Band. The jams were dynamic without superfluous meandering, and the vocal harmonies were superb. In the second set, Garcia, as he did on many occasions, came off as a heroic figure, doing his best work just when you counted him out. After the TV cameras were turned off, the band reverted to earlier form, hobbling across the finish line. But the brilliance of those six songs created an indelible memory for those on hand.

I stuck around to see more than half of the ensuing Dylan/Petty show. At the time, I was listening exclusively to Grateful Dead and Jerry Garcia Band bootlegs. There were few artists who would have kept me in Rich Stadium after the Dead, but Dylan had my respect, although I'd yet to embrace or understand the full scope of his oeuvre. I was enjoying the show as I kept an eye on the time. I had a ticket for a flight from Buffalo to Newark Airport that forced me to leave early. Leaving Rich Stadium with two small gym bags, I hitched a ride to the airport. A van of hippies heading back to Toronto picked me up. With only a few minutes until my plane took off, I started running through the airport like O.J. Simpson in a Hertz commercial. My heart was pounding as I reached the gate, and I suddenly realized that I'd left one of the gym bags in the van. I zipped open my red Converse bag and saw the plane ticket, my car keys, and a wallet with my license and cash. The other black Puma bag, which had dirty laundry, a toothbrush, toothpaste, and underarm deodorant, was headed across the Canadian border in a Volkswagen van decorated with dancing bear stickers. It wasn't a total bust for the hippies. The bag was rugged and sturdy, and the deodorant would make a nice addition to their hygiene routine. I boarded that plane with seconds to spare.

Deadheads, Dylan, and the Grateful Dead reconvened for a pair of shows at RFK Stadium in Washington, DC on July 6 and 7. The temperature at showtime was 100 degrees with hazy sunshine and stifling humidity for both concerts. Survival and hydration took precedence over transcendent music. The Grateful Dead performances were abysmal. The jams were short, the song selections were unimaginative, and Garcia's performances were consistently lethargic. Dylan seemed to deliver a better show, but I spent most of the time that he was on stage scurrying for shade in the hallways. Dylan added to the Grateful Dead's dilemma by joining them for horrible renditions of "It's All Over Now, Baby Blue" and "Desolation Row." As Dylan's abrasive voice croaked along with Garcia and Weir, it was obvious the Dead had a better handle on these songs. What happened to the confident performer from the *Hard to Handle* video earlier in the year?

After twenty-five years of abusing himself with a plethora of unhealthy habits and addictions, Garcia's stressed body was done in by the extreme weather conditions of the summer tour. Back home in

Marin, three days after the tour, a dehydrated and exhausted Garcia passed out in the bathroom of his house and was found by his house-keeper and confidante, Nora Sage. By the time the ambulance arrived at Marin General Hospital, Garcia had slipped into a diabetic coma with a high fever. For several days Garcia was in and out of the coma, in very serious condition. Garcia's doctors told him that his blood was as thick as mud due to dehydration.

For touring Deadheads the news was shocking, but based on what we'd seen over the previous three years, it should have been predictable. Garcia survived this life-threatening episode, and that was as unbeliev-able as the fact that an episode like this hadn't happened earlier. Luckily, Garcia would have a chance at recovery and a return to performing. There was no permanent nerve or brain damage.

Describing the onset of his coma, Garcia said, "I started feeling like the vegetable kingdom was speaking to me…There were these Italian accents and German accents and it got to be this vast gabbling. Potatoes and radishes and trees were all speaking to me. It finally just reached hysteria and that's when I passed out and woke up in the hospital."

While Garcia was contemplating communications with the vegeta-ble kingdom, the Dylan and Petty tour rolled close to New York City, stopping off at the Brendan Byrne Arena in East Rutherford, New Jersey, on July 21. Dylan had lost many friends and peers over the years, and these were sad times. Earlier in the year, Richard Manuel, keyboardist and vocalist for The Band, committed suicide after a Band concert at the Cheek to Cheek Lounge in Winterpark, Florida. He hung himself from a shower curtain rod in a Quality Inn Motel. And now the road had almost claimed the life of Jerry Garcia.

Dylan was a million miles from sober when he stepped out on the Brendan Byrne stage. A decent bootleg video of this show has made the rounds. Wearing matching black leather pants, vest, and fingerless gloves, Dylan smoked cigarettes, chatted with the audience, chuckled at his own comments, and smoked some more. He seemed more intent on being a talk show host than he was on performing music. At one point, Dylan rambled:

"Is it past anybody's bed time? Ha-ha, it's past mine. I should have been in bed hours ago. Ha-ha-ha. OK it's Tom Petty and the Heartbreakers right here. Benmont Tench playing the keyboards. Come on right up against that . . . .?right up against that, fence whatever it is. Yeah, you can come on right up on stage now if you want to. Lead guitar player, Michael Campbell. One of the best guitar players around. Stan Lynch, one of the finest drummers in all the USA. I know, born in the USA. Well were we all born in the USA, anybody here who wasn't born in the USA? I'd like to meet them. OK, we're gonna sing 'Happy Birthday' right now. We're gonna sing 'Happy Birthday' to the bass guitar player in this band. His name is Howie Epstein. Now you sing all those words what you want, but you sing it. What key we gonna sing it in? He's gonna choose the key himself, it's his birthday."

Following the presentation of cake with candles, Dylan kicked off a round of "Happy Birthday," and the Queens of Rhythm finished it off. Dylan introduced Al Kooper, and for old time's sake they played "Like a Rolling Stone." Dylan chuckled at his vocal sloppiness as he skipped through his most beloved song without any emotional attachment.

A few weeks after the Brendan Byrne show, *Knocked Out Loaded* was released. It was Dylan's poorest-selling album since his eponymous debut. "Brownsville Girl" was hailed as a minor masterpiece, and "Maybe Someday" and "Under Your Spell" were decent new compositions. Dylan mixed in some random covers, and the entire album suffered from lack of ingenuity and subpar production.

Twenty-five years of songwriting and recording left Dylan drained, and his enthusiasm for touring waned. After his final show of the True Confessions tour with Petty, in Paso Robles, California, on August 6, Dylan took an eleven-month break from the road. With Garcia recovering from a coma and other serious health issues, the future of the Grateful Dead was uncertain. Little did any members of the Grateful Dead, or Dylan, realize they were simply turning a page and embarking on the next thirty years of their musical odyssey.

TWELVE

THE RESURRECTION OF JERRY

" **I** 'm not Beethoven," declared Garcia when he came out of the coma. He had awareness and his hearing was fine, but doctors feared Jerry might not walk again. From talking and walking to playing guitar, Garcia would have to relearn everything. Friends and family were by his side. His ex-wives, Sara and Mountain Girl, were there, as well as his brother, Tiff, and his daughters, Annabelle, Trixie, and Heather. Deadhead Nation was praying for him and sending positive energy and healing vibes. Mountain Girl, Trixie, and Annabelle moved in with Jerry to help him coalesce.

One of Jerry's oldest friends and musical collaborators, Merl Saunders, was there to assist Jerry's recovery every step of the way. They talked and went for short walks as the pathways of Jerry's brain circuitry slowly began to function properly. When Jerry picked up the guitar again, he had to relearn chords, and Merl was patiently by his side encouraging him. "I had to do everything at least once to remind my muscles about how something worked," said Garcia. "It was the thing of making the connection between mind and muscles."

Only five weeks after Jerry came out of the coma, he called John Kahn and had him arrange some Jerry Garcia Band practice sessions. As crazy as it was unfathomable, the Jerry Garcia Band would play two club shows at the Stone in San Francisco on October 4 and 5. The 1,600 tickets sold out instantly. Garcia was getting back to doing what he loved, but sadly, there was another motivation to his hasty return. Garcia was in debt, and his bank account was overdrawn.

Considering Garcia's brush with death, the results of the Stone shows are stunning. Jerry relied on the music of Dylan to express himself on this poignant night. Garcia's first version of "Forever Young" was the second song of the night, and the two-set, twelve-song show concluded with "Tangled Up in Blue." The spirit of Dylan was with Jerry on the night of his improbable return. The following night at the Stone, JGB performed "I Shall Be Released" and "Knockin' on Heaven's Door." There were ten Jerry Garcia Band shows and an acoustic performance from Kahn and Garcia before the long, strange trip continued.

On December 15, 1986, the Grateful Dead were back in business, performing the first of three shows in the Oakland Coliseum Arena. Deadheads rejoiced when Jerry hit the stage and the band bolted into "Touch of Grey." There were collective tears of joy when Garcia sang, "I will survive," and the entire joint sang, "We will survive," in celebration. Although Jerry looked thinner and fragile, he smiled like he hadn't smiled on stage in a long time. And everyone making a living officially, or unofficially, from the band, would continue to cash in, and the Grateful Dead economy would explode beyond expectations moving forward. Garcia still needed to do a lot of work to get his guitar chops back to where they were, but just to get back to this point was impressive.

Why Garcia rushed back into performing so quickly is an interesting question. If ever he had an opportunity to at least temporarily free himself from the Grateful Dead, this was the moment. No one would have begrudged him for taking off at least six months, or a year, to get himself healthier. But the Grateful Dead had become a peaceful, hedonistic music mafia, and Garcia was the Godfather. Garcia was a kind soul who rolled and flowed with fate, and he accepted his role as patriarch of this movement born on the streets of San Francisco. It was all he'd known. Garcia's friend from Hibbing, Mr. Dylan, fought against those who tried to anoint him, stamp him, or label him. After the disappointing *Knocked Out Loaded*, Dylan's confidence was fading, yet he was free to do as he pleased. His next adventure was a journey into the Twilight Zone, as

Dylan starred in a movie as Billy Parker, an aging rock star living on a chicken farm.

Dylan's co-stars in *Hearts of Fire* were Fiona Flannigan and Rupert Holmes. The film was shot in Canada and the United Kingdom. It's an awful movie that was unanimously declared a disaster by critics. At least this film wasn't a blemish on Dylan's resume, because unlike *Renaldo and Clara*, he wasn't responsible for any part of the screenplay. However, Dylan's screen presence is the one redeeming attribute of this atrocity, and the soundtrack has a strong performance of Dylan covering John Hiatt's "The Usual." *Dont Look Back* captured Dylan as an enigmatic visionary exploding on the worldwide scene, a wiry, witty hipster simultaneously charming and challenging his audiences. Playing the role of Billy Parker didn't require much preparation. These days, Dylan was living the part.

Dylan's final public appearance of the year was in Toronto, to present Gordon Lightfoot the Canadian Music Hall of Fame Award. Looking glamorous in a white dress, Canadian country and pop star Anne Murray introduced Dylan. The cameras couldn't find Dylan in the maze of spotlights and translucent curtains. Eventually Bob appeared, and he had to walk across the front of the stage to get to the little podium on the other side for his presentation. Looking very '80s, with black gloves and prancing across the stage in a suit Prince might have worn, Dylan looked back at Anne Murray twice to make sure he was heading in the right direction. It was a very odd setup.

As Dylan arrived at his mini-stage, the loud cheers morphed into a standing ovation. Reacting as if he was still Billy Parker, the ex-rock star living on a chicken farm, Bob turned away from the audience and looked at the bank of TV screens behind him to see who this Dylan guy was. It was surreal watching Dylan watching himself on a stack of video screens with his back turned to an audience of celebrities paying homage to him. In a brief speech, Dylan mentioned that Gordon had previously turned down this award because he wanted Bob to be the one to introduce him. This is one of a series of arcane live Dylan moments that can be viewed on YouTube.

Dylan didn't have much of an agenda as 1987 began. Out on the West Coast, a revitalized Jerry Garcia immersed himself in several projects. In January, the band began to record tracks that they had been playing for several years to make a new album of originals titled *In the Dark*, which was produced in-house by Garcia and John Cutler, with input from other members of the band. To capture the essence of the Grateful Dead sound, the band set up on stage in the Marin Veterans Auditorium and played the songs as if there was an audience there. The instrumental and vocal overdubs were recorded at Club Front Studios for final mixing.

Garcia and Len Dell'Amico finished off *So Far*, a long form video of rehearsal footage mixed with live performances. There's some interesting black-and-white film and photos throughout the video, and quality camera angles of the band as they jammed. Throw in excellent sound quality, and we have a technically superb product. Unfortunately, the video doesn't capture the band's X factor. *So Far* displays second set songs in a segment just under one hour. "Terrapin Station" is reduced to just the first part, "Lady with a Fan," before it's segued into space and drums, and more space. Any music fan would find the ending of "Terrapin Station" more rewarding than a percussion duet. The Uncle John's Band > Playing in the Band opening to the video is hot. The ending combo, Throwing Stones > Not Fade Away is about as commercial as the Grateful Dead gets in concert. If you take the video away, the music is not something that a seasoned Deadhead would fixate upon, and if I was trying to turn somebody on to the Grateful Dead, there's a multitude of superior videos that capture the X factor.

Grateful Dead popularity had been on the rise all decade, and now that their beloved leader was on the mend and touring again, there was palpable excitement. The East Coast spring tour began with three shows in Hampton. I saw the following pair of shows in the Hartford Civic Center on March 26 and 27. My experience at the second gig best sums up the overwhelming glory, and occasional frustration, I'd experience on this tour.

The venue was overcrowded inside and out. The aisles and hallways were packed with spinning dancers as the Dead sleepwalked through the first seven songs. "The Music never Stopped" closed the set. Garcia's guitar playing down the stretch was stupendous. As the jam boiled, the audience roared, and Garcia found a way to feed off that energy and invented a route to extend the climax without ever becoming redundant. It was easily the best "The Music Never Stopped" I'd ever seen, and more importantly, it was evidence that Garcia was back, and there was hope that he might be better than ever.

"Touch of Grey" opened set two, and the explosion of noise and happiness from the crowd had Garcia smiling throughout. Garcia lost some steam during a flat Estimated Prophet > Eyes of the World. After drums, set two concluded with Uncle John's Band > Morning Dew. When Jerry broke into that "Dew," the collective excitement of the moment was overwhelming. Running on fumes, Jerry managed to channel his emotions through a weary voice, and the final solo thrilled us all. As the Comeback Tour rolled on, there would be those occasional tunes where Garcia would amaze, sandwiched in between average or lackluster performances. Regardless, the quality of these shows went beyond the expectations of most.

During the Comeback Tour, my musical universe was pried open by Dylan. For six years, I thrived on nothing but Grateful Dead and Jerry Garcia Band bootlegs. I was a twenty-three-year-old college student studying history at the State University of New York at New Paltz. History is an ideal major to have when your only real interest is hedonism. I'd been sharing a house for three months with my friend Phil, who was a Deadhead and Dylan enthusiast. Since we went to Dead shows together, and that was our common ground, he never pushed the Dylan issue with me. "Like a Rolling Stone" was my favorite tune, and I enjoyed the standard Dylan anthems, but I never owned any of his albums besides his two volumes of greatest hits.

I woke up on Monday morning April 6, 1987, in a fabulous mood, knowing I was going to see the Grateful Dead at the Brendan Byrne

Arena that evening. My maroon '78 Chevy Caprice Classic was in a body shop for minor repairs, so I borrowed Phil's car to score a cup of coffee. Dylan's "Tangled Up in Blue," was playing in the tape deck, but since this was just a two-minute ride, I skipped going back into the house to get a Dead tape. Whistling to Dylan's harp solo, I pulled into the parking lot of McPeady's, the local convenience store, dropped a few ice cubes into a large cup of pipin' hot black java, and drove away.

As I headed home on Route 32 North, the opening riff of the next tune sounded familiar. Dylan's voice shattered the serenity: "We sat together in the dark, as the evening sky grew dark." I couldn't believe it, but I had never heard Dylan's "Simple Twist of Fate," a tune Garcia's band covered. The cadence and intensity of Dylan's voice made my head want to spin. Garcia's version was thoughtful and poignant, but this was enormous. The acoustic arrangement was elegant and hypnotic as Dylan's voice jabbed and danced with supreme authority. I knew I was stepping into something much bigger than the tape I was listening to.

"Oh, I know where I can find you, in somebody's room. It's a price I have to pay. You're a big girl all the way," crooned Dylan. I couldn't name this tune, which had the same magical quality as its predecessors. I tried to make sense of what I was hearing ("You're a Big Girl Now"), when Dylan exclaimed, "Someone's got it in for me, they're planting stories in the press." Each succeeding notion from Dylan seemed to gobble up the one before it until the final chorus climaxed: "We are idiots, babe. It's a wonder we can even feed ourselves." I had to find out the name of this album. And if Dylan was capable of this, how about the albums that "Like a Rolling Stone" and "Mr. Tambourine Man" were on? There had to be gold in those mines. I also realized that Route 32 North had ended as I reached a traffic circle in the city of Kingston. I had driven twenty minutes past my home in a car that wasn't mine.

After I charged through the front door, Phil informed me that I was hijacked by *Blood on the Tracks*. Over the next few weeks, I hunted down every Dylan album at various record shops in Ulster County.

Dylan's oeuvre became my curriculum—gateways to alternate thinking: A Jew saved by Jesus, *Slow Train Coming*; a rebel on the road sneering at the world, *Highway 61 Revisited;* an icon airing dirty laundry, *Street Legal*; a lone voice against social injustice, *The Times They Are A-Changin'*; a carefree crooner singing love's praises, *Nashville Skyline*; a poet changing the foundation of popular music, *Bringing It All Back Home*. I even loved *Knocked Out Loaded*. Sure, it wasn't on par with those other albums, but it's a lot easier to appreciate an album like that when it's part of a massive archive.

My Dylan revelation happened exactly five years after the Grateful Dead show that changed my life in Philadelphia on April 6, 1982. These were two worlds, or genres, in the bigger universe of modern music. Dylan and Garcia, students during the birth of rock and roll, were now the two most bootlegged performers of their time. There was a fanatic with a tape recorder anytime they breathed publicly because they were essential figures in the history of American music.

Now that I was gung-ho for everything Dylan and Dead, the most incredible thing happened. It was announced that the Grateful Dead would be Dylan's backing band for a series of stadium shows over the summer, and the Dead would also perform their own show at the same concert.

THIRTEEN

DAYS OF MIRACLE AND WONDER

P lans for the upcoming tour were discussed when Dylan was on hand for the Grateful Dead's last gig of a three-night stand at the Henry J. Kaiser Convention Center in Oakland on March 3, 1987. Jerry was in a celebratory mood, opening the show with "Quinn the Eskimo," and Dylan was in the audience swaying to his song, which was performed more in the style of Manfred Mann's hit version. Dylan was also photographed backstage with the Grateful Dead by Herb Greene. Before rehearsing with the Dead in May, Dylan spent the early part of the year involved in an assortment of recording activities and guest appearances.

On February 19, 1987, Dylan, George Harrison, and John Fogerty guest appeared at a Taj Mahal concert at the Palomino Club in Hollywood. They played an unrehearsed eighteen-song set based on the formative days of rock and roll. Dylan was lead vocal on only one number, singing Buddy Holly's "Peggy Sue" with Harrison. This was their first live performance together since the Concert for Bangladesh, and it would be their last, although they'd soon collaborate as members of the Traveling Wilburys.

Around this time, Dylan wrote and recorded "Wish I Know Now What I Knew Then" with Ringo Starr and his band in Memphis, Tennessee. The song has never been released. Dylan also played harmonica on a tune at a Warren Zevon recording session. Undoubtedly, Dylan's most famous collaboration was with U2's Bono on "Love Rescue Me." The words came to Bono in a dream, and he thought it might have been part of a Dylan song, so he called Bob to ask him. It wasn't a Dylan song, but the two of them got together, finished writing the tune, and later in the year, Dylan joined U2 in the studio to record it for the album *Rattle and*

Hum. Talking about the song's meaning, Bono said, "It's about a man people keep turning to as a savior but his own life is getting messed up and he could use a bit of salvation himself."

In March, Dylan began recording his new album, *Down in the Groove*, which would be released the following summer. This album's another grab bag of originals, covers, and collaborations. Dylan found two songs that he liked from Robert Hunter's notebook and created arrangements for them. "The Ugliest Girl in the World" is a spoof on the vanity of beauty that would have been better off buried in Hunter's notebook. The other tune, "Silvio," is a song of an outlaw, or rambling troubadour, reflecting on his existence. It conjures up that Old Weird America similar to Hunter's compositions on *Europe '72*, and it has a rough Dylanesque edge to it. Some have surmised that Hunter wrote "Silvio" as a portrait of Dylan. The opening verse sounds autobiographical as Dylan sings, "Stake my future on a hell of a past. Looks like tomorrow is a coming on fast. Ain't complaining about what I got. Seen better times but who has not." Garcia chimes in on the background vocals for the pleasant studio track that could have benefited from an infusion of electric Garcia. "Silvio" achieved its potential as a fiery rocker for many years as a live staple during Dylan's Never Ending Tour.

The performances on *Down in the Groove* had a more authentic Dylan sound than *Knocked Out Loaded*, although it contained nothing as epic as "Brownsville Girl." "Let's Stick Together" and "When Did You Leave Heaven?" were spirited covers, but not the type of material one would hope for on a Dylan album. The most encouraging part of the album was the last two tracks, a quirky arrangement of the traditional tune "Shenandoah" and Albert E. Brumley's "Rank Strangers to Me." The latter tune is a chilling vocal performance—Dylan's alive inside the song. It's a bleak statement that captures the dark side, and never before could Dylan have tackled this song with so much authority. It's also a signpost on the road Dylan was heading down for his next creative outburst. "Rank Strangers" is a close relative of "Man in the Long Black Coat," Dylan's brilliant original on *Oh Mercy* (1989).

Dylan was a stranger to his own songs when he arrived at Club Front Studio in May to rehearse with the Grateful Dead for their upcoming six-show summer tour. The Dead had a list of Dylan songs ranging from obvious to obscure. Overwhelmed by the multitude of material that he had forgotten, or felt no connection to, Dylan split the studio and considered walking away from the project. In *Chronicles*, Dylan described leaving the studio to go for a walk in the drizzling rain and stumbling upon a tiny bar where some jazz cats were playing. He went into the sparsely crowded bar, ordered a gin and tonic, and observed a singer who reminded him of Billy Eckstein. The vocalist sang with graceful confidence, and was using a technique familiar to Bob to arrive at his power. Dylan doesn't go into any technical description of what the technique was, but it was something that he used to do. After this encounter, Dylan felt he could push through the obstacles he was facing, and after struggling a bit, he was willing to attempt anything the Dead threw at him. Since Dylan's descriptions of this event are vague, it's possible that this scene is nothing more than a dream.

Reflecting on the Washington, DC, shows when Dylan appeared on stage with the Dead, Garcia said, "I found myself in the weird position of teaching Dylan his own songs. It's just really strange! It was funny. He was great. He was so good about all this stuff. Weir wanted to do Desolation Row with him, y'know, and it's got a million words. So Weir says, 'Are you sure you'll remember all the words?' And Dylan says, 'I'll remember the important ones.'"

These sessions from dates in May and June produced bits and pieces from a vast landscape of music covering several decades. The Dylan material included expected classics intertwined with numerous surprise selections from Dylan's recent albums and "Walkin' Down the Line," an unreleased early composition. Dylan and the Dead explored their shared favorite artists, like Buddy Holly, Hank Williams, Johnny Cash; and there were a few completely unexpected numbers from contemporary peers. Dylan's atonal singing and odd phrasing often sounded clumsy against the Dead's methodically patient tempos. A lot of the tracks from these sessions were snippets of songs and aborted attempts. Yet, a talented sound engineer could find a way to salvage twenty-five of these tracks to create a worthwhile official release.

"The Boy in the Bubble" from Paul Simon's 1986 album *Graceland* was one of the surprise delights of this rehearsal. The arrangement was crisp and the voices of Dylan, Garcia, and Weir meshed. I don't think there was serious thought put into playing this live, but the chorus was ideal for the situation, "These are the days of miracle and wonder. This is the long distance call. The way the camera follows us in slo-mo. The way we look to us all." It would have thrilled packed stadiums of Dylan and Dead fans.

One of Dylan's best performance from these tapes was on Luke McDaniel's "Go Ahead Baby." This was the exception from a singer who for the most part sounded sloppy and detached. Dylan pleads, "Go ahead baby come awwwn! Don't keep me waiting too long." Dylan's holding notes, smoothly changing pitch, and clearly annunciating like he did at the start of his first tour with Petty.

Looking at songs that weren't played on the upcoming tour, "Gonna Change My Way of Thinking" is the standout Dylan original from the rehearsals. Musically, the Dylan and Dead are locked into the same frequency, and Dylan's fully committed to the performance, even if he can't remember the words. He gets the first verse right, and then makes up dummy lyrics before singing, "Jesus said, 'Be ready, for you know not the hour in which I come," after which he howls, "No!" The Holy Spirit is flowing through the Maestro. Words and verse sequence be damned. Feeding off Dylan's energy, Garcia uncorks a sizzling solo and the band returns to a thundering chord progression, authoritative and triumphant. Brent Mydland's filling in the gaps with soulful organ grinding. Dylan follows with the last verse, "There's a kingdom called heaven." In mathematical Garcia guitar progression, the next solo plays off its predecessor and eclipses it. Dylan passes on an opportunity to sing another verse. He forgot most of the words, but he remembered the important ones. Dylan and the Dead captured the spirit of "Change My Way of Thinking," perhaps better than the original.

Jerry and his mates tested Dylan on his recent material as they played three tunes from both *Slow Train Coming* and *Shot of Love*, and a pair of songs from both *Knocked Out Loaded* and *Infidels*. The Dead worked up a funky reggae-influenced arrangement for "In the Summertime." Had the Dylan/Dead tour found its way into a few intimate venues, this would have been a colorful addition to the set lists. In Club Front studio, they also played striking acoustic versions of "Stealin'" and "Rollin in My Sweet Baby's Arms." "Walkin' Down the Line," "When I Paint my Masterpiece," and "Folsom Prison Blues" are some of the other tunes worthy of honorable mention that weren't played on the upcoming tour. A Dylan/Dead acoustic/electric affair would have been interesting.

After the Grateful Dead played a show at Laguna Seca in Monterey in May, a thousand fans were invited to cheer the band on as they played "Touch of Grey" for an MTV video. Gary Gutierrez, who worked his animation magic for the opening scene of *The Grateful Dead* movie, conceived of having life-size skeleton puppets of each band member playing "Touch of Grey" until they transformed into the real band members for the last verse, and the rousing "We will survive" climax. Smiling all the way, Garcia looked like the healthiest gray-haired guitarist on the scene.

The video debuted on MTV on June 19. MTV executives and their audience were thrilled with the video, which was unique in the monotonous shuffle of heavy metal videos featuring long-haired musicians lusting after scantily dressed models. Suddenly, a new generation of young Americans were turned on to an alternate reality, the chill, retro Haight-Ashbury hippie party, courtesy of the Grateful Dead and Deadheads.

The first Dylan/Dead show was held on July 4 in Foxboro Stadium, home of the New England Patriots. This promising All-American affair was disappointing. The parking lots were filled early due to the onslaught of Deadheads, forcing people to park many miles from the football stadium. The year before, the Grateful Dead endured brutal heat during their final shows in Washington, DC, and they faced more of the same in Foxboro.

They opened for Dylan in Foxboro and played a sluggish and unimaginative one-set show. This was not a good omen for the upcoming Dylan/Dead set. This was Dylan's first show in eleven months, and he was rustier than an old dirt shovel in a porous toolshed. This show is only noteworthy because Dylan played his first live versions of "Queen Jane Approximately and "Joey," and he also performed "John Brown" and "Chimes of Freedom" for the first time since 1963 and 1964 respectively.

Dylan had six days off before his next appearance with the Dead. Garcia and company had business to attend to, playing a show in Pittsburg and two in Roanoke, Virginia, before reconvening with Dylan on July 10. These were optimistic times for Deadheads and the band, and nobody was questioning the sanity of what they were doing. Garcia was knocking on death's door less than a year earlier, and now he was working harder than he had all decade. Garcia's recovery seemed unstoppable, yet there were gigs like Foxboro where a lethargic Garcia simply made it to the finish line.

Nobody questioned whether the band should be on the road playing gigs in between the taxing Dylan/Dead shows. A commercial whirlwind engulfed the band. After thriving for twenty-plus years as counterculture heroes making their own rules, the band and their extended family savored the unexpected commercial success. They were on the verge of becoming an American institution—baseball, hot dogs, apple pie, and Grateful Dead. Lost in the economic windfall was Garcia's health. He never had a chance to properly rehab and recover. His wondrous comeback once again made him seem like the grandfatherly guitar Buddha.

In the Dark was released on July 6, and it peaked in the sixth spot on the Top 200 album chart. "Touch of Grey" would become the Grateful Dead's first hit single in a few months. The album brings out the essence of the songs, and the studio production is pristine. That being stated, it's not the band's best studio album because the songs aren't equal to the quality of those on *American Beauty* or *Workingman's Dead*. Time was on the Dead's side. If they had recorded these new songs back in 1983, it's unlikely the album would have turned out as good. "Touch of Grey" would not have emerged as a hit song or resonated the way it did in 1987. Most fans enjoyed "Touch of Grey" when it joined the rotation, but it was never a cherished number until the 20th Anniversary Tour.

"Black Muddy River," a Hunter/Garcia dirge, was the newest composition added to *In the Dark*. It had a traditional folk flavor, and it was typical of the songs Hunter and Garcia would compose moving forward. Bob Weir contributed two strong tunes to the album, "Hell in a Bucket" and "Throwing Stones," a politically charged second set showpiece. These songs flourished in concert back in '83 and '84. It's ironic that the Dead were getting acknowledged for music that materialized in what is perceived to be one of their darkest eras.

I recall listening to *In the Dark* on the way to Philadelphia for the second Dylan/Dead show in JFK Stadium. The cassette tape included an outtake of Weir and Barlow's "Brother Esau." The long set of music that the band played to open the festivities on 7-10-87 was a more interesting listen than the new album. Garcia's guitar forays were precise and explosive as the band opened with "Iko Iko," "Jack Straw," and "Sugaree." Other highlights included "Cassidy," "China Cat > Rider," and "Terrapin Station." A positive vibe filled the air heading into the Dylan segment.

Dylan and the Dead greeted a fired-up crowd with "Tangled Up in Blue." The Dead played it in the style of Jerry Garcia Band, and Dylan strung the lyrics out in an interesting chant that might have worked if a different band backed him. Garcia, a considerate player, was cautious about jamming and stepping on Dylan. Garcia played pedal steel guitar on "I'll Be Your Baby Tonight," something he hadn't done prior to this tour since 1970. Wearing a red jacket and black beret, Dylan was bobbing and weaving like a dazed fighter as he shouted lines and hung onto syllables uncomfortably long, in a self-mocking manner. Dylan's live debut of "Frankie Lee and Judas Priest" was solid as he managed to remember most of the words. There was still room for improvement, but the JFK show was worth seeing. As a veteran Deadhead and a neophyte Dylanologist, I was a thrilled historical witness, and I expected great things from the upcoming show in Giants Stadium.

FOURTEEN

BORN AGAIN IN THE SWAMPS

On Sunday July 12, 1987, Bonnie Tyler's "Total Eclipse of the Heart" was the number one Billboard single, and Stephen King's *Misery* sat atop the New York Times Best Seller list. Like the hobbled protagonist of *Misery*, Dylan was crippled by fame and out of touch with his muse. Ten miles east of Giants Stadium stood the majestic skyline of Manhattan, the island where the myth and legend of Bob Dylan took flight. If Dylan took the time to think about his early days in the village, it must have seemed like those events happened in another lifetime. Surrounded by highways, swamps, and sweaty hippies on this ninety-five-degree day in East Rutherford, New Jersey, Dylan would receive a lifeline from the Dead.

Instead of playing a long set before taking the stage with Dylan, the Grateful Dead returned to their standard two set format. It was a strong outing for the band, and outside of opening the second set with "Morning Dew," there was nothing exceptional about it. A great roar filled Giants Stadium as Dylan appeared on stage with the Dead by his side, and the intoxicating aroma of kind bud quelled the stench of East Rutherford.

I lost my friends so I could take in this part of the show by myself. I had an uncanny sense that this would be a special show. My recollections of this concert have been fortified by the tapes and a high-quality video. Looking scruffy cool with his acoustic guitar slinging low, Dylan wore an unbuttoned, long-sleeve gold shirt, black beret, and there was a fingerless black glove on his axe-picking hand. "Slow Train Coming" opened the journey. Dylan's posture was excellent as he strummed and sang in an engaged manner. From the left side of the stage, Garcia was enthralled, and he looked comfortable and content, as did Bob Weir in his SEVA t-shirt and Daisy Duke shorts.

Hesitation and tentativeness were not an option for Dylan or Garcia. It was as if they had made a pact before the show. At the onset of "Stuck Inside of Mobile with the Memphis Blues Again," Dylan barked out the lyrics in garbled fashion but he never backed off, and by the third verse, the storyteller fired off the lyrics as if he was awed by them for the first time. The Grateful Dead delivered an arrangement paced for Dylan's style, and they left room for two concise solos. The band would add "Stuck Inside of Mobile" to their repertoire after parting ways with Dylan, and Garcia would always take two solos. On this night, after hearing Dylan passionately holler, "Oh MAMA! Can this really be the END?" Garcia adds a third solo, setting the tone for a run of heroic performances.

Garcia makes the move to pedal steel as the only live Dylan/Dead performance of "Tomorrow is a Long Time" follows. The band serves a lovely country-tinged rendition as Dylan grumbles and growls the lyrics as if he never heard the song before. But after singing the chorus with Jerry, Bob, and Brent, and digging Jerry's steel pedal picking, Dylan finds the emotional texture and howls the last verse with a loving feeling.

Cruising along "Highway 61," Dylan chuckled when he sang, "Found a promoter who nearly fell off the floor, yeah-eah, I never did engage in this kind of thing before, yeah-eah." Dylan unexpectedly realized the irony of the lyrics as he was singing them, because he never did engage in this kind of thing before. Dylan was always the alpha male leading the musical charge. In Giants Stadium, the de facto leader was Jerry Garcia. In a 2006 interview for *Rolling Stone* with Jonathan Lethem, Dylan said, "The Dead did a lot of my songs, and we'd just take the whole arrangement because they did it better than me. Jerry Garcia could hear the song in all my bad recordings—the song that was buried there." Garcia played a mean slide guitar during "Highway 61 Revisited." As experimental as the Dead's music was, Garcia was surrounded by the same musicians, with the Jerry Garcia Band as his only other musical outlet. Performing with Dylan was the fulfillment of a fantasy, and it was an opportunity for Jerry to step outside his comfort zone.

After exiting "Highway 61," the performers attempted "It's All Over Now, Baby Blue." The last two times Dylan and the Dead tried this in '86, the results were disastrous. Once again, the timing of Dylan's singing/shouts were awkward, but he advanced confidently, and by the second verse he found a way to match his rapid-fire phrasing to the Dead's leisurely arrangement. As Garcia sang, "And it's all over now, baby blue," Dylan blasted everything but the last two words, and waited for Garcia to catch up, and with the same cadence as before, hollered, "Baby Blue!" Without altering his approach, Dylan made it happen. And Garcia expressed his love of the moment with a second solo. In Grateful Dead history, this is the only "Baby Blue" with two solos, just as the earlier "Stuck Inside of Mobile" is the only one with three solos.

Something was happening as Dylan and the Dead launched "Ballad of a Thin Man," a third consecutive foray into Dylan's visionary mid-'60s music. There's intense pride on the faces of Weir and Garcia as they hear Dylan deliver all the right lyrics. Garcia plays licks in response to what Dylan's singing. The timing of all the musicians is uncanny as Brent strikes some powerful chords after Dylan blasts the "contacts among the lumberjacks" bridge. Dylan acknowledges Brent's contribution with an emphatic, "Oh yeah!" Garcia's exquisite, mind-melting ending solo creates a vibe of psychedelic confusion. There's a little bit of Mr. Jones in all of us.

After the Dead help Dylan revive "John Brown," an unreleased anti-war tale from Dylan's early days, twilight faded into darkness as the musicians tuned-up against a background of flickering cigarette lighters. One of the massive video screens hovering over Giants Stadium lit up with the image of Garcia as his axe announced the coming of "Wicked Messenger" from *John Wesley Harding*, a number that Dylan had never played live. One of Garcia's bands, Legion of Mary, covered

"Wicked Messenger" a handful of times in 1975. Dylan stepped up to the mic and bellowed, "There was a wicked messenger from Eli he did come!" His visceral, preacher-like vocals matched the biblical bent of the song. If Dylan's attentive singing was any indication, he was moved by the Garcia's cascading blues riff and the thunderous sound of the band. When Garcia heard Dylan howl, "The soles of my feet, I swear, they're burning," his nimble fingers wiggled across the fretboard like dancing sausages. Dylan swayed and staggered across the stage, mesmerized by Garcia's outburst. I was awestruck in the audience— a moment of instant revelation—one of the hottest guitar solos I ever heard. "If you can't bring good news then don't bring any," sang Dylan, and the Dead closed it out by pounding the blues-infused melody line one more time. Garcia and Weir stood proud. Dylan looked possessed. Mission accomplished.

I had no idea of the historical ramifications of the performance (Dylan's debut of "Wicked Messenger"), or the mid-life creative malaise that Dylan was experiencing, but I felt like I'd just witnessed a healing. This exceeded any preconceived fantasy of what I thought might happen with Garcia and Dylan on stage. The following presentations of two of my favorite songs, "Queen Jane Approximately" and "Chimes of Freedom," were slightly off the mark, although "Chimes" had a scintillating final vocal flurry from Dylan.

The tune that echoed through my head following the concerts in Foxboro and JFK was the epic gangster tune from *Desire*, "Joey." In my brief tenure as a Dylan connoisseur, I'd overlooked the power of this tune. By Dylan's side, Garcia crooned the chorus with conviction: "Joey, Joey. King of the streets, child of clay. Joey, Joey. What made them want to come and blow you away?" And with the Dead pounding the chord progression in a resounding manner, this "Joey" destroys the album version. As Dylan stood on a stage built over the end zone of a football field, where it was rumored that Teamsters boss Jimmy Hoffa was buried, Dylan took on the persona of a mobster and told the tale of Joey Gallo as if he were a sworn witness.

From the cradle, "Born in Red Hook Brooklyn," to the grave "One day they blew him down in a clam bar in New York," Dylan casts a spell over Giants Stadium, holding his guitar like a rifle as he stares straight ahead and sneers. All five verses are rendered in perfect sequence, and Dylan delivers the facts with the swagger of a raconteur in a social club. As Dylan performs, the projection machine rolls in the minds of the audience. Dylan was viscerally reconnected to a song he had left for dead.

In a 1991 interview with Paul Zollo, Dylan said, "To me, that's a great song. Yeah. And it never loses its appeal…That's a tremendous song. And you'd only know it singing it night after night. You know who got me singing that song? Garcia. Yeah. He got me singing that song again. He said that's one of the best songs ever written. Coming from him, it was hard to know which way to take that. [Laughs] He got me singing that song with them again… But, to me, Joey has a Homeric quality to it that you don't hear every day."

Garcia's guitar prowess was on display again during "All Along the Watchtower," which I thought would end the most thrilling set of music I'd ever witnessed. As the smoldering remains of the last jam touched down, Dylan hollered, "Thank you. Grateful Dead!" Dylan played 36 shows in 1987, and the only other time he spoke to the audience was when he said, "Shalom!" after playing "Highway 61" in Tel Aviv on September 5. Dylan was obviously moved by the performance of the Dead on this night. He strummed a few chords, and then Bob's next spoken/sung words were, "Come gather 'round people, wherever you roam." I believe Jerry and friends were caught off guard by this, but they were happy to work overtime. Jerry filled in the space between Dylan's timeless lines with lively licks. As I stood amongst the faithful in Giants Stadium, lunatic tears of joy rolled down my face. This moving rendition of "The Times They Are A-Changin'" still chokes me up every time I hear it.

Unbelievably, after a five-hour production, the Grateful Dead came out with Dylan for a double encore, and Dylan played guitar during "Touch of Grey." "We will get by-eye-eye, we will survive" never sounded better than hearing Weir and Garcia sing it with Dylan in between them. "Knockin' on Heaven's Door" was the gentle farewell to the wondrous affair. It was a lazy version, but it was amazing they were still playing. I was a reasonably fit twenty-four-year-old, and I was on the verge of collapse.

Following a week of rest, the Dead and Dylan headed west to play their last three concerts in Eugene, Oakland, and Anaheim. I'm not sure what happened, but the budding momentum of the tour crashed. The Eugene show wasn't much better than Foxboro, and the other shows were plagued by inconsistencies. The July 24 show in Oakland was the best of that pack. The versions of "I Want You" and "Knockin' On Heaven's Door" are essential listening.

In 1989, a compilation was released from this tour. Unanimously, critics trashed and bashed *Dylan & the Dead*. It's an awful album, and Dylan was responsible for selecting the tracks. The Dead put together suggestions for the album, and most of the tracks were from the Giants Stadium show. Dylan nixed their input. When Garcia visited Dylan in Malibu to discuss the mixing of the album, he found Bob listening to the tapes on a boom box. The released album was an unconscious act of self-sabotage, and the Grateful Dead suffered the collateral damage. If they weren't going to build an album around the Giants Stadium show, no album was the prudent option.

Dylan & the Dead fueled the criticism of Dylan fans who didn't care for the Grateful Dead's style. Clinton Heylin, who wrote *Behind the Shades*, an informative biography on Dylan, ranted against the Dead's influence on Dylan by writing, "Deadheads have sought to take credit, on behalf of their band, for the change that was about to come, even though the lessons Dylan took from the shows included how not to tour, what audiences to avoid, and who not to play with." Other renowned Dylan scribes, like Paul Williams and Greil Marcus, were generally dismissive of this tour, and the music of the Dead in general.

For Deadheads, understanding Dylan was easier than the other way around. Garcia had been turning his base on to a steady dose of Dylan all the way. On the other hand, Dylan didn't play any Dead tunes, and up until 1986, their music hadn't influenced Dylan's work. Although, the first time Garcia played with Dylan in 1980, Bob introduced him by saying, "I'm a great admirer and fan of his and support his group all the way."

Understandably, the Dylan crowd was more snobbish towards the Grateful Dead than vice versa. Listening to tapes of the Dead/Dylan shows wasn't going to win over Dylan devotees, since only one of the six performances was worthy of lavish praise. Dylan fans with no previous Deadhead experience were probably put off by the throngs of hedonistic hippies eager to dance and cheer for anything. And if they were introduced to a Dead concert between 1987 and 1995, they weren't seeing the band anywhere near their prime. Regardless, these were two worlds spawned from similar times and places, spurred on by the same musical roots and inspiration. In a cosmic twist of fate, after years of benefitting from Dylan's creations, the Grateful Dead opened the door to the second half of Dylan's career, and arguably, had the greatest influence on his music since Woody Guthrie.

FIFTEEN

DETERMINED TO STAND

In a 1991 interview with Robert Hilburn, Dylan said, "You're either a player, or you're not a player. It didn't occur to me until we did those shows with the Grateful Dead. If you just go out every three years or so, like I was doing for a while, that's when you lose touch. If you're going to be a performer, you—you've gotta give it your all."

Dylan's a performing artist, and the Dead showed him, and reminded him, that he had to continually dedicate himself to his craft. During their two tours together, Dylan also observed the Dead's unique blueprint, a master plan for organically growing a fan base. Dylan was keenly taking notice, and in 1988, he'd launch his own Grateful Dead-style tour. There was still something missing though. At a 1997 press conference Dylan said, "The spirit of the songs had been getting further and further away from me. Probably because I'd been playing these songs with a lot of different bands, and they might not have understood them so well...I know it influenced me until I started playing with the Dead and I realized that they understood these songs better than I did at the time."

Dylan still had to clear the hurdle of relating to his own songs. It sounded like he had tapped into the essence of "Wicked Messenger" and "Joey" when he played them on 7-12-87 in Giants Stadium with the Dead, but perhaps, in Dylan's mind, he credited the Dead. Those weren't his arrangements. Reflecting on his state of mind before his final tour with Tom Petty in *Chronicles*, Dylan wrote, "Tom was at the top of his game and I was at the bottom of mine. Everything was smashed... My own songs had become strangers to me, I didn't have the skills to touch their raw nerves…There was a hollow singing in my heart and I couldn't wait to retire and fold the tent."

Dylan's final excursion with Tom Petty & the Heartbreakers was named the Temples in Flame Tour—30 shows across Europe. The tour commenced with a seventeen-song outing in Tel Aviv on September 5, 1987. Two nights later in Jerusalem, Dylan played thirteen songs, and none of these songs were played at the previous concerts. This kind of full-scale set list revamping was unprecedented for Dylan, and a direct result of his Grateful Dead experience. Dylan's sets continued to be adventurous for the remainder of his tour with Petty.

Dylan's singing was expressive, but rougher than his previous outings with Petty. Paul Williams, author of a trilogy of books that chronicle Dylan's career as a performing artist through 1990, raved about several of the shows from this tour. The best part of this tour for Dylan fanatics was that Dylan was mixing up the set lists and winging it on stage. Dylan took more chances than most artists, but now, like the Grateful Dead, his fans would be entertained by the results of the set lists.

On October 5, 1987, at a concert in Locarno, Switzerland, Dylan experienced a career-changing epiphany that he first explained to David Gates in a 1997 *Newsweek* interview and he later wrote about in *Chronicles*. It was a fiercely windy evening at the Piazza Grande Locarno, and in the thick of a song, Dylan suddenly couldn't sing—his mouth opened and nothing came out. "There's no pleasure in getting caught in a situation like this," said Dylan. "You can get a panic attack. You're in front of thirty thousand people and they're staring at you and nothing is coming out."

Dylan doesn't identify the song when this incident happened. After listening to the tapes, I surmise it may have occurred in a gap where Dylan misses a few lines in the second song of the concert, "Like a Rolling Stone." Dylan fought through the stressful situation, and suddenly, he was revitalized. "Everything came back, and it came back in multidimension. Even I was surprised. It left me kind of shaky…It was like I'd become a new performer, an unknown one in the true sense of the word. In more than thirty years of performing, I had never seen this place before."

In the interview with David Gates, Dylan gives a clearer vision of what happened when he stepped up to the mic and he couldn't sing: "It's almost like I heard it as a voice. It wasn't like it was even me thinking it. *I'm determined to stand, whether God will deliver me or not.*" And all of a sudden everything just exploded every which way. And I noticed that all the people out there—I was used to them looking at the girl singers, they were good-looking girls you know? And like I say, I had them up there so I wouldn't feel so bad. But when that happened, nobody was looking at the girls anymore. They were looking at the main mic. After that is when I sort of knew: I've got to go out and play these songs. That's just what I must do."

It was time for Dylan to rise from the Billy Parker stage of his career. He wasn't a washed-up rock star. He was the innovator who changed the face of music numerous times. Everybody was staring at him; not at the girls, Petty, or the Heartbreakers. There was no escaping or diminishing his iconic stature. Surrendering to Jesus and spreading the word of God wouldn't free him from his fate. In the same interview with Gates, Dylan said, "I find the religiosity and philosophy in the music. I don't find it anywhere else. Songs like 'Let Me Rest on a Peaceful Mountain' or 'I Saw the Light'—that's my religion. I don't adhere to rabbis, preachers, evangelists, all of that. I've learned more from the songs than any kind of entity. The songs are my lexicon. I believe the songs." Amen.

That's a compelling statement that Dylan aficionados, Deadheads, and music zealots can relate to. Music is religion for most of the people who fall into these categories. In 1966, when John Lennon said that "We're [the Beatles] more popular than Jesus now," it caused a furious uproar. Many considered it a tongue-in-cheek comment, but the power of song in people's lives is much more powerful than they are willing to recognize or admit. In Dylan's moment of panic on stage in Switzerland, he trusted in the power of song; those that he had created.

If the Grateful Dead could pack stadiums year after year working out of their songbook and covers that they reinvented, the possibilities for Dylan were limitless. He never had to write another song, he could just slip into his back pages and breathe life into tunes that were collecting dust in his canon. With his extreme knowledge of the wider American songbook he could perform night after night and his act would never have to grow old or get stale.

The Grateful Dead continued to give it their all after the Dylan/Dead tour. On August 22 and 23, they played a pair of gigs at the Calaveras County Fairgrounds, Angel's Camp, California. Their old amigo, Carlos Santana, came out and jammed a couple of songs with them on each night, including a sizzling "All Along the Watchtower," where Jerry and Carlos traded leads.

There was at least a Dylan tune or two in every Grateful Dead set list. Taking advantage of their time with Dylan, by early 1988, the Dead debuted seven new Dylan songs at their shows: "All Along the Watchtower," "Queen Jane Approximately," "Maggie's Farm," "Stuck Inside of Mobile with the Memphis Blues Again," "Ballad of a Thin Man," "When I Paint My Masterpiece," and "Knockin' on Heaven's Door." The last two songs mentioned were already covered by the Jerry Garcia Band. At the Dead shows, Bob Weir was singing all these Dylan numbers except for "Heaven's Door." His spin on Dylan songs wasn't as unique as Jerry's, but he brought a lot of energy to them—and remembered the lyrics better than the man who wrote them.

Grateful Dead mania peaked as the band headed east for their fall tour of '87. When the Dead started their unprecedented five-night run at Madison Square Garden, "Touch of Grey" soared up to the tenth spot on the Billboard Hot 100 chart, and would peak in the ninth slot. The Grateful Dead had their first hit single as they joined the likes of Whitney Houston, Michael Jackson, Whitesnake, Huey Lewis, and Bananarama in the elite hit-makers club of September '87.

Following their first two shows at Madison Square Garden, Garcia and Weir paid a visit to NBC Studios to appear on *Late Night with David*

Letterman. Middleweight Champion Sugar Ray Leonard, who had just come out of retirement to upset Marvelous Marvin Hagler, was the other guest. It made for a nice pairing—Sugar Ray and Jerry, the comeback icons. With his sharp wit and jovial demeanor, Garcia looked good, but if you compare this appearance to his last appearance on Letterman's show in April 1982, he appeared to have aged twenty years in just five. Weir hadn't aged a day since 1982.

Garcia and Weir joined Letterman's band, led by keyboardist Paul Schaffer, and played "When I Paint My Masterpiece." I've always been baffled as to why Weir sang lead vocals on "Masterpiece." He did a respectable job with it, but the Garcia Band version was much better. After some relaxed and witty conversation with the host, Weir showed Letterman an old parlor trick. Weir, Letterman, Schaffer, and Biff Henderson gathered around Garcia and gave TV land the illusion that they were lifting Garcia out of his chair—a bit of silly magic. What happened the following night in Madison Square Garden was truly miraculous.

Emotions were running high for Garcia's first set of New York City's performance since the coma, and the Friday night September 18 ticket was a hot commodity. The first set merrily rolled along, and after a strong version of "Birdsong," it ended abruptly after six songs. Experienced Deadheads expected an eight- to eleven-song opening set, but shorter sets were no longer a surprise. Dead crowds were boisterous, optimistic, and appreciative on this tour, especially in New York.

On this evening, the packed house in the Garden continued to aid the band, and eventually all the emotion was returned in one of the most stunning live spectacles I've ever seen. As of the publication of this book, videos of 9-18-87 MSG can be found on YouTube. The show can also be found on the 80-CD box set, *Thirty Trips Around the Sun*, released in 2015 as part of the Grateful Dead's 50th anniversary celebration. The massive box set contains one show from each of the Dead's thirty years, and 9-18-87 MSG effectively represents a glorious year. However, if you really want to experience this show, I suggest listening to an audience tape. The audience in conjunction with the band is something to behold.

The funky groove of "Shakedown Street" ignited set two. There was group singing, clapping, and dancing as a euphoric vibe gripped the crowd. It was a routine version, but NYC Deadheads embraced it as if it were a stairway to a new enlightenment. "Man Smart, Woman Smarter" kept the dance party flowing, and the audience was duly pumped for this popular but pedestrian tune. Weir screamed a solo chorus in falsetto that led to a resounding finish. The audience imposed its energy and will on the band and there was no turning back.

A split-second after the last "The women are smarter that's right," chant, Garcia strummed the chord progression of "Terrapin Station." The aural sensation was as pure as heaven's rain, and there was bedlam in the Garden. I was fifteen rows away, watching Garcia dig in, focused, judiciously channeling the excitement in the air. Every line meant something to almost everyone in the audience, and Jerry was the shaman, collectively getting everyone off. The ending refrain rang out like a royal rhapsody. Jerry and Brent chased each other with gleaming leads as Lesh, Weir, Hart, and Kreutzmann hammered the thunderous arrangement. "Terrapin" was excellent, but the energy in the building was absurd. You could sense something special was imminent after the Drums > Space segment.

An ordinary "Goin' Down the Road Feelin' Bad" set the stage for "All Along the Watchtower." This was my first "Watchtower" without Dylan, and there was a Garden roar as soon as the riff was identified. Garcia's first solo made everybody's hair stand on end, and Weir shrieked, "No reason to get excited!" It was at that point that I asked myself, *What if they play 'Morning Dew'?* I flashed back to that time I saw my first "Morning Dew" in Philadelphia, and somehow, this moment would be bigger. After all Garcia had been through, and where the Dead were now with the success of "Touch of Grey," did Garcia have the audacity to pull this off? The anticipation was unbearable. The thought of "Morning Dew" emerging from "Watchtower" was almost too much to bear.

"Watchtower" fizzled into a few seconds of no man's land. If the next song were "Black Peter," "Sella Blue," or "Wharf Rat"—Garcia songs that fell into that slot—it would have been a letdown, and it would have taken me a few minutes to get into it. The moment demanded the Holy Grail. Garcia had no path but the "Dew," and he bent a warning note before striking into the sanctified anthem. To be in the thick of that audience, and to experience the collective euphoria, is the realization of the ultimate power of music, which is beyond anything from any other realm. It was as if New York was healing Garcia, and Jerry just announced that everyone had a winning lottery ticket.

Garcia delivered what we desired. He sang soulfully and spiritually, bestowing it upon his devotees like a soothing prayer. This is where the enthusiastic wisdom of New York Deadheads factored in. They knew every nuance of the song and treated it like a religious anthem, only expressing their joy in response to Jerry. You could hear a pin drop as Jerry growled, "Where have all the people gawwwwn TODAY!" And then the silence was parted by the unified approval of his followers. "Morning Dew" is an apocalyptical song of survival after a nuclear war, but hearing Garcia sing it after coming back from a near-death experience gave the anthem deeper resonance.

Phil's bass rattled the arena as Garcia leaned forward and shredded a shrill solo. Singing from the heart of humanity, Jerry crooned: "I guess it doesn't matter anyway" four times, each cry more sorrowful than the last, and each ensuing eruption from the audience, louder. The entire Garden was shaking from the last roar; it was as if a Knick just hit a three-pointer at the buzzer to win the NBA Championship. Usually Garcia builds his "Dew" solo deliberately, but due to the overwhelming emotional explosion, he went for the jugular—down on the lower part of the fretboard, a blizzard of notes. Standing there was surreal.

How was Garcia going to execute and extend this jam when he started with a climactic tirade? This is where the man excels, inventing pathways that never existed before. At one point he makes a circular motion with his hand as if he's waving a magic wand, and then Garcia seemingly discovers a frequency that never existed before, the highest possible notes on the fretboard, and peels them off with speed and precision before the band joins him for the final fanning chord. The heroism is complete with a final: "I guess it doesn't matter anyway."

Weir cut the tension in the building, breaking into "Good Lovin'." Halfway through the song there's a subtle shift in the chord progression, and Garcia starts singing "La Bamba." It was a great surprise for many on hand, although a healthy percentage of the audience knew they had done this combo for the first time a week earlier in Providence. The Grateful Dead were now featuring two top ten hits, because the Los Lobos version of "La Bamba" topped the Billboard charts a few weeks earlier. The crowd was thrilled and the band segued back into "Good Lovin'" and finished the show with a "Knockin' on Heaven's Door" encore.

This was one of those nights where you had to be there. The night of 9-18-87 was one of the best shows of the year, but not an all-time classic. The "Morning Dew" was tremendous, but the band played some better versions in the 1972 to 1977 era. But for many of us there, this Watchtower > Morning Dew was the most electrifying musical experience of our lives. The crowd imposed its will on Garcia, and Jerry absorbed the energy gave it right back to us—improvised collaboration between band and audience. For one evening, we all believed that Jerry was completely healed and better than ever, and days like these would go on forever.

After finishing the East Coast tour in Philadelphia on September 24, the Dead played three gigs at the Shoreline Amphitheatre in Mountain View, California, in early October, and then Jerry headed back to New York City. Garcia was booked to play eighteen shows between October 15-31, at the Lunt Fontaine Theatre. Billed as Jerry Garcia Acoustic and Electric, Jerry on Broadway was arranged by Bill Graham, who was seen out in front of the theatre before shows. The acoustic band included Kahn and Garcia's old friends David Nelson and Sandy Rothman. The acoustic set was followed by electric JGB, consisting of Kahn, Melvin

Seals (keyboards), David Kemper (drums), and Gloria Jones and Jackie LaBranch on vocals. The residency included five days when there was a matinee show as well as an evening concert.

The acoustic sets were delightful, as Garcia had an opportunity to reconnect with his bluegrass roots. The mixed sets featured an occasional Dead song like "Ripple" or "Deep Elem Blues (traditional)," but for the most part, Garcia and friends turned the crowd on to roots music: "Blue Yodel #9," "Swing Low (Sweet Chariot)," "Diamond Joe," "Spike Driver Blues," "Two Soldiers," a tune that Dylan would cover on a future album, and "Drifting Too Far from the Shore," the song that had Dylan wondering if he was born to the right parents when he was growing up in Hibbing. The Jerry Garcia Band played more gospel numbers than ever before, and they added two Van Morrison songs to the rotation, "And it Stoned Me" and "Crazy Love." These songs were my indoctrination to the world of Van Morrison. Within a few months, every Van album was part of my collection.

What a glorious and strenuous year it was for Garcia. The toll of playing matinee and evening shows with two different bands on Broadway, and the Dylan/Dead shows along with a normal allotment of Dead shows, may not have been the right recipe for someone recovering from a life-threatening illness and twenty-plus years of substance abuse. Dylan and Garcia were determined to stand, and now their survival skills were paramount.

SIXTEEN

HANDLE WITH CARE

Inspired to return to public service and perform his songs, Dylan unexpectedly put a pause on his plans due to a freak accident that injured his hand. "It had been ripped and mangled to the bone and was still in the acute state—it didn't even feel like it was mine," Dylan wrote in *Chronicles*. "It was like a black leopard had torn into my tattered flesh. It was plenty sore. After being on the threshold of something bold, innovative and adventurous, I was now on the threshold of nothing, ruined."

Dylan wrote that the injury happened in 1987, and talked of being laid up in January, disappointed that his ensuing spring tour might be canceled. It's obvious he's talking about the 1988 tour, but surrounded by a legendary cast, he played guitar and sang "Like a Rolling Stone" when he was inducted into the Rock and Roll Hall of Fame on January 20, 1988. The accident might have happened after that ceremony, because there's no record of any public appearances or recording sessions between January 20 and his Traveling Wilburys rendezvous in April. It's an unusual period of inactivity for a restless soul. Regardless of whether the accident was before or after January 20, it was during this period of recovery that Dylan started writing again, and these terrific songs would end up on his next album, *Oh Mercy*.

Among those inducted into the Rock and Roll Hall of Fame with Dylan were the Beatles, Beach Boys, Woody Guthrie, Lead Belly, and Les Paul. One of the memorable moments was Bruce Springsteen's induction speech for Dylan. Bruce said, "When I was fifteen and I heard 'Like a Rolling Stone,' I knew that I was listening to the toughest voice that I had ever heard...a guy that had taken on the whole world and make me feel like I had to, too. The way Elvis freed your body, Bob freed your mind." Paying homage to Dylan's latest works, Springsteen added, "To this day, where great rock music is being made, there is the shadow of Bob Dylan over and over again...If there was a young guy out there writing 'Sweetheart Like You,' writing the *Empire Burlesque* album, writing 'Every Grain of Sand.' they'd be calling him the new Bob Dylan." It was a thorough induction speech hitting all the right notes, putting Dylan on Mount Rushmore without putting him out to pasture.

Dylan couldn't have fathomed that after paying his dues for twenty-six years on the road to the Rock and Roll Hall of Fame, he hadn't even reached the halfway point of his career. He would go on to play more shows in the second half of his career than the Grateful Dead did during their Long Strange Trip from 1965-1995. Of course, this was a silly and implausible notion for anyone to ponder back in 1988, but the new Dylan was on the cusp of a remarkable rebirth.

Jerry Garcia never changed masks. Year after year, it was the same musicians by his side and the same tie-dyed masses out there, getting larger and larger and becoming more supportive. It didn't matter anymore how good the band was playing; everything was groovy and greeted with rapturous applause. Commenting on the crowds at the shows he was doing with Petty, Dylan said, "I'd see people in the crowd and they'd look like cutouts from a shooting gallery, there was no connection to them." In March of 1988, as I heard Deadheads explode in ecstasy to mediocre music, I felt little connection to the scene. I wondered if Garcia felt the same way as Dylan did on certain nights, as if he was playing for spinning hippie puppets.

The Dead's spring tour of '88 had few shows that impressed me. At this point I was satisfied with a couple of hot jams per show, something worthy of repeated listens. There was a hot "Mississippi Half Step" in Atlanta, a killer "All Along the Watchtower" in Hampton, and a smoking "Fire on the Mountain" at the Brendan Byrne Arena. But after seeing three abysmal shows to end the tour in Hartford, the idea of putting in all this effort to watch Garcia deteriorate before my eyes didn't make sense.

The coma did take something out of Garcia's creativity on certain songs. The more intricate jams of "Let it Grow," "Scarlet Begonias," and "China Cat Sunflower" didn't shine as they had before. In the Jerry Garcia Band, hard-hitting jam songs like "Let it Rock," "After Midnight," "Rhapsody in Red," and "Sugaree" were replaced by soothing spiritual numbers. Garcia had aged physically beyond his years, and his insane workload and inability to kick his drug dependencies guaranteed a slow and steady decline, even though the band rebounded for some quality runs over the next two years.

As fans drifted in and out of the Dead touring scene, an unconditional love and allegiance to the band and Garcia remained. No matter how drugs negatively affected Garcia's playing, Deadheads cherished the good times, and they never ranted against the direction the band was heading. Sure, after experiencing the Wall of Sound in '74, there was disappointment for some in the stripped-down sound system and the tepid jams when the Dead returned to action in '76, but their loyalty remained in place. Nobody shouted "Judas!" at Garcia or angrily protested the direction of the band. It was a world unto itself that defied the standard rules and conventions of rock and roll and it kept growing, even when the music went through periods of stagnation and decline. It was the opposite of Dylan's love/hate relationship with his fans.

Physically and mentally on the mend, Dylan was ready to roll when he received the fateful call from George Harrison, inquiring if he could record a B side for a single in Dylan's Point Dume home studio. After recording "Handle with Care" with Harrison, Roy Orbison, Tom Petty, and Jeff Lynne, the supergroup—and record executives—knew there was potential for something special. They decided to make an album, *The Traveling Wilburys Volume 1*. With Dylan's tour starting in June, the Wilburys decided to write and record the album in a ten-day span in May, at the home and recording studio of Dave Stewart of the Eurythmics.

An uncanny comradery continued through these recording sessions as five legendary singer/songwriters strummed acoustic guitars and set up microphones and recording equipment in Dave Stewart's kitchen. Jim Keltner, the percussionist for these sessions who was dubbed "Buster Sidebury," placed microphones on the fridge and rattled the doors with his drumsticks. From song lyrics to vocals, everyone contributed freely, although Petty admitted he was a bit intimidated when he was auditioned for lead vocal on a song right after Roy Orbison. There was tremendous reverence for Roy, and a giddy feeling of disbelief that he was in the band.

Having an ex-Beatle and Roy in the room must have put Dylan at ease—all eyes were not focused on his every gesture. Although, George was fascinated as he watched Bob write a large chunk of "Tweeter and the Monkey Man." Harrison said, "The way he writes the words down, like very tiny, like a spider's written it, you know, you can't hardly read it. And that's the amazing thing. It's just unbelievable seeing how, how he did it."

Being in the company of great singers forced Dylan to be attentive to his vocal performance. Dylan was coming off one of his roughest years as a singer; his voice was uneven, nasally, and whiny, and it sounded like he'd rather not be singing. Instead of being intimidated, Dylan's voice offered a wonderfully gruff counterpoint to Orbison. And an engaged Dylan made Petty seem like an apprentice. As consistently smooth as Harrison and Lynne were, Orbison and Dylan are the standout voices of the Traveling Wilburys.

Paul Williams was an outstanding Dylan analysist, but I found his criticism of "Tweeter and the Monkey Man" harsh: "To my taste the song that resulted is significantly lacking in charm; and Dylan's delivery of the narrative as lead singer is void of presence or conviction." I believe the opposite. The dynamic that makes this song special is Dylan's singing. He could have used dummy lyrics with the driving energy and sharp cadence at play here. Even though the tune was constructed quickly, he sang brashly, as if this were an urgent tale. "Tweeter and the Monkey

Man" is a light-hearted outlaw New Jersey adventure that includes the titles of two Springsteen songs, "Mansion on the Hill" and "Thunder Road," and there are allusions to Dylan songs: *You can hear them tires squeal* ("Sweetheart Like You"), and *in Jersey anything's legal as long as you don't get caught,* which is similar to *in Patterson that's just the way things go* ("Hurricane"). Steeped in Americana, "Tweeter and the Monkey Man" is not so much a parody of a Springsteen or Dylan song as it's a parody of the Traveling Wilburys and the song-making process they found so engaging. "Tweeter and the Monkey Man" makes my double CD collection of Dylan's best songs of the decade.

"Dirty World," a Prince parody with Dylan on lead vocals, follows "Handle with Care" on the *Traveling Wilburys Volume 1*. Dylan deadpans Prince in his own style with a bold and charming vocal. With its energetic bluster, playfully overt sexuality, and the campfire singalong finale, "Dirty World" is a zany piece of the Wilburys puzzle, but not the type of tune Dylan would bring to life at one of his shows. "Congratulations," the other song Dylan sings lead on, is an outtake set of lyrics that Dylan brought with him to the sessions, and the only song that wasn't organically created on the spot. If Dylan was determined to stand and get back to the place he once was, these sessions were a great workout.

There's a magical flow to the album, and a camaraderie that's distinctive to this group. These were the right musicians coming together at the right time. As they had perfectly layered "Handle with Care" with the right voices in the right spots, they accomplished the same effect on "Last Night," as Orbison belted out another unforgettable bridge, "I asked her to marry me, she smiled and pulled out a knife. 'The party's just beginning,' she said, 'it's your money or your life.'"

Prior to "Tweeter," the eighth track, "Margarita," captured the joyous, freewheeling spirit of the album—everything they threw against the wall was bound to stick. It's a simple '50s-style pop tune with a one-word chorus, and Dylan grumbles the main verse with pizazz, "It was in Pittsburgh late one night. I lost my hat, got into a fight. I rolled and tumbled till I saw the light. Went to the Big Apple, took a bite." With that rough voice busting in, it sounds like Dylan just stepped out of a barroom brawl. Even in a simple throwaway tune, Dylan was on his game.

Petty takes the lead on the feel-good finale and gives a shout-out to Jimi Hendrix, "Maybe somewhere down the road when somebody plays, Purple Haze." "End of the Line" took on a haunting tone when Orbison died of a heart attack three months after the album was released. Yet, like "Touch of Grey," it's a triumphant song of survival.

Well it's all right, even if you're old and grey
Well it's all right, you still got something to say
Well it's all right, remember to live and let live
Well it's all right, the best you can do is forgive
Well it's all right, riding around in the breeze
Well it's all right, if you live the life you please
Well it's all right, even if the sun don't shine
Well it's all right, we're going to the end of the line

This record captures a time in the lives of five musical legends who had paid their dues, seen some tough times, and had just tasted the sweet smell of success or were on the threshold of something momentous. This is the coolest pop record of its kind. An album can be simple, humorous, spontaneous, and, one of the greatest albums of all time. This can't be classified as a Dylan album, and I wouldn't dare rank it with his ten best albums, but I'd find a spot for it in my Top 100. Like the famous *Seinfeld* episode when Jerry and George pitch a show about nothing to an executive at NBC, great music, like great TV, doesn't have be about anything or have some important message.

Down in the Groove was released on May 31, 1988, and it gave little clue of what Dylan had been through lately and where he was headed. Critics had reached a point where they didn't take pleasure in bashing a subpar Dylan album anymore, and the music-buying public ignored

Dylan's latest effort. But after graduating from Grateful Dead University, having his performing epiphany in Switzerland, writing many of the songs that would be on *Oh Mercy*, and recording what would be a smash hit record with the Traveling Wilburys, Dylan launched the second half of his career.

SEVENTEEN

STRIKE ANOTHER MATCH GO START ANEW

There are five chapters in *Chronicles*, and in each one, Dylan writes about either a developmental stage of his career or a significant turning point. He turned readers on to his influences and the cast of characters that surrounded him at crucial periods of his life. Fans wanting to know what inspired his great anthems, and how he came to write so many anthems in such a short period of time, were sucked deeper into the endless web of Dylan intrigue. He didn't reveal the inspiration behind "Chimes of Freedom," or tell us who "Mr. Tambourine Man" was, and he probably never will. Chapter four, "Oh Mercy," is a colorful take on his mind-set at the start of what would eventually be known as the Never Ending Tour, and the *Oh Mercy* sessions with Daniel Lanois in New Orleans. Surprisingly, this is the longest chapter in the book, and it tells us the significance of this period to Dylan.

Feeling disconnected from live performances of his older material, Dylan acknowledged that for his audience, "It must have been like going through deserted orchards and dead grass." He also realized that in addition to changing his approach, he needed to reach a new audience. "In many ways my audience was past its prime and its reflexes were shot. They came to stare and not participate." Touring with the Dead, he saw an ideal prototype crowd. Few Deadheads were disappointed that he didn't play harmonica, an acoustic set, or "Like a Rolling Stone." Dylan didn't necessarily want to be followed from city to city by pranksters in tie-dye. He was seeking a more open-minded crowd that hadn't stamped and labeled him, and was willing to be in the moment with his music.

Dylan told Elliot Roberts (promoter of the Dylan/Dead and Petty tours) that he wanted to play around 200 shows a year, and more or less, visit the same towns on a three-year schedule. It sounded like a crash course on organically cultivating an audience, as the Dead did for the past twenty years. On *Down in the Groove*, released a week before Dylan started his first tour of 1988, there was a message on the sleeve of the album: "If you are interested in receiving information about Bob Dylan concert dates, artwork, album releases, preferential seating at concerts, home videos, etc., please write to…" On the inside sleeve of the live album *Grateful Dead* (1970), there was a similar call for fans to reach out to the band for more info and unite. Dylan wanted to put his fate in the hands of new fans, stating, "I would have to rely on word of mouth. I'd rely on that like my life depended on it."

Dylan's new band, the smallest group he ever toured with, consisted of G. E. Smith on guitar, Kenny Aaronson on bass, and Chris Parker on drums. Smith was responsible for putting the band together after passing an audition set up by Elliot Roberts. Smith and a few guys from the SNL band were waiting for Dylan in an uptown New York club that was closed off for the audition. Dylan showed up wearing a hoodie, sunglasses, and fingerless gloves. "We were nervous, this was Bob Dylan," said Smith. Early in the session, Dylan asked Smith if he could play "Pretty Peggy-O," and after they gelled on that tune, Dylan knew this was the guy to lead his band.

Concord (6-7-88) and Sacramento (6-9-88), California, were Dylan's first gigs with G. E. Smith. On opening night they played thirteen songs; six electric, followed by three acoustic with just G. E. and Bob, and then the band returned for three electric tunes and an encore. This was the pattern for the rest of the year except that the number of songs per show increased as the tour moved along. On opening night, Dylan played four songs live for the first time: "Subterranean Homesick Blues," "Absolutely Sweet Marie," "Lakes of Pontchartrain," and Dylan's version of "Driftin' Too Far From Shore." His mission was to stand and deliver these songs, and the other tunes that defined who Dylan was, to the masses. The following night in Sacramento, of the twelve songs played, ten were different from the night before. The tone for the tour was set.

On June 24, Dylan played at the Garden State Performing Arts Center in Holmdel, New Jersey, and I was there. I had seen six Dylan concerts, but number seven was my first without the Grateful Dead in the house. The National Anthem was played over the PA before Dylan, Smith, Aaronson, and Parker stormed the stage with "Subterranean Homesick Blues." It was an electric ambush, possibly the way Dylan always heard it in his mind. Dylan snapped off the lyrics with the same pacing as the original, and G. E. unleashed searing Telecaster leads between verses, backed by the romping and stomping of Aaronson and Parker. The music had the confrontational attitude of Dylan's '66 European tour, but the '88 audience in New Jersey was settling in, trying to figure out who Dylan was and why they were there.

It was an aggressive show that left me startled and breathless at times. The versions of "Driftin' Too Far from Shore" and "Silvio" rocked three times harder than the studio tracks. Dylan opened the door for Smith, allowing him to make a huge impression. There were no long journeys from Smith, but he had a handle on Dylan's music and his solos cut to the bone. Dylan's phrasing was emphatic, a major improvement from the year before. The song of the night, and most nights on this tour, was the set ending, "Like a Rolling Stone." *How does it feel to be on your own?* The words resonated as I was standing on a hill in Holmdel, New Jersey, looking down on Dylan's gritty band. The passion of Dylan's vocals, backed by the psychotic sting of Smith's leads, came off like electroshock therapy. Like the original, this version screamed of the liberation of someone who hit rock bottom and found insane pleasure in knowing that this was the best thing that ever happened to him. He was on the path to unforeseen glory. The song couldn't possibly be better than the original track, but the tale may have been more visceral to the performer.

Nine days after my rendezvous with Dylan in Holmdel, I rounded up a posse of friends and drove nine hours to see a pair of Grateful Dead shows in Oxford, Maine. Over 100,000 Deadheads invaded the space in and around the Oxford Plains Speedway. By 1988, ecstasy was as popular as LSD, and thousands of people were there just to be part of the scene or to sell something. I was a creature of habit because I didn't crave this scene, I was just hoping for a few hot solos.

The show on 7-2-88 began with a promising "Iko Iko" "Jack Straw" pairing. Lack of intimacy was the overwhelming factor diminishing my enjoyment of the hot "Straw" solo. The sound in the speedway was merely adequate, and I was so far from the stage that I didn't even feel like I was at a concert. The first set featured three new songs from their next album: "Blow Away," "Victim or the Crime," and "Foolish Heart." It took me a few decades to find pleasure in any of these songs, and on this night, I loathed that they unloaded these songs in succession.

The second set was average until the Dead played All Along the Watchtower > Morning Dew as they had in Madison Square Garden on 9-18-87. The excitement and execution levels weren't on par with the magical night in the Garden. They closed out the set with "Sugar Magnolia" and encored with "Quinn the Eskimo." I saw many of the songs I wanted to see, and it was a much better performance than the last shows I saw in Hartford; yet, I wondered if my time and energy might be better spent elsewhere.

The following day, as I was feasting on a two-pound lobster at a luncheonette somewhere in the middle of Maine, my friend Perry, the lead guitarist from a Dead cover band called the Lost Boys, put his newspaper down and said, "Hey, it says here that your boy Dylan's play-ing in Old Orchard Beach tonight." Immediately, I knew that's where I needed to be. I testified about how great Dylan was at the Garden State Performing Arts Center and suggested we skip seeing the Dead again that night. It didn't take much convincing. Weary of the Dead scene himself, Perry decided to join me for the twenty-minute drive to see Dylan in Old Orchard Beach. A feeling of exhilaration surged through me as I staged my Grateful Rebellion. *Strike another match go start anew, it's all over now, Baby Blue*. Howdy Old Orchard Beach, so long Oxford Plains.

By coincidence, I was dressed like Dylan's campaign manager. I was wearing a baby blue Members Only jacket with a Dylan pin, and underneath was a Dylan t-shirt from the Holmdel show. We scored tickets and a couple of jumbo brews, and made our way to the front of the stage to wait for Dylan. Once upon a time, seeing the Jerry Garcia Band was this intimate and easy, and getting tickets for Dylan and the Band was mission impossible. Amazing how this whole thing had reversed.

Dylan stepped on stage in a suave black suit with silver buttons. I could have reached over and shined his shoes. Mr. Smith, the ponytailed axe master, stepped up by his side and they attacked "Subterranean Homesick Blues." I thanked the heavens for the cosmic fate that delivered me to this Maine resort town nestled alongside the Atlantic Ocean. The ending of the set featured overly emphatic vocals on "You're a Big Girl Now" and a "Like a Rolling Stone" thriller. Dylan rewarded the electrified but sparse crowd with a triple encore of "A Hard Rain's A-Gonna Fall," "Silvio," and "All Along the Watchtower." During the last five songs, Dylan reeled through the years: 1975, 1965, 1987, 1962, and 1968. Bolstered by Smith's aggressive picking, he was fulfilling his Locarno prophecy.

Dylan played six songs that I didn't hear at the Holmdel show. As far as I knew, the Grateful Dead was the only major band out there mixing up their set lists on a nightly basis. If this was the way Dylan was operating, switching up his set lists, I had to see more. Although the concerts were on the short side, they were action packed. At a Grateful Dead show I endured startling amounts of downtime in hopes of hearing a few historic solos from Garcia. There was the endless tuning up, drums and space, intermission, several songs that I'd heard too often to appreciate, and those pesky new songs that would be on their next album, *Built to Last*. And there was the erosion of Garcia's talent, which I was too much of a critic to ignore. His guitar and vocals were notably better in '87. In 1988 I'd traveled to Atlanta, Hampton, East Rutherford, Hartford, and Oxford, Maine, to see eleven concerts, yet nothing was as thrilling as seeing and hearing Dylan close range in Old Orchard Beach as he howled, "And I'll tell it and think it and speak it and breathe it. And reflect it from the mountain so all souls can see it. Then I'll stand on the ocean until I start sinkin'. But I'll know my song well before I start singin'." It made me weep.

Recalling a night when there were several music luminaries on hand to see Dylan in London, and G. E. was playing "Mr. Tambourine Man," Smith said, "There's a line in there where he says, 'Just to dance beneath the diamond sky with one hand waving free.' I started to cry, making sure my face is out of the light because tears are running down…I'm here with Bob Dylan, and he's singing 'Mr. Tambourine Man.'" In the same interview, Smith talks about the time he was waiting with his bandmates for Dylan to arrive at their first rehearsal. "We were nervous, this *was* Bob Dylan. I can't compare his iconic stature to anyone now in similar, in music, and what Bob meant…He was the guy who influenced the Beatles."

The enormity of Dylan's art touched me in a profound way that night. It's one thing to collect his albums and simply lose yourself in the wonder and awe of that. As an obsessive music fan who followed Garcia, I sensed that Dylan was on the cusp of something important, and my time would now be better spent pursuing Dylan than the Dead. At the very least it was a more intimate experience, without all the superfluous hoopla of the Dead scene that seemed to be veering away from the true spirit of the music.

On September 2, 1988, I caught a Dylan show at the Orange County Fair in Middletown, twenty minutes from my college town in New Paltz. I enjoyed the gig with a gang of college friends and Dylan fans from the Woodstock area. This performance was longer and better than the other two I saw earlier in the summer. There were raging versions of "Absolutely Sweet Marie" and "Seeing the Real You at Last," tunes that Dylan didn't play at Holmdel or Old Orchard Beach. People danced wildly during "It Ain't Me Babe," part of the quartet of encores. Smith and Dylan strummed a lively acoustic arrangement, yet it was still surreal watching people swing dance as Dylan shouted, "It ain't me babe. No, no, no, it ain't me babe. It ain't me you're looking for…BABE!"

I hadn't given up on the Grateful Dead, but that changed after a subpar eight-show residency in Madison Square Garden. I was hoping there would be some magic at the 9-18-88 show, a year after the legendary Watchtower > Dew night, but the band bombed. The sets and the jams were short. My friend Phil and I passed time by observing and commenting on the odd behaviors of Deadheads. As they band slogged through a comatose Wharf Rat > Throwing Stones > Not Fade Away ending, Deadheads clapped and chanted, "You know our love will not fade away!" as if that was the sole purpose of coming to the show. On nights like this, I could see how a Dylan fan, or rock fan who had never seen the band before, would come away unimpressed and wondering what all the fuss was about.

Two nights later the Dead played a much better show with a "Morning Dew" to end the set, although it wasn't the type of show that would make it into my listening rotation—one and done forever.

Following a successful two-part tour of the United States and Canada, six more Dylan shows were scheduled: two in the Tower Theatre in Upper Darby, Pennsylvania, and four in New York's Radio City Music Hall. I saw the first two nights at Radio City and missed the third night, the same day that the *Traveling Wilburys Volume 1* was released. On my hour-and-a-half drive from New Paltz to New York City to catch the final show on October 19, I listened to the Wilburys album twice, and the second time around, I couldn't believe what I was hearing. I wasn't exposed to much hype about the album, and I didn't think Dylan would play an integral role on it. I thought this was a goofy CD I was obliged to buy because Dylan made a cameo on it. Since *Down in the Groove* was the only new Dylan material released since I'd become a fan, I was elated by the unexpected magic of the Traveling Wilburys.

I picked up my Deadhead friend Doug and convinced him to tape that night's show. I was an accomplice to sneaking the equipment in, and we taped ourselves a classic. A few years later, a soundboard recording of this show made the rounds amongst collectors, but I was enjoying a great audience recording the day after. Doug was an experienced taper, recording more than 200 Dead shows in his prime.

Set lists of the Radio City shows only varied slightly. Dylan saved the best for last. After blazing another "Subterranean Homesick Blues" opener, Dylan performed one of my favorites, "I'll Remember You." His voice was hoarse and his presence inside the vocal was unrelenting. The fifth song of the electric set was "Bob Dylan's 115th Dream," a *Bringing It All Back Home* number that Dylan debuted a week earlier at the Tower Theatre. The performance was decent but the gesture was immense.

Dylan sounded like a crestfallen raconteur as he spouted "Gates of Eden" to commence the acoustic set. For these shows, Dylan inserted "With God On Our Side," into his acoustic sets. After Dylan played his final show of the previous tour, which ended in New Orleans on September 25, Dylan met with producer Daniel Lanois to discuss collaborating on Dylan's next album. Lanois invited Dylan to watch a Neville Brothers session for their *Yellow Moon* album, and this is where Dylan heard Aaron Neville belt out "With God On Our Side" with this added verse:

In the nineteen-sixties, came the Vietnam War.
Can someone tell me, what we were fighting for?
So many young men died, so many mothers cried.
Now I ask the question, was God on our side?

Knowing a good thing when he hears it, Dylan chronologically added that verse to his versions in Radio City, and the new lyrics received loud cheers every night. The three-song electric set was overwhelming. A tight "Silvio" was followed by Dylan saying, "Thank you! I was really honored . . . last year the Amnesty Tour chose a Bob Dylan song as their theme song. A song called 'Chimes Of Freedom.' This year, to my great surprise, they chose another Bob Dylan song. Actually that one was last year, 'I Shall Be Released' was the one they chose this year. Anyway, I guess they're gonna have another Amnesty Tour next year. I think they're gonna use another Bob Dylan song called 'Jokerman.' But I'm trying to get them to change their mind, trying to get them to use this one." As Dylan spoke, G. E. and the band thundered a regal introduction for "In the Garden." The song raged forth, Dylan singing like a jaded preacher and the band hammered a chord progression like Led Zeppelin. I was rattled by the rumbling force. My previous concept of "In the Garden" was the soft version from *Saved* that seemed feckless compared to what was going down in Radio City. And after the guitar jam of the night, Parker slammed the rifle-shot drumbeat signifying another '88 "Like a Rolling Stone" stampede.

Dylan's encore was a potent five-song set starting with "Wagoner's Lad," a traditional tune from the Harry Smith *Anthology of American Folk Music*. Dylan's rugged phrasing resonated, especially when he grunted, "My horses ain't hungry, and they don't need your hay. Sit down beside me for as long as you stay. I'll go to Montana if moon show the light, but my pony can't travel this dark road tonight." Bob savored every syllable. It was as Dylanesque as anything he'd performed that night.

I had a desire to hear a certain Dylan song I'd never heard before, and as "Wagoner's Lad" ended, I whispered in Doug's ear (we were taping), "Lonesome Death of Hattie Carroll," and presto, Dylan played it for the first time during the Radio City run. "Knockin' On Heaven's Door" started out as an acoustic duet and it ended as an electric version. Halfway through, Dylan and G. E. traded acoustics for electrics, and Aaronson and Parker kicked in. "All Along the Watchtower" and "Maggie's Farm" closed out the incredible night.

In no time at all, *The Traveling Wilburys Volume 1* went platinum, becoming Bob's best-selling album of the decade. Dylan's last performance of a triumphant year was as part of the Bridge Benefit, an all-acoustic evening of music organized by Neil Young at the Oakland Coliseum on December 6. On this date twenty-six-years earlier, Dylan recorded "A Hard Rain's A-Gonna Fall" in Columbia studios. In Oakland, Dylan and Smith tore through a six-song set that started with intense versions of Jesse Fuller's "San Francisco Bay Blues" and the Woody Guthrie classic "Pretty Boy Floyd." Later that night, Dylan learned that Roy Orbison died of a heart attack. Lefty Wilbury was only forty-nine.

EIGHTEEN

FORGET THE DEAD YOU LEFT

K *nocked Out Loaded* and *Down in the Groove* sound like focused albums delivered by an artist determined to give his fans a high-quality product when compared to *Dylan & the Dead,* released on February 6, 1989. Dylan was responsible for selecting the tracks, and it's difficult to understand his line of thinking here. Maybe he wanted to continue to lower critical expectations by completing a trilogy of disappointing albums, setting the stage for a great comeback album. Two of the seven tracks are from the Foxboro show, including an uninspired version of "Joey," when he could have used the stunning version from Giants Stadium. There are blown lyrics strewn all over the recording, and it was a tedious selection of songs.

The Grateful Dead thought along the same lines as this author, and wanted to use mostly songs from the Giants Stadium show. When Garcia visited Dylan at his home in Malibu to discuss the album, he found Dylan listening to the tapes on a cheap boom box. Dylan insisted that his voice be mixed down in the recording, and this didn't make the album any more appealing. A fitting title for the album would have been *A Summer Blunder with Dylan & the Dead*. For most Dylan fans, this was the first time they heard anything from this tour, and they wouldn't be seeking any more. Maybe down the road, a Dylan bootleg series release featuring some cleaned-up tracks from the Club Front sessions along with the Giants Stadium show can put a positive spin on this historical collaboration that helped shape Dylan's Never Ending Tour.

Dylan/Dead relations took their strangest turn six days later, when Bob joined the Dead on stage for the second set of their show on February

12 at the Great Western Forum in Inglewood. Dylan played guitar out of the spotlight in between Garcia and Weir as the band opened with "Iko Iko." That was followed by unusual selections: "Monkey and the Engineer," "Dire Wolf," "Alabama Getaway," "Cassidy," "Stuck Inside of Mobile with the Memphis Blues Again." Most of these were tunes that the Dead played in the first set, and the band had never played an electric "Monkey and the Engineer" before. Dylan added meager backing vocals in places, and showed no interest in singing his own song. The music had no spark, and it was bizarre to see Dylan this passive on stage. (This can also be seen on YouTube.) After the Dead finished off the second half of their set, Dylan re-emerged for a "Knockin' On Heaven's Door" encore, and grunted the lead vocal. It was fine for a novelty version, but Dylan's odd phrasing clashed with the lush, methodic pacing of the Dead's version of "Heaven's Door."

The day after his guest appearance, Dylan phoned the Grateful Dead office in San Rafael to ask if he could join the band. This was a serious request. The band members voted on the proposition, and if the vote were unanimous, Dylan would have been a member of the Grateful Dead for at least a tour. One no vote shot down the dream. Weir has publicly stated that he voted to give it a go, and we know how Garcia voted. The no vote likely came from Lesh or one of the drummers, and it was a great business decision, nothing personal. Dylan tried to fit in as one of the boys the night before, and it was awkward at best. Even in a legendary line-up like the Traveling Wilburys, Dylan was a huge presence. The Dead would have had to, on some level, restructure what they were comfortable doing, and there was little benefit to having Dylan in the band, except for the fact that Garcia and Weir greatly admired Dylan.

For an artist who had stood his ground and delivered his songs consistently the year before, this was an odd detour. Maybe Dylan was hurting from Roy Orbison's passing, and perhaps he was drinking too much in the late '80s. A part of him was still weary of carrying the load of being Bob Dylan. As much as I would have loved to see Dylan as a member of the Grateful Dead for a while, the no vote worked out for all involved. The Grateful Dead stepped out and had a stellar year of touring, bouncing back from the inconsistencies of '88. And Dylan headed down to New Orleans to record *Oh Mercy* with Daniel Lanois.

Bono had introduced Dylan to Lanois, one of the hottest producers of the day, best known for his work with U2. Upon meeting Lanois, Dylan described him as "*Noir* all the way—dark sombrero, black britches, high boots, slip-on gloves—all shadow and silhouette—dimmed out, a black prince from the black hills." Dylan settled down in New Orleans, renting a large house, and Lanois assembled the band. Among the key musicians were Mason Ruffner (guitar), Cyril Neville (percussion), Willie Green (drums), and Tony Hall (bass). Lanois set up one of his infamous makeshift recording studios. Dylan found the offbeat atmosphere stimulating. It was not the same old vibe of a sterile New York City recording studio.

Lanois and Dylan were strong-minded individuals with big ideas, and naturally this led to conflict and disagreement, but their mutual respect for each other ensured the success of this endeavor. It was rough going early on as they struggled finding the right tone and tempo for "Political World." After a long day of near misses, Lanois smashed a metallic Dobro on the floor. This might have been the right time for Dylan to start working on "Everything is Broken," the third track of *Oh Mercy*.

The struggles continued in the Victorian mansion on Soniat Street as the sessions produced mixed results. Lanois was a hands-on producer who played many instruments, and he was possessed in his pursuit of making a great record. "He would have done anything to make a song happen—empty the pans, wash dishes, sweep the floors," said Dylan. The turning point of the sessions came in the middle of March as they were working on "Where Teardrops Fall." Saxophonist John Hart, who hadn't contributed much during the sessions, stepped up and played a jaw-dropping, spiraling solo at the end of the song. Dylan knows a transcendent moment when he hears one, and he knew this was a keeper. Hart's presence and appearance reminded Bob of the Reverend Gary

Davis, and Dylan's demeanor changed. "All of a sudden I know that I'm in the right place doing the right thing at the right time and Lanois is the right cat."

Throughout the sessions, Lanois would suggest to Dylan that the record could benefit from a song like "Masters of War," "Girl from the North Country," or "With God on Our Side." That rocket left the launching pad decades ago, but while in New Orleans, Bob wrote two songs crucial to the foundation of *Oh Mercy*, "Man in the Long Black Coat" and "Shooting Star." "Black Coat" is a microcosm of the album—haunting and brooding, mysterious and vividly vague. The song launches with a foreboding chord sequence that echoes as crickets chirp in the background. Dylan's restrained harmonica blasts warn of the mayhem to come. The second harmonica line accentuates the melody and dials up the suspense.

This song was performed in the right city, by the right artist, at the right time in his career. Dylan evokes a serene landscape in the opening verse: *Crickets are chirpin', the water is high/ There's a soft cotton dress on the line hangin' dry*. And then there's the devastation brought on by the man in the long black coat: *Windows wide open, African trees/ Bent over backwards from a hurricane breeze*. It's the type of song you can picture Dylan writing in New Orleans, although there's no obvious reference to the city. The man in the black coat has a face like a mask. The singer allows you to picture him as you please. Dylan's delivery is grouchy and raw—authentic voicing that fit the mood of the song against Lanois's layered rhythms. Dylan brings the bridge to a climax: "People don't live or die people just float. She gone with the man in the long black coat." It's a line that resonated with fans, but Dylan wasn't happy with it, and in *Bob Dylan Lyrics (1962-2012)*, he changed the "People don't live or die" line to "I went down to the river, but I missed the boat." I think that line misses the boat. On Dylan's initial writing of "Black Coat," the line was *People don't live or die, people just are*. Obviously, that doesn't rhyme with boat, but Dylan's fixation with one of the most memorable lines of this album is vexing.

"Shooting Star" is the other *Oh Mercy* composition created in New Orleans. "Under the southernmost magnolia, I started feeling something about a song called 'Shooting Star,' a song I hadn't written yet," commented Dylan. "I could vaguely hear it in my mind. The kind of song you hear when you're wide awake in your head and see and feel things, but all the rest of you is asleep." With its soothing melody and reflective/sentimental tone, "Shooting Star" is the ideal lullaby to conclude *Oh Mercy*. A fiery biblical bridge connects the verses and gives the tune that bittersweet taste that Dylan loves dishing out. The prettiest harmonica solo of the album brings the music to a poignant conclusion, like a prayer with a good night kiss.

Oh Mercy begins with some haunting guitar riffs that gradually increases in volume and intensity. Before Dylan sings a word, you can feel his presence. This is a Dylan record! His mature voice shatters the silence: "We live in a political world/ Love don't have any place/ We're living in times where men commit crimes/ And crime don't have a face." Dylan's delivering his State of the Union address. This isn't a classic protest song, it's a scathing commentary on corporate greed and lack of compassion in society. In this political world, "Courage is a thing of the past," or as Dylan sings in "Black Coat," "People don't live or die, people just float." It's a gripping opener and well worth the growing pains that Dylan and Lanois went through early in the sessions.

The sequencing of songs is sublime as the second track, "Where Teardrops Fall," ends with the sobbing sax solo that's followed by "Everything is Broken," which opens like the theme of the TV show *Batman*. Dylan offers a list of broken things that rhyme, yet I hear it as a vital cog in this album, not some kind of throwaway song. "Ring Them Bells" follows. This gorgeous piano composition with biblical references has as much spirituality as anything from the born-again era. Dylan offers this clever line: *Time is running backwards and so is the bride*.

After "Black Coat," the balladeer tries to put out the torch of a past love in "Most of the Time." *I can't even be sure/ If she was ever with me/ Or if I was ever with her.* The haunting appears to be eternal, but the last verse is surprisingly empowering as Dylan defiantly sings, "I don't compromise and I don't pretend. I don't even care if I ever see her again. Most of the time." A nice acoustic take of this song appears on *The Bob Dylan Bootleg Series Volume 8*. The Lanois makeover on *Oh Mercy* is perfect within the context of the album. A song of self-reflection, "What Good Am I?" follows. The music almost comes to a standstill as Dylan's voice carries the load. It's the type of song any of us can place ourselves inside and ask, what good am I? "Disease of Conceit" is another musically sparse song with biting lyrics, and well placed on the heels of "What Good Am I?"

Dylan poses a different question on the penultimate track, "What Was It You Wanted?" *Ask not what I could do for you, but what do you want from me?* On my first couple of listens, I thought it was a man/ woman romantic entanglement, and then it dawned on me; it's about the endless stream of requests from fanatics wanting something from Bob Dylan. The song begins with that mysterious and murky Lanois sound and develops at a gripping pace. Dylan blows sharp, stinging harmonica solos. "Shooting Star" is the rewarding finale of the thirty-minute New Orleans masterpiece.

This road trip to New Orleans turned out to be more productive than touring with the Grateful Dead, even if the shows would have been wildly successful. I'd rate *Oh Mercy* Dylan's best album of the decade, even though the *Infidels* sessions produced an abundant harvest of quality tunes. During these sessions with Lanois, some fabulous songs were not included but were used on future albums: "Series of Dreams," "Dignity," "Born in Time," and "God Knows." One or more of these tunes could have been squeezed on to *Oh Mercy*, but the finished product had great balance, flow, and strength. This is a mature and timeless work from a master who was comfortably expressing himself in his own bold style. Nobody was making music like this in 1988, and nobody would again, until Lanois and Dylan got together for *Time Out of Mind* nine years later.

Although this wasn't something he learned from Garcia, Dylan had been taking a more Jerry-like approach to developing his music. Garcia had always sat back and worked with the musicians and circumstances that surrounded him. Throughout most of his career, Dylan was an artist possessed, always chasing inspiration, and frequently changing the personnel and scenery around him. *Blood on the Tracks*, *Desire*, and *Street Legal* all featured different musicians, and the '74 Comeback Tour, the Rolling Thunder Revue, and the '78 World Tour all differed drastically. Jesus became Bob's next source of inspiration.

Now Dylan was relying on, and trusting, those around him. Petty & the Heartbreakers played on *Knocked Out Loaded*. He trusted in the arrangements of the Grateful Dead as his backing band. Elliot Roberts assembled the Smith/Parker/Aaronson group for his tour. When Dylan wrote the lyrics to many of the songs for *Oh Mercy*, he didn't rush into a studio and record them. He took Bono's advice, contacted Lanois, and patiently waited for the right time to get together with him, and then trusted in his producer to assemble the musicians and create an ideal setting. Even the Traveling Wilburys adventure came about organically.

The Grateful Dead rebounded from a sluggish end to 1988. The new year would be heralded as the band's best since Jerry's coma. Surprisingly, for the first time in thirteen years, there was no Northeast spring tour. On the East Coast, the Dead only played in Atlanta and Greensboro. My first chance to see the band that year was an up-close and personal experience courtesy of pay-per-view TV. Their Summer Solstice show from June 21 at the Shoreline Amphitheatre was televised for a small fee, and broadcast for free on FM. I had a bunch of friends over to my pad in New Paltz and served a spread of chicken wings and fish tacos, and whipped up several batches of banana daiquiris.

It was an old-school show with hot versions of "Cassidy," "Deal," "Eyes of the World," and a brilliant "Morning Dew," during which I knocked over a tray of Tostitos and salsa. Clarence Clemmons joined the band on sax during the second set, and there were no new songs from their upcoming studio album. It was a pleasure to experience a live show without a huge road trip and dealing with the overcrowded masses—win-win all around.

I went truckin' eight hours up to Buffalo to see the Dead on July 4th, and caught a pair in Giants Stadium on July 9 and 10. This summer tour was a strong one for the Grateful Dead, and all the shows were video-taped. The two best official DVD releases from this tour are *Down Hill from Here* from the Alpine Valley Music Theatre, and *Crimson, White and Indigo*, from JFK on July 7. My gripe with the shows I saw were the new songs that would be on *Built to Last*, which took up spots that used to be occupied by better tunes. The band was executing in a concise and peak state, but Garcia still could only get the wow factor going here and there. After my last show at Giants Stadium, I only saw the Grateful Dead four more times. The last time I was in awe of Garcia's playing in the moment occurred during "Morning Dew" on 7-10-89.

Giants Stadium was engulfed in a wild lightning storm towards the end of the first set. The Neville Brothers joined the Dead on stage during set two, and the Cajun mojo rolled during "Iko Iko," which was followed by a fair "Watchtower" that segued into "Morning Dew." Once a rare tune, "Morning Dew" had become a staple that you could count on seeing once every four shows. This is another show available on YouTube, and this "Dew" is extremely view worthy. Garcia sings four rounds of "I guess it doesn't matter anyway" from a place of pain, as if he just had a root canal. The grand jam takes off with cascading, playful licks. Then Garcia strikes a ringing chord as if he's clocking in for work, and he changes the creative flow of the solo. Suddenly his fingers are scrambling east and west, north and south, and he traces his footprints backwards. After all the "Dew" jams I've heard, there's no other like this. Garcia moves into the climactic finale, but the band is slow to follow, apparently stunned by Garcia's virtuosity. Jerry's heroic talent could daze those sharing the stage. One section of a jam could make everything all right. The Dead and the Nevilles sent everyone home happy with "Sugar Magnolia" to close the set, and a "Knockin' on Heaven's Door" encore.

Shaking things up during tour '88, Dylan played unpredictable originals like, "I Dreamed I Saw St. Augustine," "One More Cup of Coffee," "The Man in Me," and "Song to Woody," as well as an eclectic mix of covers, "Trail of the Buffalo," "Man of Constant Sorrow," "I'm In the Mood for Love," "Nadine," and "Give My Love to Rose." Dylan began his 1989 touring year in late May as he played in Europe through the end of June. Dylan toured with the same musicians as he had the previous year until Kenny Aaronson had to leave the band to get treatment for skin cancer. On June 10, 1989, at a concert in The Netherlands, Tony Garnier replaced Aaronson, and Tony has remained Dylan's bassist for twenty-nine years and running. The 6-10-89 show happens to be a monster, featuring a "Shelter from the Storm" with stunning shifts in tempo and texture of sound. Dylan is playing harmonica again, something he skipped entirely the year before. The 6-10-89 "Like a Rolling Stone" is a ferocious attack—an unreal release of energy and aggression—Dylan's way of welcoming Garnier to the band.

Dylan was back touring the United States in July, and I headed back to Old Orchard Beach to see him on July 15. These were pre-Internet days so I had no idea what to expect. I was relieved to see G. E. in the band again, and when Dylan played harmonica, I was thrilled on a chilly night in Maine. Dylan's master plan was to play the same towns year after year and attract a new fan base, and without realizing it, I was a willing test subject. The three-song *Bringing It All Back Home* acoustic set of "Love Minus Zero/No Limit," "She Belongs to Me," and "Mr. Tambourine Man" made the Maine excursion highly worthwhile. Following Dylan had become much more exciting than following the Grateful Dead.

I drove from Maine to Bristol, Connecticut, the following day to see Dylan in Lake Compounce Festival Park, where I met up with Dylan fanatics from Woodstock. *Oh Mercy* wasn't scheduled for release until October, and consequently, Dylan wasn't previewing any of those songs yet. On a steamy summer evening with the sun still blazing, Dylan came out with the hood of his sweatshirt over his head, shades, and harmonica rack in place. The third and fourth songs were "I Believe in You" and "I Don't Believe You," respectively. A spiritual affirmation was followed by the ballad of a spurned lover as Dylan had fun lining up songs with similar titles. Dylan's pacing was quick, confident, and at times, reckless. The year before it seemed like Smith was leading the band. This year Dylan was doing his thing, and the band had to be on its toes. The surprise tune at this show was Gordon Lightfoot's "Early Morning Rain."

I caught six unique and satisfying shows on this leg of the tour. The best of the batch was at the Garden State Performing Arts Center where I saw my first show of the Never Ending Tour the year before. Dylan was showing up in the same towns and I was doing my part, spreading the news—word of mouth. I convinced Deadhead Doug to sneak his equipment in to tape the show. Doug respected Dylan, but he was a Garcia loyalist all the way. Doug was with his girlfriend taping in the fifth row, and I was shuffling on the lawn as Dylan opened the show with his first live performance of "Trouble" from *Shot of Love*. Dylan's group rocked it violently, and swiftly segued to a tender version of Van Morrison's "One Irish Rover." Dylan's vocals burned intensely against the casual arrangement, spurring Smith to finish the song off with a spiraling solo. The band slammed into "I Don't Believe You" and Dylan unleashed an authoritative harmonica solo. It sounded as good as it did with The Band in 1966. It was one of those nights when Dylan pushes himself and his band, and every risk is rewarded.

I've enjoyed listening to this show for many years since that night, and I owe thanks to the dogged perseverance of Doug, who improbably battled off a female usher to successfully finish taping this show. During the fourth song, "Just Like a Woman," the trouble begins. As a tribute to tapers everywhere, I've transcribed their conversation from the tape as Dylan played on five rows away.

Usher: Can I see what you have in there? What do you have in that bag? Why is there a red light on?

Doug: I got a flashlight.

Usher: If it's a tape recorder, shut it off right now... I have to take the tape. I'm going to get a security guard. I have to get a security guard, then. Give me the tape, or I'll get a security guard.

Doug: I don't understand. What's wrong?

Usher: Is that a tape recorder?

Doug: No, it's a camera with a flashlight blinking.

Usher: If it's a camera, why is the light on? Listen, if it's a camera, let me see it, or I'll have to call a security guard over.

Doug: The light's not even on. Don't worry; I'll shut it off.

Usher: I know, but you're not listening to me. You still have to check it with a security guard.

Doug: I'll shut it off. Don't worry.

Usher: Yeah, but even if you shut it off ...

Doug: OK. I'll shut it off.

Usher: I'll call a security guard if you don't come with me now and check it in. You're not listening to me. (In the midst of this bickering, Dylan was twenty feet away, blowing a lyrical harp solo.)

Doug: I don't understand what the big deal is.

Usher: There are no cameras or anything allowed in the theatre. I have to check that with a security guard.

Doug: It's not a camera.

Usher: What is it?

Doug: It's a flashlight. I told you already.

Usher: Can I see it then, sir? Whatever it is, I have to check it with security.

Doug: Miss, believe me. It's nothing; it's not worth the hassle. It's just me and my girlfriend. I swear to God, it's nothing. Please trust me.

Usher: I don't care what it is. You have to check it with a security guard.

Doug: I'll come back tomorrow.

Usher: No, you can't come around tomorrow.

Doug: I don't see what the big deal is.

Usher: It's not allowed. If it's a camera or anything, anywhere, or recording device, it must be checked in with a security guard.

The usher suddenly disappeared as if Doug wished her off to a cornfield. I would have folded under that pressure. Doug spoke to the usher in hushed tones, doing his best to protect the audio integrity of the tape. He was a master taper all the way, still interested in turning out a quality tape under serious duress. The other live Dylan debut that night was a lovely acoustic rendition of "When Did You Leave Heaven?" from *Down in the Groove*.

G. E. Smith's solo soared during "I Shall Be Released," setting the stage for a manic "Like a Rolling Stone." The garbled lines gushed out of Dylan. During the extended instrumentals, Dylan stomped around the stage and occasionally stopped for a guitar hero pose. "Mr. Tambourine Man" was pleasing as the final encore. Bob's cadence had comic texture: "I'll come following, ah . . . you!" What a fabulous performance. And for the foreseeable future, Mr. Dylan, we'll be following, ah you!

NINETEEN

OH MERCY

*O**h Mercy* was released on September 18, 1989, exactly two years after the Dead's iconic performance in Madison Square Garden when "Touch of Grey" was a top ten hit. The reviews for *Oh Mercy* were stellar across the board, and since this was my first time experiencing an album of Dylan originals, my anticipation and expectations were epic. Adding to the allure of the release was the album cover featuring graffiti art taken from a building in Manhattan, and the enticing title… *Oh Mercy*.

I purchased the album the day of its release at Rhino Records in New Paltz. Fifteen minutes before the store opened I sat in my car, eyes glued on the door, blood pressure rising. The long-haired, heavy metal cat who worked the morning shift pulled the store keys from the pouch of his hoodie and opened the door. I didn't want to scare him by immediately pouncing on the poor lad, so I gave him a half-minute before charging in and proclaiming, "I'm here for *Oh Mercy*."

"You're here for oh what?" chimed the clerk, as if I'd asked him when the next train from Ronkonkoma would be pulling into the station. After I explained the gravity of the situation, that I was there for the new Dylan album, the attendant said, "I don't know, dude, let me check, I only work here part-time."

That's when I saw them, *Oh Mercy* CDs behind the counter, lined up on a shelf—pretty maids all in a row. I ripped the cellophane off and freed the CD for listening before I got to my car. I was rocking out to "Political World" on the short drive home. A few hours later, as I listened to *Oh Mercy* for the third time, I realized I wouldn't be attending classes that day, and I just might not see the inside of a classroom for the rest of the semester.

The following Monday, tickets for a Dylan performance at the Mid-Hudson Center in Poughkeepsie were going on sale. Since this was only 15 minutes from New Paltz, I headed out to Poughkeepsie at 2:00 a.m. I showed up with a blanket and squatted next to the box office door on a frigid evening. I fell asleep as the sun began to rise, and when I woke up there was a line of about twenty folks behind me. They weren't sure if I was a bum or a Dylan fan. When the ticket window opened, I was rewarded with six front row tickets, dead center. A reporter from the *Poughkeepsie Journal* was waiting to interview me for a story about Dylan's return to the Hudson Valley. When I opened the paper the following day, there was a photo with me fanning out my front row tickets below my smiling face. The caption read:

OH MERCY!
Howard Weiner, 26, of New Paltz, New York, displays his front row tickets for Bob Dylan's concert at the Mid-Hudson Civic Center on October 20.

It was quite a thrill to see my name below "OH MERCY!" Just as I had great fortune during my early days of following the Grateful Dead, this was confirmation that I was on the right path. I wasn't writing about this or anything else at the time, but I knew I was witnessing essential music history that, for the time being, I would pass on by word of mouth. Before the Poughkeepsie gig, Dylan kicked the tour off with four shows at New York City's Beacon Theatre, and I was there for the last three.

Dylan's run at the Beacon began on October 10. That night I was at Shea Stadium for a Rolling Stones concert in support of their new album, *Steel Wheels*. The Stones were also playing Shea Stadium on the 11th, but I picked the right night to be there. Eric Clapton joined the Stones for a mind-blowing blues assault on "Little Red Rooster." It was a phenomenal show with an elaborate stage production. *Steel Wheels* was their most rocking album in a long time. Even though their set lists didn't differ much, I could have gone to see this show five nights in a row.

The *Oh Mercy* songs debuted on the tour's opening night at the Beacon Theatre were "Everything Is Broken," "Most of the Time," and "What Good Am I?" This trio was also performed the following two shows. These were strong shows that I enjoyed very much, but my memory of them was obliterated by Dylan's astonishing performance on Friday the 13th. Dylan stormed the stage in a gold lame suit and pointy white boots. My evening unfolded like a surreal dream as I watched the proceedings from the front row of the balcony with my Woodstock friend, Blaise. We smiled all night as we watched Dylan and his bird nest hairdo wiggle away below.

Dylan opened with the *Empire Burlesque* rocker "Seeing the Real You At Last," which segued into "What Good Am I?" Possibly influenced by his time with the Dead, Dylan was segueing songs more than ever before. Dylan went to *Infidels* for his third song, "Man of Peace," and followed with his live debut of "Precious Memories" from *Knocked out Loaded*. Dylan infused the night with a breathless pace as he stood and delivered his newer songs without regard for what people may have wanted to hear. Aware of the city he loved, Dylan turned the clock back to his Greenwich Village days with an acoustic set that began with "Don't Think Twice It's Alright," and one for his hero, the man who drew him to New York. "Song to Woody" was a loving gesture, and it struck the right emotional chord for those on hand.

"Everything Is Broken" filled the Beacon with bawdy rock and roll again. There could be no mistaking Dylan was sentimental on this final night at the Beacon as he followed with "I'll Remember You." The final three electric songs came off like a communal exorcism. The stacks of speakers hanging like worms in front of the Neo-Grecian décor were smoking from G. E.'s nasty blues leads during "It Takes a Lot to Laugh, It Takes a Train to Cry." Earlier Bob played one for Woody, now he pivoted into one for Jesus, "In the Garden." I hadn't seen this one since the Radio City shows. Dylan blitzed through "Like a Rolling Stone" to end the set. It was hurried until he neared the finish line, and then the Transcendent One lingered in the triumph of his consecrated anthem by tacking on a three-minute harp solo before departing.

It was too much to process as I sat there in the front row of the balcony for the world premiere of "Man in the Long Black Coat" as the first encore. The pulse, vibration, and rumbling force made me feel unsafe in the front row of the balcony. Pure ecstasy might catapult me into the orchestra pit below. This is where things got weird. In the thick of "Leopard-Skin Pill-Box Hat," Dylan placed his guitar down, sang a verse, and then grabbed his mic and went for a stroll while playing harmonica. Bob stepped to the front of the stage and got down on his knees while keeping the harp solo alive. Suddenly, he dropped the harmonica to the ground like a Wise Guy dropping a gun after a hit, and nonchalantly walked off the stage and into the crowd. He shook hands with a few stunned fans in the front row and shuffled out the exit door to the right of the stage onto West 75th Street.

The house lights stayed on as the band continued to play, and I'm pretty sure that Dylan didn't inform the band if he was coming back. The jam stumbled to a confused ending and the crowd applauded, and wondered if Bob would return. But there was not a word heard; goodbye, not even a Shabbat shalom. Folklore states that the man in the gold lame suit hopped on a bicycle and pedaled to his Manhattan apartment.

Billed as Formerly the Warlocks, the Grateful Dead kicked off their fall '89 tour in Hampton, Virginia. Without much advance notice, the billing helped minimize overcrowding at the Hampton shows. Fans were rewarded with special performances of songs that hadn't been played for many years. At the 10-8-89 show, Deadheads were treated to Help on the Way > Slipknot! > Franklin's Tower for the first time in four years, and there was an old-school, "And We Bid You Goodnight" encore. The big payoff came on 10-9-89 when they broke out "Dark Star" for the first time in five years, and later in the second set played

"Death Don't Have No Mercy" for the second time in nineteen years. They encored with "Attics of my Life," the first performance of that *American Beauty* ditty in seventeen years.

The Grateful Dead headed north for a five-night run that began on October 11 in East Rutherford. The Stones, Dylan, and the Dead were all playing in the New York City area that night. Due to my preoccupation with Dylan, I didn't see any of the Dead shows. I didn't miss much until the final night. On Bob Weir's forty-second birthday, October 16, 1989, Grateful Dead magic rippled through the Brendan Byrne Arena as they seamlessly segued and looped beloved jamming songs: Dark Star > Playin' > Uncle John's Band > Playin' > Drums > I Will Take You Home > I Need a Miracle > Dark Star > Attics of My Life > Playin' Reprise. It was a helluva of a second set loop, and the show was officially released as a double CD, *Nightfall of Diamonds*, in 2001.

There's nothing quite as gratifying as casually walking to your seats in the front row of a major concert, especially if you earned it the old-fashion way, by freezing your ass off and squatting on a city sidewalk for seven or eight hours. It was another wild night with Dylan in the Mid-Hudson Civic Center on 10-20-89. This venue is a faceless dump better suited for professional wrestling or roller derby, but Dylan was in fine spirits as he kicked the festivities off with "The Times They Are A-Changin'."

I had a stare-off with Dylan as he sang, "What good am I…while you softly weep, and I hear in my head what you say in your sleep, and I freeze in the moment, like the rest that don't try." Dylan avoided direct eye contact with me the rest of the night, but for those thirty seconds we were frozen in the moment.

In 1998, during Dylan's Grammy Award-winning speech for *Time Out Of Mind,* Dylan spoke of a night in Duluth when he went to a Buddy Holly concert and Buddy looked right at him, and somehow Buddy's spirit was in the recording studio when *Time Out Of Mind* was recorded. Eyeballing Dylan was a peculiar experience, almost uncomfortable, like staring at the sun.

During '89 Dylan was full of surprise, and later in the show he played piano for the first time on stage in several years on "When You Gonna Wake Up" and the wondrous live debut of "Ring Them Bells." Being reasonably close to Saugerties and Woodstock may have spurred a moving performance of "Tears of Rage," a song created in the basement of the most famous pink house in music. It was an amazing night, and I savored these shows because Dylan was pushing his art and his audiences to the brink.

A week later I caught my final show of the tour at the RPI Fieldhouse in Troy, New York. From the standpoint of quality performances, this was the best show of the tour. Dylan continued to pepper his sets with unexpected choices. My favorites on this night were "Lenny Bruce," "Mama You've Been On My Mind," "A Hard Rain's A-Gonna Fall," and "My Back Pages." Dylan was pounding the keys again for the debut of "Disease of Conceit," in the encore slot. The nineteenth and final tune of the night, "Maggie's Farm," had an extraordinary instrumental ending. These were the best of times for the early days of the Never Ending Tour.

The Grateful Dead released their latest, and what would be their last studio album, *Built to Last*, on Halloween. It was all tricks and no treats. The album consisted of eight new original compositions that the band had been playing live, and four of them were Brent Mydland songs. Brent did a superb job fitting into the band and replacing both Keith and Donna Godchaux. However, these tunes didn't capture the essence of the Grateful Dead sound, and really should have been on a solo Brent album. Even though the chord progression is basic and the lyrics are mediocre, it's hard to deny that "Blow Away" is an energetic song. Weir's contributions are "Picasso Moon" and "Victim or the Crime." Although it's not a great song, "Victim or the Crime" features Garcia's best guitar work on this album. There are three Hunter/Garcia songs; "Foolish Heart," "Standing on the Moon," and "Built to Last." I can't say I love any of them. "Foolish Heart" has a nice feel to it and a decent jam, hardly qualifications for a Dead classic. Many Deadheads thought highly of "Standing on the Moon." Hunter's lyrics are strong and Garcia sings with feeling, but these slow-moving ballads seemed to be all that Garcia was interested in cranking out. "Built to Last" is a sluggish number that never resonated with me. This material seemed to reinforce that Garcia was fading and getting older.

This album was disappointing coming after *Oh Mercy*. I hoped *Built to Last* would have a new original that wasn't previously played live, or a few quirky instrumentals. This album was a carbon copy of *In the Dark* with inferior songs. It didn't seem like there was anything holding *Built to Last* together. It lacked purpose. After several listens, I gathered a group of Dylan/Dead friends for a *Built to Last* listening party in my New Paltz pad. I desperately wanted to like the album, and I wondered if any of these cats could find something they liked about the album. After we obtained a nice valium, weed, and wine buzz, we listened and reached a unanimous lame CD verdict. I ejected the CD and stepped into my backyard and tossed the disc like a Frisbee, deep into the woods. Let the squirrels, skunks, and raccoons figure that one out. *Built to Toss* would have been a more fitting title.

Except for *In the Dark*, the Grateful Dead's success was never built around, or due to, album sales. The Grateful Dead machine was a highly profitable and unstoppable force—as long as Jerry could keep on keeping on. In the face of economic prosperity, the band tried to stay true to its roots, but overwhelming demand dictated that they play larger venues, and ultimately, intimacy was sacrificed.

On the other hand, Dylan appeared to be the youth of 1,000 summers as the '80s ended. His experience with the Dead brought him back to life, and his career as a performing artist exploded without the commotion attached to Garcia's comeback. Thanks to an article published in *Q Magazine* by journalist Andrew Deevoy, Dylan's tour that began in 1988 was now being called the Never Ending Tour. With Garcia and Dylan both closing in on their fiftieth birthdays at the dawn of a new decade, the only thing for certain was that if they continued their touring ways, the road ahead would be filled with glory, heartache, and pain.

TWENTY

DEATH DON'T HAVE NO MERCY

After seeing Dylan walk out into the crowd and exit through the side door of the Beacon Theatre, it was hard to imagine a more surreal concert experience, but Dylan topped that during his first show of 1990 at Toad's Place, a club with a 700-person capacity in New Haven, Connecticut. Toad's Place had some history. Back when the club opened in 1975, Muddy Waters, Johnny Lee Hooker, and Koko Taylor performed there. Before they hit the big time, U2 played at Toad's three times between 1980 and 1981. And before the Rolling Stones embarked on their Steel Wheels tour, they played a half-hour set there on August 12, 1989. Without advance publicity, Dylan slipped into Toad's with G. E. Smith and crew and performed a four-set, fifty-song extravaganza to prepare for his upcoming tour of Brazil, Paris, and London.

This was both a public practice session and a show foreshadowing his upcoming tour. In Toad's, Dylan debuted three *Oh Mercy* tunes, "Political World," "Where Teardrops Fall," and "What was it You Wanted?" "Political World" was performed three times, and "Teardrops" twice. In a rare move, Dylan played "Wiggle, Wiggle," a tune that would be on his next album, and he served up his first Traveling Wilburys tune, "Congratulations." There were a series of surprise covers that included Springsteen's "Dancin' in the Dark" and the opening number of the night, Joe South's "Walk a Mile in my Shoes." This was an incredible time. Dylan was giving it his all, and really cutting loose in a way that he never had before. The shows in Brazil, Paris, and London all had sets of twenty songs or more. Dylan delivered his best on February 8, 1990, at the Hammersmith Odeon in London. The Dylan was on fire all night, bopping around as if he was under the influence of some high-grade Peruvian yeyo.

The Grateful Dead had abandoned the notion of fun club gigs with outrageous set lists long ago. Their last such gig was on October 16, 1981, at the Melkweg in Amsterdam. Following a cancelled concert in Paris, the band rented some equipment and headed to Amsterdam. On that evening they played an acoustic and electric set, breaking out rarities like "Hully Gully," "Gloria," and the first "Turn on Your Love Light" since the passing of Pigpen.

My first Dead show of 1990 was on March 26 at the brand-new Knickerbocker Arena in Albany. This show was sabotaged by five of the worst songs from *Built to Last*, and consequently, my passion to see the band continued to dwindle. If only I could have had faith and made it to the Nassau Coliseum on March 29.

Branford Marsalis, the younger brother of Wynton, and the most talented improviser of his legendary jazz family, showed up with his saxophone to sit in with the Grateful Dead on 3-29-90. After jamming with the band during "Birdsong," the penultimate song of the opening set, Branford thought his evening was over. "We came off the stage and everybody said 'Boy, that was great.' We chatted for about 10 minutes and I said 'Look, thanks for letting me play.' They said 'Oh, no, where you going? Stick around, play the rest of the show.'"

The second set began with "Eyes of the World," a tune usually appearing three or four songs into the set. Maybe Garcia sensed this was the type of tune Marsalis could swing to. Branford wasn't familiar with many Dead tunes. After listening to the chords and rhythms, he swiftly checked in with some light riffs and built from there. "Eyes" starts with a manageable pace, perfect for Branford to feel his way through. Standing tall on the right side of the stage between Garcia and Mydland, Branford picks up on the mojo and stirs in dreamy melody lines that match the texture of the tune. Garcia, a gracious host, likes what he hears and plays off Branford's idea before stepping up to sing. Branford's confidence grows as he plays off Garcia's vocals with breezy leads.

Garcia pounces on the first solo in a way that sets the stage for Marsalis—here you go, Branford, here's everything you need to know, the DNA of "Eyes." As Branford blows chords that add to the swinging rhythm, he's absorbing Garcia's lesson. Without any visual or verbal cue, Garcia steps off and Branford glides in. With the ease of Coltrane, Branford's blowing and everybody in the Nassau Coliseum's glowing. There's an incredible surge of emotion in Branford's playing, as if he was waiting for this specific moment his entire performing career. Deadheads are caught up in the rapture of the solo; this is the hottest jam of the show.

Branford is putting licks together à la Garcia, in a language that the band and the fans understand. The Maestro scales the mountain and steps off as Garcia and Mydland pick up the conversation. Garcia throws out a lead, Branford answers, and Mydland plays off that, and then Branford reverses the process. Garcia sings: "There comes a redeemer, and slowly too fades away." A huge roar fills the arena. Whether you call it jazz, rock, or fusion, it's absolutely sublime, and Marsalis has pulled off the best solo by a guest in Grateful Dead history.

The first seven minutes of this "Eyes" is so stunning, it obliterates the remaining ten minutes. Once I hear Garcia start singing that second verse, I find myself skipping back to the beginning of the track to hear Branford's brilliance again, as opposed to letting it play through. Garcia introduces some Midi effects during the second solo as his guitar licks take on a sax-like quality. Starting in late '89, several members of the band played around with this new Midi technology. I understand their fascination with the technology, but it sounded gimmicky, and it took the place of authentic jamming. Branford did his thing as the band cruised through "Estimated Prophet," and then he was startled by reaction when the crowd realized they were segueing into "Dark Star." "They started playing the song and the audience went absolutely ape shit," said Marsalis. "They went bananas. I'm looking at them going bananas and I'm going, 'OK, this must be an anthem.' Then I got all these telephone calls on my private number [from] Dead Heads. The phone would ring and I said 'How'd you get this number?' and they'd say 'Don't worry about it, we're harmless, we just love the music.'"

In a televised interview with Dave Marsh, Marsalis said, "The first time I played with them at the Nassau Coliseum was a very special night." Branford played with the band four more occasions, with their last jam coming on December 16, 1994. There's lots of worthwhile music on these occasions, but nothing clicked like 3-29-90. Garcia's decaying virtuosity and health factored into the diminished results at these other shows.

Aside from having four songs on the new album, Brent's contributions on stage were bolder than ever before. Later in the year, *Without a Net*, a double live CD featuring performances from the spring '90 tour, was released. This collection includes the Branford "Eyes of the World," and you can hear Brent's comfort level interacting with Marsalis and Jerry. After the Grateful Dead performed three shows at the World Music Theatre in Tinley Park, Illinois, in late July, Mydland returned home to the East Bay suburb of Lafayette, California.

On July 26, Mydland injected himself with a speedball. The potency of the cocaine and morphine mix killed him almost instantly. Brent was thirty-seven years old. The overdose appeared to be accidental, not a suicide. Primarily a drinker, Brent began using harder drugs over the past few years as he dealt with family problems and depression. Although he'd been with the band for ten years, he always felt like the "new guy." He was the youngest member of the band, and he didn't have the breadth of cultural experience that his mates did as they bonded and came of age in San Francisco.

People around Jerry at the time of Brent's death noticed he was deeply saddened. In a *Rolling Stone* interview, Garcia said, "It was heartbreaking when Brent died, because it seemed like such a waste. Here's this incredibly talented guy—he had a great natural melodic sense, and he was a great singer. And he could've gotten better, but he just didn't see it." Looking at the videos from the summer '89 tour, it's obvious Garcia and Mydland developed on stage chemistry, often smiling and nodding at each other in approval. There were several junctures over the previous ten years where the band should have considered taking a break from touring to rejuvenate. Now the Grateful Dead Machine was big business, and a hiatus was not an option. Auditions for Brent's replacement began immediately.

Before revving up the Never Ending Tour again in May, Dylan finished recording the tracks for his new album, *Under the Red Sky*, in April, with producers Don and David Was. The album was released on September 11, the same date that *Love and Theft* would be released eleven years later. There were more negative reviews than positive ones for *Under the Red Sky*. The opening track, "Wiggle, Wiggle," featuring Guns n' Roses axe man Slash, is a short and simple rock assault with Dylan listing things that wiggle, like he listed things that are broken in "Everything is Broken." The ensuing title song is built around nursey rhymes, as is the last tune, "Cat's in the Well." The album is dedicated to Dylan's four-year-old daughter, Desiree Gabrielle Dennis-Dylan. However, this is not a light-hearted album. The nursery rhymes mask more complex ideas.

Dylan's delivery of the final line is stunning: "Good night, my love, may the Lord have mercy on us all." A lot of the themes on this album resemble those of *Oh Mercy*, but the performances are raw and unique. It's a slightly shorter album than *Oh Mercy*, and there's no definitive songs like "Man in the Long Back Coat," but *Under the Red Sky* has several strong numbers, and it's a cohesive work of art.

I was initially disappointed with the album. After a dozen listens, I began to crave it. The mix of Dylan on accordion, Al Koper on keyboards, and George Harrison on slide guitar gives "Under the Red Sky" a rich sound texture as Dylan howls lines like, "This is the key to the kingdom and this is the town. This is the blind horse that leads you around."

"Born in Time," a reworked *Oh Mercy* outtake, is another charming performance, sentimental and mystical, reminiscent of "Simple Twist of Fate." The other *Oh Mercy* extra, "God Know," is revamped into a rocking spiritual number accented by skillful strumming and picking from Stevie Ray Vaughn, who also appears on "Cats in the Well." Two weeks before the release of *Under the Red Sky*, Stevie Ray Vaughn was killed in a helicopter crash after playing a concert at the Alpine Valley Music Theatre. Stevie Ray had beaten back his drug demons, and at the age of thirty-five was thriving in a state of blissful sobriety. But the inherent dangers of being on the road cut down one of the greatest blues guitarists in his prime.

Elton John makes a guest appearance on "2 X 2," which is the least appealing song on the album. My distaste for the song has nothing to do with Elton, it's just a track that drones on without any noteworthy developments. "Handy Dandy" is an enticing performance with crisp vocal delivery, a keyboard riff similar to "Like a Rolling Stone," and evocative lyrics that invite the listener to apply the descriptions as they please. When Dylan sings, "He's been around the world and back again/ Something in the moonlight still hounds him," it's easy to imagine Bob writing that line after his brief tour of Brazil, Paris, and London.

The fabric of *Under the Red Sky* is an amalgamation of many musical styles, and the lyrics are striking in places, but it's Dylan's commitment to the performances that makes this work. If Dylan would have walked into a studio with these ideas a few years earlier, he probably would have come away with another *Knocked Out Loaded*.

Dylan was back on the road in May, kicking off a tour where the bulk of the shows were played in Canada before he headed to Europe for nine dates at summer festivals. Consistently throughout his career, Dylan has committed to being an international performing artist, building and keeping a worldwide audience, while the Grateful Dead only made occasional attempts to spread their music overseas.

Dylan still had Jerry and the boys on his mind as he returned to North America to start another tour that began in Canada and ended in Arizona. He played his first Dead cover, "Friend of the Devil," in Merryville, Indiana, on August 27, 1990. This selection made sense since this was the most Dylanesque song in the Dead's canon.

Dylan returned to the Northeast for another residency at the Beacon Theatre, but a few days before, on October 13, 1990, Dylan appeared at the Eisenhower Hall Theatre in West Pont, New York. Since the "Voice of his generation" was playing at the United States Military Academy, this show was reported on in many newspapers and magazines from the *New York Times* to *Rolling Stone*. Heightening the tension around the show was Iraq's invasion of Kuwait on August 2. It was beginning to seem inevitable that the United States would soon be dropping bombs, and possibly sending troops to the Middle East.

I was there in West Point on that rainy Saturday night, exactly one year after the Beacon show when Dylan walked into the crowd and split out the side of the theatre while the band was still playing "Leopard-Skin Pill-Box Hat." On this evening, a similar dash through the crowd was unlikely, since the first several rows were filled with uniformed cadets. A strange vibe filled the air as I walked from my car into Eisenhower Hall. It didn't seem like the type of place that should be hosting a rock and roll show of any kind. Everything in the area was orderly, clean, and sterile, and the ushers were cadets.

I don't recall the smell of marijuana filling up the air when the lights were turned down. Dylan transformed the atmosphere by launching into an electrified "Tangled Up in Blue" that had a Jerry Garcia Band feel. Dylan wore a black ushanka with a badge on the brim, and a dark suit with a scarf. It was a throwback to his scruffier appearances with the Grateful Dead. Cesar Diaz, Dylan's guitar technician, was on stage auditioning with the band on and off throughout the electric portion of the show. Dylan had been holding live auditions on stage for G. E. Smith's replacement since the last tour. There were no hard feelings between the two, they just couldn't work out a financial deal for Smith to remain in the band for the fourth year of the Never Ending Tour. By auditioning his guitar technician, Dylan was again operating in an organic Grateful Dead style by trying to work with those around him, as opposed to completely changing his band and going in a different direction.

A brooding version of "Man in the Long Black Coat" was followed by the controversial song choice of the night, "Masters of War." In his *Rolling Stone* review of the show, Alan Light wrote, "'Masters of War,' his most vicious anti-military song, made for a decidedly uncomfortable moment; while the band ripped into a blazing arrangement, Dylan seemed to swallow the lines 'I hope that you die/And your death'll come soon' in the face of real-life aspiring masters of war. The song met with a cool response from the cadets down front." While I'd agree that the band ripped a blazing arrangement assessment, I didn't notice a cool response or anything uncomfortable about the reaction. After all, the cadets are just instruments of the masters of war, or just pawns in their game. "Masters of War" has always been considered a protest song, but the more I hear Dylan play it through the years, it comes off as an astute assessment of the way things inevitably are in the modern, or political, world. The fiery pace and guitar solos made it a vigorous rock and roll workout. It's a number that was heavy in the rotation at the time, and you know Dylan isn't the type of artist who would back down from playing it because some might view it as controversial.

Considering the audience, "Gotta Serve Somebody" was an interesting choice to close the electric set. The acoustic sets now featured Tony Garnier on standup bass and Chris Parker contributing brushed drums. "Don't Think Twice It's Alright" benefitted from the acoustic quartet treatment. The ramped-up instrumental coda with the playful harmonica solo whipped the crowd into a frenzied state. The new acoustic presentations freed Dylan to take more chances.

"Under the Red Sky" kicked off the next electric set, and without a keyboard player, the song gained intensity and lost sentimentality. The ensuing "Wiggle, Wiggle" turned out to be an unexpected highlight as ten rows of cadets jumped out of their seats, danced around, and tossed their caps in the air. Most of these young cadets were likely fans of Guns n' Roses or the Red Hot Chili Peppers, and when Dylan was playing "Masters of War" they probably didn't know the song, or where unable to understand his garbled singing. The electric set concluded with "I'll

Remember You," "All Along the Watchtower," "I Shall Be Released," and "Like a Rolling Stone." Surprisingly, the West Point show was better than any of the next five at the Beacon Theatre.

Dylan's last two New York City stops at Radio City Music Hall (1988), and the Beacon (1989), were filled with transcendent music, drama, and there was an air of personal triumph for Dylan. The 1990 Beacon shows were the end of the G. E. Smith era, and the constant shuffling of guitarists adversely affected the momentum of the concerts. Dylan's playing was energetic and sloppy. He was blazing into a new stage of his touring career without a game plan, except to stand and keep delivering these songs.

After the death of Brent Mydland, the Grateful Dead marched forward with the only strategy they've ever known. They had the good fortune of temporarily landing Bruce Hornsby, a talented jazz musician with a successful solo career, to play piano with the band as they transitioned to a permanent replacement for Brent Mydland. Bruce Hornsby & the Range opened for the Grateful Dead on a few occasions. At one of those shows in Buckeye Lake Music Center on June 25, 1988, Hornsby came out and played accordion on "Sugaree." Hornsby was familiar with the Dead's music, and his presence was an immense spiritual lift following the loss of Brent.

Some of the talented players considered to replace Brent were Bill Payne (Little Feat), Chester Thompson (Santana), Tom Constanten, and Merl Saunders. The band chose Vince Wellnick, who played with the Tubes and Todd Rundgren. The Dead liked his style, and he was easily the best harmony singer of those auditioned. Recalling how they broke the news to him, Vince said, "I got a call from Bobby and the first thing he said was, 'Is your insurance paid up?'" It was a warped joke from Weir about the string of bad luck that had befallen those who have played keyboards for the Grateful Dead.

Six weeks after Brent's death, Wellnick made his debut as the Dead's fall tour began in Richfield, Ohio, on September 7. Vince was a talented player, but the sounds and texture of his electronic keyboard were awkward. There was a carnival-like tone to a lot of his playing that didn't blend well, and was distracting at times. Bruce Hornsby came to the rescue, joining Wellnick and the Dead on September 15, 1990, during the second show of their six-night Madison Square Garden run. Hornsby's appearance inspired Garcia, who played tremendously throughout the MSG residency. The 1990 shows were clearly better than the 1988 MSG shows. Hornsby was with the band as they played their final tour of Europe in October. Heading into the new year, it looked as though the Grateful Dead could roll on indefinitely.

On October 29, 1990, Dylan fans were blessed with some more new music from their hero with the release of the *Traveling Wilburys Volume 3*, their second and final album. Without Roy Orbison, and the sparks of spontaneity from their first sessions, matching the artistic and commercial success of their debut album was going to be a tough task. The album didn't spawn any hit singles or popular MTV videos, and it didn't have the easy listening flow of its predecessor. Dylan changed his name from Lucky to Boo Wilbury. Boo was the standout performer of *Traveling Wilburys Volume 3*. Harrison, Petty, and Lynne came to these sessions and gave it their all, yet Roy's absence took a toll. They missed his improbable voice, which was the ideal counterpart to Dylan, but most of all they missed the man. Just being in the same room with Roy Orbison created an irreplaceable gestalt.

Harrison, Petty, and Lynne meshed in a way on this album that almost made their performances bland or flat. The group tried to recapture the Wilbury sound, when they might have been better off heading in a new direction. "Seven Deadly Sins" features Dylan's best vocal from either album. After the second verse, Dylan misses and slurs the first few words of the chorus, yet his performance is so authentic in the spirit of the song that they wisely decide to use this take without overdubbing. Dylan's lovesick growling of the deadly sins brushes against the pitch-perfect harmonies of the other Wilburys in this striking '50s-style doo wop number. The other irresistible number here is "New Blue Moon." Lynne, Petty, and Harrison start the song off with impeccable group singing as Dylan waits in the weeds, and then disturbs the peace by singing, "Too many moons have come and gone and none of them were blue. Too many times the sun came up, but it came up without you, you, ya, you, who whoo!" A million people could have been auditioned to sing this line, and none of them could have ever sounded like Dylan does here. He's slurring words together, elongating syllables, and improvising an ending that is dramatic and funny. I can't think of another singer who could attempt or invent something like this and pull it off. Most of us hoped for more from the *Traveling Wilburys Volume 3*. Thankfully, we got an encore.

TWENTY-ONE

IN THE MIDDLE OF NOWHERE

As Dylan closed in on his fiftieth birthday, the Recording Academy decided to honor him with a Grammy Lifetime Achievement Award. It was time to make amends for never honoring him with an Album of the Year Grammy for one of his visionary albums. The ceremony was held at the Radio City Music Hall on February 20, 1991, and fear was in the air. The Gulf War was under way and the United States and its coalition partners were busy flying sorties and bombing the Iraqis out of Kuwait. Gary Shandling hosted the awards show, and Jack Nicholson was on hand to introduce Dylan, as he did at Live Aid. It didn't seem possible, but what happened next was weirder than Live Aid or *The Shining*.

Nicholson appeared devilishly handsome in a black tuxedo as he began his intro by saying, "With the possible exception of Boston Celtic Kevin McHale, he was the most famous person ever to leave Hibbing, Minnesota." Jack's offbeat yet stellar introduction, during which, he called him "Uncle Bobby," led into a montage of Dylan footage that began with "The Times They Are A-Changin'" and ended with "Series of Dreams." Nicholson had a few more flattering words before turning the stage over to Dylan and his band. Behind the stage there was a huge backdrop of Dylan's face from the cover of *Biograph*. A thrashing garage band sound introduced the chord sequence to "Masters of War." Wow! In the middle of the Gulf War it was a ballsy choice, and I found it to be more of a State of the World address rather than a condemnation of America's involvement in the war or the Iraqi aggression.

Uncle Bobby looked hip wearing a white top hat with black trimming, black shirt, bow tie and purple jacket. He played an acoustic, and there was a red lightning bolt on his guitar strap. Dylan had a harmonica rack around his neck although he didn't blow a note. Three days of film montages couldn't have prepared a national TV audience for what they were about to hear. With eyes tight-shut, Dylan stepped up and unleashed the lyrics of his song in a phlegm-filled growl. He was the first performer in Grammy history to gargle a song as opposed to singing it. There was absolutely no emotional attachment to what he was gargling. The words came off as meaningless, and before he let John "J. J." Jackson, the new guitarist, play a solo, his last word trailed off in a nasally whine. Garnier on bass and Ian Wallace on drums were cooking, but Jackson's solo went nowhere and an odd, maniacal smile spread across his face. Oh, how G. E. Smith would have killed on this solo! Dylan must have been thinking there must be some way out of here. If only the Principal Pederson were on hand, he could have cut the power and pulled the curtain as he did in Hibbing High.

There was stunned applause, and eventually a standing ovation from the assembled music luminaries as Dylan laid down his guitar and harmonica rack and headed to the stage to receive his award. Nicholson went to meet Dylan, and the two almost passed each other like strangers in the night. As they stopped to acknowledge each other, Dylan offered Jack a handshake. Not noticing the gesture, Jack left him hanging and just patted him on the shoulder. Although, the genuine admiration they had for each other was palpable. As the two moved to the front of the stage, the ovation for Dylan became louder, and Dylan turned to Jack and started applauding for him. Jack applauded for Uncle Bobby, and gestured that this was his ovation, and his moment.

Nicholson said, "Thank you, for the constant state of restlessness that has enabled you to seek newer and better means of expressing the human condition with words and music; for living your creative life fearlessly and without apology, and leading the way no matter how the times change, the National Academy of Recording Arts and Sciences joins a worldwide network of grateful fans in presenting you this Grammy Lifetime Achievement Award. Congratulations!"

As Jack was speaking, Dylan was swaying uneasily, and fidgeting with his hat and his hands. Dylan took his Lifetime Award plaque from Jack, spun around and looked for an exit, but a pair of foxy presenters in multi-thousand-dollar gowns blocked his escape route. Dylan was possibly sick, intoxicated, or both. It appeared as if he woke up with a hangover and popped three Quaaludes before hitting the stage. Regardless, he now had to improvise a speech that he never planned to deliver.

Dylan said, "Thank you. Well, alright, yeah. Well…my daddy didn't leave me too much. You know he was a very simple man, and he didn't leave me a lot but what he did tell me was this…"—Dylan nods as he looks at the Grammy and nervous laughter consumes the room—"He said so many things [real laughter]. He said, 'Son, you know it's possible to become so defiled in the world that your mother and father will abandon you. And if that happens, God will always believe in your own ability to mend your own ways.' Thank you."

Dylan rallied from an embarrassing episode to charm the crowd and give Dylanologists a passage to fixate over. The "It's possible to become so defiled" proclamation has been over-analyzed for its biblical connotations. Dylan fans had to be anxious watching this ceremony live. Looking back at the video, it's amazing how cool Dylan looked even in this arcane situation. As he swayed and fidgeted, he looked like the adult version of Huck Finn. There's a legendary glow around this man even in his darkest hours.

Dylan's first tour of 1991 began in Switzerland in late January, with John Jackson and Cesar Diaz on guitars, and Ian Wallace handling drumming responsibilities. Before returning to the states for the Grammys, Dylan played in Belgium, Holland, Scotland, Ireland, Northern Ireland, and London. Dylan was jetlagged and worn-down by the night of his Grammy performance, but Dylan fans in Europe reported that Bob seemed intoxicated throughout the tour, and the new line-up was easily the worst of the Never Ending Tour.

Easing the early year disappointment of Dylan fans was the release of *Bob Dylan: The Bootleg Series Volumes 1-3 (Rare and Unreleased)*

1961-1991. Serious collectors had heard some of these tracks, but for most of us, this collection was a cause for celebration, and an affirmation that Dylan's genius went well beyond the scope of his released albums. Volumes two and three are sublime. The alternate take of "Idiot Wind" is less aggressive-sounding than the released version, but the raw expression of pain is intense and beautiful. The best of the elite batch of songs are "Let Me Die in My Footsteps," "Farewell Angelina," "She's Your Lover Now," "Angelina," "Someone's Got a Hold of My Heart," "Foot of Pride," and "Blind Willie McTell." The box set ended perfectly with "Series of Dreams," as if Dylan intentionally created and saved this *Oh Mercy* outtake for this occasion.

My first Dylan show of the year was at Albany's Palace Theatre on May 8, 1991. I wasn't privy to any inside information, and I was a decade away from surfing on the Internet. I hoped that G. E. Smith would emerge from the side of the stage, but that never happened. John Jackson was the lone lead guitarist. Smith's absence was enormous.

I didn't realize it at the time, but this was one of the best Dylan shows of the year. He must have been inspired by his proximity to Woodstock and the ambiance of the beautiful theatre. The highlights of this eighteen-song show were catching my first versions of "Visions of Johana" and "Shooting Star." I can say with certainty that 1991 was Dylan's worst year of touring. But out of this messy year there were still several good shows, and a plethora of outstanding performances.

After touring Europe in June, Dylan's Summer Tour began at the Tanglewood Music Shed on July 4. The Boston Pops Orchestra ignited this star-spangled celebration in Lennox, Massachusetts. I was at this show, and I got caught up in a scary ordeal of my own doing. My hippie friends didn't have tickets, so they scampered over a six-foot fence with barbed-wiring, and they suggested that I do the same because there was a tremendous line getting into the place. I had tickets, but my faculty to reason deserted me. I was a good athlete, but not much of a climber. As I reached the top of the fence, I placed one foot on the other side, and my mesh gym shorts became entangled in the wire. With my manhood precariously dangling over the razor-sharp wires, the mother of all adrenaline rushes kicked in and with one movement, I freed my shorts and flung myself off the top of the fence and struck a clean landing on the ground below. I narrowly averted disaster, but I had a six-inch slash on my calf muscle. Luckily, it was a surface cut that only required a tetanus shot the following day. It was a miracle I wasn't getting stitched up in a hospital, or worse.

The Dylan show was hideous. I couldn't identify the opening song. A few years later, I saw a set list in the Dylan fan magazine *Isis*, and learned that the mystery song was "New Morning." The show was so bad it's not even review worthy. I saw another show a week later at the Garden Performing Arts Center, and it was another evening of slop.

The only interesting part of these shows was the silly between-song banter. Between "Wiggle Wiggle" and "I'll Be Your Baby Tonight," Dylan said, "That's my ecology song for tonight. It's all about fishing. Well, here is one of my older songs, not to be confused with Whitney Houston's new song. It's got the same title. It's not the same thing, though."

Between "I'll Be Your Baby Tonight" and "When I Paint My Masterpiece," Dylan quipped, "That's my attempt to do one of Whitney Houston's songs. Actually, it sounds more like hers than mine. Anyway, this is some kind of foreign language one." Oh the horror! It isn't all that funny when you pay money to go see one of the most accomplished performing artists, but this between-song goofiness was fascinating. Usually when Dylan's talking too much on stage, it's a sign he's detached from what he's doing. As Dylan stated in that interview with Cameron Crowe, "Sometimes you feel like a club fighter who gets off the bus in the middle of nowhere, punches his way through ten rounds, vomits up the pain in the back room." At these shows, Dylan was vomiting up the pain.

Now and then, Dylan's garrulous outbursts of 1991 were the precursors to great art. In München, Germany, on June 21, Dylan offered this creative intro: "Here's a song about . . . Sometimes, like just today, somebody was coming to my hotel and stopped me on the street and he grabbed me around the shoulders and said, 'Mr. Zimmerman!'"—pronounced with a thick German accent!—"These kind of things kind of shake a person up sometimes. And long ago somebody said the same thing. He didn't know me and he got run over by a streetcar, in the middle of the street. It was a sad thing, but there wasn't anything for me to do but go back and write this song. And after it was written, that's when it was sung." Dylan proceeded to reel off a stunning acoustic version of "Don't Think Twice It's Alright." Dylan and Garcia had this uncanny ability to rise out of the muck and create transcendent music out of nowhere. And luckily, there were always fanatics on hand with microphones and sometimes, cameras. I've had the pleasure of viewing a quality DVD of this München show.

Garcia had road woes in 1991 as well. According to Blair Jackson's biography *Garcia*, an anonymous source from the Dead's inner circle reported that Garcia had on several occasions expressed his displeasure with the way things were going and wanted to take a break. At one meeting, Garcia said, "Am I the only one who thinks that stadium shows suck?" Everybody else seemed to embrace it as simply the way things were. The truth that nobody wanted to embrace was that Grateful Dead economics was becoming more important than artistic vision. In a 1989 interview, Garcia explained that seeing music in stadiums is "not a pleasant experience generally. I don't see why anyone would go to more than one of those shows myself."

The stadium experience is especially sobering for those who saw the Jerry Garcia Band in small clubs and intimate venues. My last Grateful Dead stadium gig was on June 16, 1991, in Giants Stadium. As soon as the band would hit a recognizable part of a jam, the audience would go ape shit, drowning out the sound and making it more difficult, or unnecessary, for the musicians to extend the jam. Anytime Hornsby and Garcia traded leads, the place would explode as if the Messiah had just touched down in Giants Stadium. The show was decent, but I didn't have the desire to ever see them in a stadium again.

Brent's death took a toll on Garcia. There are conflicting reports as to the extent of Jerry's drug use after the coma, but Garcia began using Persian again regularly after Brent's overdose. In a 1991 interview with James Henke of *Rolling Stone*, Garcia said, "Brent dying was a serious setback—and not just in the sense of losing a friend and all that. But now we've got a whole new band, which we haven't exploited and we haven't adjusted to yet. The music is going to have to take some turns. And we're going to have to construct new enthusiasm for ourselves because we're getting a little burned out."

Some of the most honest commentary on Garcia's problems came from Bruce Hornsby: "I remember we played nine nights at Madison Square Garden [1991] and I thought except for a couple of really great nights, to me it was really a dogshit run. Garcia was in this place I couldn't understand." If Hornsby, who had only been jamming with the band for a year, felt that way, imagine how hardcore connoisseurs of the Dead's music felt. I spent years of my life listening to nothing but Garcia in his prime. The novelty of being part of the Grateful Dead scene lost its attraction to me long ago, and watching Garcia's talents decline as he aged rapidly before my eyes destroyed my appetite for more shows, although I did see one more for old time's sake on the Grateful Dead's final tour.

One from the Vault, a double CD of a 1975 Grateful Dead show from the Great American Music Hall in San Francisco, was released in 1991, and it kicked off a lucrative business of officially issuing concerts from the band's fecund archive. This initial release sold 150,000 copies. Since the band's merchandise company issued the CD, the profit margin was terrific, and the releases kept coming. Twenty-five years later, fans are still devouring these releases. Some of this music reached the general listening public, but due to the overload, these CDs did little to help the Grateful Dead's legacy, except amongst their faithful.

Jerry Garcia Band, a two-CD collection of performances from the 1990 JGB run at the Warfield, was released in 1991. Garcia's performance of "Senor" is stunning. The soulful harmonies of his backup singers and the mysterious ambiance of music set the stage for a yearning vocal from Garcia and a lyrical guitar solo where every note is filled with emotional resonance. I prefer the abundance of guitar work from the Garcia Band from the early '70s and '80s, but this collection captures different sides and sounds of Garcia: ballads, rockers, spirituals, Dylan covers, and a Beatles tune.

In addition to the JGB outlet, Garcia reunited with his old friend, mandolinist David Grisman, for a recording session and tour. Their first album, *Garcia/Grisman* (1991) featured "The Thrill is Gone," "Friend of the Devil," "Russian Lullaby," "Rockin' Chair," "Two Soldiers," and some arrangements from Grisman with an assist to Garcia. This is a solid exercise in bluegrass-styled music, but their best albums, *Shady Grove* and *So What*, were released after Garcia's death.

For all his lifelong experimentation and years of improvisation that led to one of the most heralded archives of music by any performer, Garcia never strayed from his San Francisco musical family. It was as if Jerry were under lock and key, and there were only a few musicians he could tour with. A tour with Hornsby, Dylan, or Santana was out of the question. There was no Traveling Wilburys chapter for Jerry. Secretly, the Dead family feared the what-if-Jerry-left scenario, but ultimately, Jerry could have said, "Fuck it. I'm taking a break and then I'm going on tour with Dylan." Jerry was addicted to the comfort of the Grateful Dead world as much as he was appalled by it at times. Dylan was a lone wolf all the way; Garcia, not so much.

Dylan's band gelled and improved as his little tour rolled along. There was no room to fall because they had pretty much bottomed out. On October 6, 1992, a 30th anniversary celebration concert was held at Madison Square Garden to honor Dylan's recording career with Columbia Records. When Neil Young took the stage, he dubbed the proceedings, "Bobfest." Also on hand to perform at the gala were George Harrison, Eric Clapton, Johnny and June Cash, Kris Kristofferson, The Band (without Robbie Robertson), Stevie Wonder, the Clancy Brothers, Roger McGuinn, Tom Petty, Willie Nelson, Lou Reed, and many more.

The house band consisted of G. E. Smith, Steve Cropper, Donald "Duck" Dunn, Booker T. Jones, Al Kooper, and Jim Keltner. Out of the many worthwhile highlights, Eric Clapton's guitar tirade on "Don't Think Twice It's Alright" reigned supreme.

It was a long night, and Dylan looked weary when he hit the stage for acoustic versions of "Song To Woody" and "It's Alright Ma." An iconic cast joined him for three more encores. Dylan, McGuinn, Harrison, Clapton, Young, and Petty, all sang a verse each on a superb rendition of "My Back Pages." Watching this on pay-per-view TV made for a great night of entertainment, but based on Dylan's performance, I wasn't sure he'd worked his way out of the malaise that had befallen him the year before.

Garcia's not the type of guy who would just show up at a major event at Madison Square Garden on his own, even for a Bobfest. But two months earlier, a few days after his fiftieth birthday, Garcia became ill. He refused to let his girlfriend, Manasha, call for an ambulance. Garcia received some in-home treatment, and it was later diagnosed that he had an enlarged heart and chronic lung disease. Garcia spent a couple of months recovering before returning to action with the Dead for a Halloween '92 show at the Oakland Coliseum.

Dylan had Jerry on his mind at the start of a show in Wilkes Barre, Pennsylvania, on November 1, 1992. The first song of the night was the Garcia/Hunter composition "West L.A. Fadeaway," and the seventh and last song of the electric set was the Hunter/Dylan arrangement of "Silvio." In between those songs, Dylan played "Pretty Peggy-O," "All Along the Watchtower," "Positively 4th Street," "Tangled Up in Blue," and "She Belongs to Me," all tunes covered by either the Grateful Dead or Jerry Garcia Band. Dylan had an inspired run of shows in November. It was as if Bobfest reminded Dylan of how important he was to fans, legendary peers, and stars on the rise.

Dylan's new studio album, *As Good As I Been to You* came out on November 3rd. Some critics credited this album for returning Dylan to his roots, and the songs that inspired him as he rolled to fame as a young man in Greenwich Village. If he did need to reconnect to his folk past, that already happened. Since Dylan launched the Never Ending Tour, many shows featured traditional covers that could be linked back to his Dinkytown/Greenwich education—songs such as: "Eileen Aroon," "Lakes of Pontchartrain," "Pretty Boy Floyd," Wagoner's Lad," "Barbra Allen," "Man of Constant Sorrow," "Trail of the Buffalo," "Pretty Peggy-O," and more.

On the heels of *Oh Mercy, Under the Red Sky,* the Bootleg Series, and the two Wilburys CDs, I was extremely disappointed with *As Good as I Been To You.* This was my personal *Self Portrait.* This was an album thrown together because Colombia Records asked for something and Dylan had nothing to offer but covers. Dylan's guitar playing on *As Good as I Been to You* is solid, as are the covers of "Jim Jones" and "Blackjack Davey." However, Dylan's voice on this album sounds true to the way he sounded live at the time, which wasn't a good thing. Dylan could walk into a studio and play thirteen songs like this on any given day.

World Gone Wrong, Dylan's 29th studio album, which came out in October 1993, was a stronger effort, with better performances and a unified purpose. There's an eerie feel to the album, and many of the songs have Dylanesque lyrics. The title track and "Blood in My Eyes" fall into that category. If Dylan could have introduced his audience to eight more tunes like that, this would have been a great album.

Dylan plays a pleasant version of the folk ballad, "Love Henry." He also covered his first Blind Willie McTell song, "Broke Down Engine." Dylan surprised his fans by writing the liner notes for *World Gone Wrong,* which won a Grammy Award for best Traditional Folk Album of the year. Sales for this album and *As Good as I Been To You* were poor. With these albums, Dylan fulfilled his obligations for a recording contract that he'd signed five years prior.

Soon after giving us *World Gone Wrong,* Dylan scheduled four acoustic shows at the Supper Club, in Manhattan, which would be filmed for a TV special and an ensuing album release. This was to be Dylan's version of the popular MTV Unplugged Series. Dylan has never released video or audio from these Supper Club shows, and a year later he would appear on the MTV Unplugged. Although the Supper Club material has remained in the vault, these shows should be an essential part of any Dylan bootleg collection.

The Supper Club dates are a turning point for the Never Ending Tour. In 1993, Dylan's band, which now included Bucky Baxter on pedal steel guitar and Winston Watson on drums, was an improved unit, but the shows suffered from stagnant set lists and tediously long instrumentals and song endings.

The first three years of the NET were an exciting rebirth for Dylan—new compositions to explore, old classics to rediscover. He walked off the stage and into the crowd at the Beacon and played the longest show of his career at Toad's Place three months later. The next three years he became that club fighter again, the gritty, blue-collared guy who shows up in the middle of nowhere and vomits in a dingy locker room. Dylan was desperate to break out of that syndrome, and an intimate club in New York City was the perfect setting. To top it off, this was a free show. The day before the concerts, Tower Records gave away 150 tickets for each of the four shows. Free tickets and musical intimacy were two things that Deadheads would never see again while Jerry was alive.

Dylan's voice was attentive to everything he sang, and the band was locked in tight from the opening number, "Absolutely Sweet Marie." In the thick of that opening show there were inspired performances of "Tight Connection to my Heart" and "Queen Jane Approximately." The hour-long set/shows had surprises like "One More Cup of Coffee," and each set had a stellar version of "Ring Them Bells" and a few selections from *World Gone Wrong*. These sublime performances are shocking when compared to his recent output. Dylan knew he couldn't look to Jesus or Jerry to bail him out. It's as if on these nights, he proclaimed a mantra that he would growl on an album nineteen years down the line: *I ain't dead yet. My bell still rings.*

Japan was the sight of some extraordinary Dylan performances in 1994. On February 16, Dylan played his first acoustic "Masters of War" since 1963. This historic tidbit is much more compelling since Dylan was playing in Hiroshima, the city obliterated by the first atom bomb of World War II. It was a somber arrangement sung in an understated tone—clearly different than the defiant tone of the original or the rough-shod, unattached treatment he gave the song on the night he received his Lifetime Achievement Award at the Grammys.

Dylan was back in Nara, Japan in May, for three nights of appearances at The Great Musical Experience, which also included performances by Joni Mitchell, Ry Cooder, Jon Bon Jovi, and INXS. Dylan's contribution to the interactive musical experience was the same on all three nights: "A Hard Rain's A-Gonna Fall," "Ring Them Bells," and "I Shall Be Released." All the performances were backed by the New Tokyo Philharmonic Orchestra. Bob's renditions of "Hard Rain" were probably inspired on the first two nights, but since the final show on May 22 was televised, this "A Hard Rain's A-Gonna Fall" is considered by many Dylan fans to be the best ever performance of his sanctified anthem.

Dylan's strumming an acoustic guitar and as he sings, an excited roar for "Hard Rain" surges from the crowd. The orchestra, conducted by Michael Kamen, starts to back Dylan after the first line, and the emotional power of the lyrics multiplies. Dylan sings a line and then the orchestra responds majestically, as if they're framing each thought and emphasizing the importance. When he wrote "Hard Rain" during the Cuban Missile Crisis, Dylan noted that each line was the beginning of a new song that he didn't have time to write. And the orchestral framing of each line let the song resonate in a way it never did before.

Standing in front of the orchestra, Dylan looked handsome and self-assured as he annunciated clearly and stretched syllables with succinct timing. In many of Dylan's transcendent performances you can see the nervous energy running through him. In Nara, his stage demeanor is cool and elegantly refined. Dylan's in control, and the distinct improvisation coming from the heart is deeply moving. The music arrangement from the orchestra is fixed, but the Dylan Magic seems to be affecting the emotional texture of their playing. On the last verse, Dylan raises the pitch of his voice to advance the tension. This is a version that can make a grown man cry, and could make an infant stop crying to listen. Dylan sang as if he was the chosen collective voice of humanity. Historically, Dylan has tried to downplay the importance of his songs. On these two occasions in Japan, Dylan resoundingly affirmed the significance of his art.

Dylan's 1969 Woodstock snub is the most infamous no-show in the history of music. Dylan decided to make amends and bring his band to Woodstock '94, a twenty-fifth anniversary celebration of the original event. The two-day festival held in Saugerties, New York, drew 350,000 fans. Dylan played on the final night, August 14, and was slotted between Porno For Pyros and the Red Hot Chili Peppers. Oh, how the times were changing.

As he did during the year, Dylan opened up with "Jokerman" and played impressively throughout a typical but abbreviated set due to the time slot. I had soured on seeing Dylan live after the 1991 debacles that I witnessed, but I was pleasantly surprised when I watched this on pay-per-view. My Dylan boycott was over. A deliberate "It's All Over Now, Baby Blue," the final song of the acoustic set, was followed by raging versions of "God Knows," "I Shall Be Released," and "Highway 61 Revisited" that fired up the younger crowd waiting on the Red Hot Chili Peppers. It was a good show, and just another night in Never Ending Tour history.

The Grateful Dead machine rolled on as if there were no other options. Garcia continued to play despite a litany of drug and health issues, including carpal tunnel syndrome of the left hand and forearm that had been bothering him for a couple of years. A younger generation of fans would endure vocal miscues and blown or aborted guitar solos. Amazingly, American audiences still could not get enough of the Grateful Dead. I shouldn't throw stones though; there are many '70s Deadheads who must wonder why I went to so many shows when Garcia was zonked on Persian in the '80s. Although, there's no doubt Jerry was a better guitarist in '84 than '94.

"Liberty," "Lazy River Road," "Days Between," and "So Many Roads" were the new Hunter/Garcia tunes that the band had added to the rotation. There were a few mild attempts to start recording these songs for a new album, but just making it through his Dead and JGB touring commitments drained Garcia. Hunter's lyrics were quality, as always, and Garcia poured his soul into the performances. These slow ballads fit Garcia well, and esteemed Dead critics have praised these songs. I've never enjoyed these compositions, in part because I haven't been able to separate them from the time period from which they emerged. Garcia could no longer play or create music as energetic as "Help on the Way," "Scarlet Begonias," "Terrapin Station," or even "Touch of Grey," which was born four years before Garcia's coma.

Dylan and the Dead were reunited on the stage at Madison Square Garden on October 17, 1994. This was their first get-together since February 12, 1989, which was followed by Dylan's request to become a member of the Grateful Dead. Dylan was in town to play at the Roseland Ballroom the following night, so he dropped by for a "Rainy Day Women #12 & 35" encore. Dylan seemed to be in fine form as he began to sing, but his vocals were barely audible as he sang into Weir's microphone. Apparently, Dylan's mic gets turned up much louder at his shows. Garcia took a weak stab at singing a verse, Vince played some lame keyboard, and another Dylan/Dead debacle was in the books. Individually, Garcia and Dylan had created some of the most memorable moments in the history of Madison Square Garden. Together, the soul brothers bombed. One was on his way up, and the other was on his way out.

TWENTY-TWO

INEVITABLE FAREWELL

A tragic and ill-fated year for Garcia began with a single-car accident on Highway 101 in Marin County on January 19, 1995. Garcia smashed into the divider several times, but he was not seriously hurt, and police found nothing illegal in Jerry's loaner BMW. The tours rolled on. A few Jerry Garcia Band shows were canceled because of complications of a jellyfish sting, combined with continued carpal tunnel issues. Even in these troubled times, transcendent music still rolled from his soul. The Jerry Garcia Band went into a studio and recorded a stunning version of "Cigarettes and Coffee" for the movie soundtrack of *Smoke*. On tour with the Dead, Garcia performed a few moving versions of "Visions of Johanna." There was a longing in his voice as he sang the song off monitors, which were now necessary. The ghost of electricity howled in the bones of Jerry's aging face.

In 1995 I was living in Kingston, New York, and two lady friends were keen on taking a road trip to Vermont to see the Grateful Dead, and since Dylan was opening, I decided to lead the expedition. The ladies already had tickets for the show. When we arrived in Highgate, Vermont, I couldn't find a ticket to get into this huge outdoor venue. I'd have no problem getting in though, because there were thousands of scavengers prepared to rip down fences so they could get into the concert for free. Once I heard that a huge swath of fence was dismantled, I joined the freeloaders. This was the first of five shows where Dylan opened for the Dead, and he looked youthful and sounded rejuvenated. This was my first time seeing both Dylan and Garcia since the summer of '91, and I was in tears when Dylan blazed through a hot "Like a Rolling Stone" to

close the set. Dylan has an abundance of admirable traits, but his apti-
tude for staging comebacks, and just surviving, is unparalleled in the
world of entertainment.

I found my lady friends when the Grateful Dead took the stage.
We had a gay ole time shuffling on the grass to a typical first set. I set
the critic in my mind to rest and enjoyed the ambiance of a beautiful
Vermont evening, and soaked in the vibes of the peace-loving Deadhead
faithful. When I moved closer to the stage for the start of the second set,
the music crashed and burned.

I never heard the Dead play "Here Comes Sunshine" before, and if
I would have heard them do this in the '80s, I would have been deliri-
ously happy. As they opened the set with this nugget, I was appalled.
Jerry looked like a skeleton puppet, and his performance was equally
frail. The next song was a weak Vince number, "Samba in the Rain,"
and a few songs later Garcia croaked "He's Gone." The pain was too
much to bear. I knew Jerry wouldn't be alive much longer. I informed
my companions that it was time to split, even though there would be an
ensuing drum solo and another half-hour of music. "He's Gone" was the
right tune to say goodbye on.

Dylan opened for the Dead four more times; twice in Giants Stadium,
and twice in RFK Stadium. On their final night, Garcia grabbed his axe
and joined Dylan on stage. This was just like their first time on stage
together in 1980, when Jerry joined Dylan on his stage in the Warfield.
Garcia added a solo to one of his favorite Dylan tunes, "It Takes a Lot
to Laugh, It Takes a Train to Cry," and the results were much better
than the last few times Dylan tried to join the Dead. Garcia would have
benefited from leaving the Dead to do something with Dylan more than
the other way around. It was never meant to be. Garcia was the don of
his rock and roll mafia. He could do JGB shows with Kahn, but family
business took precedent over anything else. It was fitting that Jerry and
Bob shared this final moment together in the nation's capital.

The Dead's summer '95 run was dubbed the Tour from Hell. There
were massive gate crashing incidents at multiple venues. Three Dead

fans were struck by lightning in Washington, DC. There were no fatalities. A serious death threat on Jerry Garcia forced house lights to be turned on the entire show in Deer Creek Amphitheatre in Noblesville, Indiana, on July 2. There was a heavy law enforcement presence there, and they skirmished with thousands of fans who tore down the rear fence of the venue. The following night's show was cancelled. One hundred fifty Deadheads were injured when a porch on a campground collapsed after a show at Riverport Amphitheatre near St. Louis on July 5. And there are the immortal dates; July 9 was Jerry Garcia's last performance, and August 9 was the day he died.

The Grateful Dead's final show in Chicago's Soldier Field had a few memorable performances, including a double encore of "Black Muddy River" and "Box of Rain." *When I can't hear the song for the singer/ And I can't tell my pillow from a stone/ I will walk alone by the black muddy river/ And sing me a song of my own… But it's just a box of rain or a ribbon for your hair/ Such a long long time to be gone and a short time to be there.* These lyrics suited the occasion.

The highlight of the show was "So Many Roads." Garcia served up two moody solos—that conjured up feelings of a long journey being completed. Garcia sang from a weary heart, "All I know the sun don't shine. And the rain refused to fall. And you don't seem to hear me when I call." Garcia sang, "So many roads to ease my soul" repeatedly, giving everything he had left, as if he knew this was the end. Garcia released the final anguish inside of him with growls that gave everyone in Soldier Field chills. It was the transcendent moment from this night, symbolic of a spirited soul who dedicated his life to sharing his brilliant talent with those who cherished it most.

A few days before the inevitable, John Kahn recalled this conversation with Garcia. "He told me he was an old man. He was trying to explain to me how bad he felt. I was saying, 'Naw, c'mon. It's not that bad. You'll be okay.' And he was saying, 'No really.'…But there was something really wrong with him. He wasn't getting enough oxygen. He told me the hardest thing was just getting out of bed in the morning."

Garcia checked into Serenity Knolls Treatment Center on August 8, 1995. At 4:23 a.m. the following morning, Jerry Garcia was pronounced dead after the staff nurse tried to resuscitate him. Dressed in grey sweatpants, white socks, and a blue polo shirt, Jerry had just turned fifty-three.

There was a massive outpouring of grief. Garcia had become a major American icon. Many important luminaries, including President Bill Clinton, spoke on the loss of Garcia. But it was Bob Dylan who, in a press release the day after his death, put the perfect eulogy for Jerry into words:

There's no way to measure his greatness or magnitude as a person or as a player. I don't think any eulogizing will do him justice. He was that great, much more than a superb musician, with an uncanny ear and dexterity. He's the very spirit personified of whatever is Muddy River country at its core and screams up into the spheres. He really had no equal. To me he wasn't only a musician and friend, he was more like a big brother who taught and showed me more than he'll ever know. There's a lot of spaces and advances between The Carter Family, Buddy Holly and, say, Ornette Coleman, a lot of universes, but he filled them all without being a member of any school. His playing was moody, awesome, sophisticated, hypnotic and subtle. There's no way to convey the loss. It just digs down really deep.

It was an astute eulogy that stated everything that needed to be said about the man, and his music, in a paragraph. Writers and critics like to rank and categorize, but there's no way you can rank an idiosyncratic talent like Garcia. Dylan referenced The Carter Family, Buddy Holly, and Ornette Coleman, and the names could have just as easily been Bill Monroe, Chuck Berry, and John Coltrane. Jerry identified the magic in the songs of the greatest performers of his time, and those that came before. Instead of imitating what he liked, or becoming a member of a certain school of playing, he absorbed the music, and let the influences come out in his own arrangements. If he was covering a Dylan piece, Garcia would take a magnifying glass to it and dig in deep. Garcia would hear the essence of the song and color it in. He never played a

Dylan song like Bob would play it, but he always maintained a pulse on the essence of the song. In the Church of Garcia, when he played "Tangled Up in Blue" you could hear Coltrane, Ray Charles, Albert King, Mike Bloomfield—there was gospel singing and a brass band marching—funk, soul, R&B, and hard rock—waves of rapturous sound that paid tribute to Dylan's song. It was his way of saying, look at how great this is! Let's explore and salivate over every moment. His sublime playing shredded the constraints of time. Jerry Garcia had no equal.

There was massive speculation as to whether the Grateful Dead would carry on, even though replacing Garcia seemed impossible. Four months after Garcia's death, the band had their first official meeting on how to carry on. Billy Kreutzmann didn't show up for the meeting, effectively vetoing the idea of the band having any future. On December 8, 1995, on the fifteenth anniversary of John Lennon's murder, the Grateful Dead announced that they had disbanded.

I wasn't the least bit surprised when I heard of Jerry's death, and at first, I was emotionally detached from the loss. Watching Jerry deteriorate over the last few years was like watching a loved one slowly die from cancer. After hearing the news, I got together with a friend and listened to some Dead tunes that afternoon, but I shed my first tears that night watching it on the evening news. The following day I heard an obscene 1980 "Jack Straw." Garcia's fingers traveled up and down the fretboard—a blizzard of sound. Overcome by emotion, I pulled off the road and had a therapeutic cry/sobbing session. During his best twenty years, Jerry gave his fans an eternity of music. The only performer I can think of who has ever given that much of himself to his fans is, you guessed it, Bob Dylan.

Dylan's first appearance following the passing of Garcia was during a concert to celebrate the opening of the Rock and Roll Hall of Fame in Cleveland. The sensational array of performers included James Brown, the Allman Brothers, Bruce Springsteen, Johnny Cash, Carole King, Aretha Franklin, and Robbie Robertson, just to name a few. Bruce Hornsby was on hand for a tribute to Garcia. He kicked off the performance with a moving piano presentation of "Lady with a Fan" (opening movement of 'Terrapin Station') and transitioned into "I Know You Rider" as the band kicked in. It was a Garcia-styled performance without trying to copy any Grateful Dead licks. "Scarlet Begonias" concluded the tasteful tribute.

Dylan looked phenomenal in a gold jacket armed with an electric guitar as he took the stage with his touring band. Dylan opened with "All Along the Watchtower." The sanctified guitar anthem covered by so many was the ideal selection. Dylan played some lead guitar, something he'd been doing with increasing frequency, and the mix of sounds from Jackson, Baxter, and Dylan fused into a sufficient jam. Dylan confidently delivered "Just Like a Woman," "Seeing the Real You at Last," and "Highway 61 Revisited" before calling out a special guest.

"Thank you. A buddy of mine's gonna come up and perform one of my songs. Bruce Springsteen. Let me hear you say Broooce!" Bruce and Dylan's trusted confidante, bassist Tony Garnier, laughed in awe of Dylan's deadpan delivery. He announced Springsteen with a hilarious twist, and the "Let me hear you say Broooce" bit brought a smile to anyone watching. When Dylan's got the mojo rolling, a simple introduction can be extremely entertaining.

Whatever damage he did to his reputation with his '91 Grammy debacle and a subpar showing at his 30th anniversary concert was being reversed thanks to a series of stunning TV performances. The NET had been gaining steam since the Supper Club dates, and Dylan had either quit drinking booze or cut back significantly.

Dylan's first NET performance after the day Jerry died was at The Edge, a Ft. Lauderdale nightclub. The spirit of Garcia and the Dead infiltrated the fourteen-song set. Dylan played "Friend of the Devil," "West L.A. Fadeaway," and "Silvio." He performed two of his own numbers that were Jerry Garcia Band favorites, "When I Paint My Masterpiece," and "Tangled Up in Blue," as well as two other tunes that JGB covered, "It's Too Late" and "That Lucky Old Sun." A few nights later, another Hunter/Garcia tune, "Alabama Getaway," became part of Bob's live rotation.

Dylan talked about all the universes Garcia filled in his touching eulogy. If you add in all the universes that Dylan has filled throughout his career, then these two men are responsible for passing on an essential archive of American roots music and simultaneously opening new directions in music without forsaking the essence of their influences.

Still out of the loop of finding out about Dylan developments because I didn't yet own a computer, I was elated when I saw Dylan play "Friend of the Devil" and "Alabama Getaway" on May 1, 1996, at the Mid-Hudson Civic Center in Poughkeepsie, which was ten miles from my pad in West Park, New York. I had a pre-show gathering of about twenty people at my place, and within an hour, my guests must have lit up fifty joints. The next day I had a half-ounce of roaches laying around my place.

The concert totally restored my faith in Dylan. One of the highlights was catching "This Wheel's On Fire," which Dylan had played live for the first time a few weeks earlier. Dylan closed the show by singing the evening's mantra, "Everybody must get stoned." Jerry was gone, but Dylan pulled himself out of a dark hollow.

Larry Campbell replaced John Jackson on lead guitar as NET kicked off its ninth year in 1997. Jackson had grown over the years, but Campbell was a better guitarist, and a versatile talent well-schooled on multiple string instruments. I was supposed to be at the April 18 show in Albany, but my friend bailed on going at the last minute due to an unseasonable ice storm. I really regretted not going when I learned that a day after Dylan's fifty-sixth birthday, he was hospitalized with a serious heart ailment. The condition turned out to be pericarditis, an inflammation of the sac around the heart. It was caused by a fungal infection that originates from bird droppings in certain Midwestern and Southeastern states. Bob's theory was that he had possibly breathed in the toxic spores on a motorcycle ride down South while on tour. Doctors brought the condition under control with drug therapy. It was an extremely painful hospital stay for Dylan, who was released in June. Upon leaving the hospital, Dylan stated, "I'm just glad to be feeling better. I thought I'd be seeing

Elvis soon." That remark immediately reminded me of Garcia's comment when he emerged from his coma, "I'm not Beethoven!"

Just like Garcia, Dylan was back in action quickly, playing a show just two months after his illness, in Lincoln, New Hampshire, and breaking out "Tough Mama" for the first time in twenty-four years. Even though Dylan was fifty-six and Garcia was forty-five at the time of their illnesses, Dylan was in much better shape, and his return to the road would slowly strengthen him. Well before Dylan's hospitalization in January, he had a major recording session with Daniel Lanois in Criteria Studios in Miami. In addition to Lanois, Tony Garnier, and Bucky Baxter, some of the key musicians brought in for the sessions were Augie Meyers (organ, accordion), Jim Dickerson (keyboards), Brian Blade and Jim Keltner (drums), Duke Robillard (guitar), and Cindy Cashdollar (slide guitar). The ensuing album, *Time Out of Mind*, would thrill critics and fans. Just like the good will accorded Garcia and the Dead following Jerry's coma comeback, everybody loved the Dylan comeback angle. As different as the careers of these icons seemed on the surface, upon closer inspection, the parallels and coincidences linking them is uncanny.

Time Out of Mind; the title is apropos. Augie Meyers' creaky organs chords beat like a heart gone cold, and a weary voice proclaims "I'm walkin' through streets that are dead. Walkin', walkin, with you in my head." It's a stunning opening to the album. The singer sounds like he might have been a companion of Lead Belly, Brownie McGee, or Hank Williams. The sparse music is brittle. You can't quite get a handle on the era it's coming from; could be the '20s, '30s, or '40s. It has a Southern roots feel and it's an authentic voice from the past, but the album was created by Bob Dylan and a group of musicians in a studio in 1997. That's time out of mind alchemy. It happens instantly and repeatedly throughout this extraordinary collection of songs.

"Dirt Road Blues" is a quirky shuffle that creates atmosphere and scenery—a character from the Dust Bowl era, perhaps. Nothing's is as it seems here. "Standing in the Doorway," a resplendent dirge, borrows some phrases from old-school blues numbers. If Garcia were alive he would have covered this tune, made it fifteen minutes long, and relished every syllable. The deliberate pacing of the first three songs creates a hazy vibe, and wisely, Dylan breaks the trance with "Million Miles." It's 3:00 a.m. in a faceless saloon and all the patrons are gone, but the lovesick bluesman plays on: "I'm drifting in and out of dreamless sleep... Gonna find me a janitor to sweep me off my feet." The blues guitar and organ are seductive and the band is cooking. "Rock me pretty baby rock me all at once. Rock me for a little while. Rock me for a couple of months. And I'll rock you too. I'm trying to get closer but I'm still a million miles from you."

"Can't Wait," the tenth track of the album, follows the beautiful ballad, "Make You Feel My Love." It's now 5:00 a.m. and we're back in that saloon, and the lovesick bluesman is out of his mind. As the band grinds on in an ominous tone, the singer's voice is as desperate as his language. "The air burns...Well your loveliness has wounded me. I'm reeling from the blow...I'm doomed to love you. I been rollin' through stormy weather...The end of time has just begun. Oh honey, after all these years you're still the one." There's grouchiness in the voice. He's making the listener feel his love.

Mortality is an essential theme of *Time Out of Mind*, especially on the elite songs "Not Dark Yet" and "Tryin' to Get to Heaven." I can sense Jerry Garcia's presence on Dylan's mind in "Tryin' to Get to Heaven." There's obviously the "I'm just going down the road feeling bad" reference that will also have Dylan fans thinking of Woody Guthrie. "They tell me everything is gonna be all right. But I don't know what 'all right' even means," sings Dylan as if he's puzzled by the concept. Legends trapped by fame, Garcia and Dylan will never know what "all right even means." The music of this spiritual number is uplifting as the narrator travels through the middle of nowhere on a journey that he hopes will lead to heaven before the door is closed. Dylan's between-verses solo is hypnotic and heavenly.

"Not Dark Yet" might be the same character from "Tryin' to Get to Heaven" seven years down the line. Dylan's delivery of, "Well my sense of humanity is going down the drain. Behind every beautiful thing, there's been some kind of pain," is chilling—time stands still. This is the bleakest song on the album, and consequently great art. This singer has been all around the world, is still haunted by past loves, and he's coming to grips with his impending fate. "Don't even hear the murmur of a prayer. It's not dark yet, but it's getting there."

"Highlands," the epic sixteen-and-a-half-minute *Time Out of Mind* closer, touches on the same themes as "Not Dark Yet," and it sounds almost autobiographical hearing Dylan sing it. With references to Neil Young and Erica Jong, the song's unfolding closer to the present, although the repetitive Charlie Patton blues riff keeps the music grounded in the past. The narrator is a prisoner in the mysterious modern world who can't tell the difference between a real blonde and a fake, and he longs to trade places with the young men drinking and dancing with the fine-looking women in the park. "Highlands" is the longest recorded song of Dylan's career, and he manages to keep the sprawling narrative compelling, especially in the beginning and end.

Just as the Grateful Dead had taken a seven-year break between *Go to Heaven* and *In the Dark* (studio albums comprised of original compositions), Dylan did likewise between *Under the Red Sky* and *Time Out of Mind*. Dylan no longer felt compelled to run into the studio on a yearly basis. He'd already amassed an overwhelming oeuvre of albums and songs, and he was content to perform those compositions until he had something new to say. This album benefited from Dylan's new-found patience and diligence, as would his future studio ventures.

Time Out of Mind was cut from the same cloth as *Oh Mercy*, but the songs better fit this performer at this time in his life, and Dylan and Lanois had a better feel for each other this time around. People adore an inspiring comeback story, and Dylan gave fans and critics exactly what they were looking for. Dylan was finally the sentimental favorite. As critics hailed him for his "comeback" with *Blood on the Tracks*, they took equal pleasure in bashing *Renaldo & Clara* and *Street Legal*. This time all sentiments were with Dylan as he showed up to perform at the

40th annual Grammy Awards at Radio City Music Hall. *Time Out of Mind* was a heavy favorite to win Album of the Year. The only question seemed to be whether Dylan could atone for his awful 1991 Grammy showing. Regardless, Dylan at the Grammys equals must-see TV.

Kelsey Grammer introduced Dylan, and noted that he was already a double Grammy Award winner on the night for Best Male Rock Performance, "Cold Irons Bound," and *Time out of Mind* was voted Best Contemporary Folk Album. Looking dapper in gray suit with a black collar and armed with an electric guitar, Dylan's voice was strong and he appeared focused and confident. There was a group of hipsters dressed in black, swaying in a half-circle around Dylan's band. "I see, I see silhouettes in the window," sang Dylan at the start of the second verse. In a few seconds, he'd be seeing something much stranger. A thin, shirtless young intruder with the words SOY BOMB painted on his pigeon-chest suddenly appeared, dancing spastically behind Dylan. At first it must have appeared that this strange man was part of the act because nobody attempted to remove him from the stage. After singing the first chorus line, Dylan shot a look of bewilderment, as if to say, "Where the fuck is security?" Finally, somebody rushed out and hauled Soy Bomb offstage. Dylan remained calm, and channeled his adrenaline into a dazzling guitar solo and finished the song off like a triumphant hero.

Three presenters took turns announcing the nominees for Best Album of the Year. Appearing as if he didn't know who Dylan was, rap artist, Usher said, "Time Out of Mind, Bill Dylan, I mean Bob Dylan." The other two presenters were John Fogerty and Sheryl Crow. Fogerty announced Dylan was the winner, and Crow hooted and hollered for the man she adored. There was a thunderous standing ovation for Dylan, and at first, it appeared like he wanted to split without a speech. But Dylan stepped up and thanked Lanois and Mark Howard for the distinctive sound of the album, and thanked many of the musicians. There was a wonderful cadence to the speech. And he finished with a shout-out to Buddy Holly and Robert Johnson:

"And I just want to say that when I was sixteen or seventeen years old, I went to see Buddy Holly play at Duluth National Guard Armory and I was three feet away from him . . . and he looked at me. And I just have some sort of feeling that he was—I don't know how or why—but I know he was with us all the time we were making this record in some kind of way. In the words of, you know, the immortal Robert Johnson, 'the stuff we got'll bust your brains out,' and we tried to get that across."

It was an extraordinary night, and redemption for his 1991 Grammy nightmare. Few stars have made the art of receiving an award as difficult or as entertaining as Dylan. Jerry Garcia was equally uncomfortable with these situations. He was a no-show when the rest of his mates were on hand for the Grateful Dead's 1994 induction into the Rock and Roll Hall of Fame. Garcia wasn't besieged with these kind of awards, but if he lived, it would have been a different story.

The remaining members of the Grateful Dead slowly began to tour with their own groups. Bob Weir's band, Ratdog, was the most visible, and prolific at first. By 1999, Phil Lesh was touring with a powerful group featuring guitarists Derek Trucks and Warren Haynes, known as Phil & Friends. As the years rolled on, the personnel of Phil's band was always changing, but the mission was to carry on the jamming tradition of the Grateful Dead by revisiting songs from the band's repertoire, with a predilection for psychedelic tunes from their Haight-Ashbury days. Phil & Friends toured with Bob Dylan for seventeen dates in October and November of 1999. Lesh opened and Dylan closed, and at some shows, Phil came out to play encores with Dylan's band.

Many Deadheads hungered for the likes of Ratdog and Phil & Friends, and others, like myself, missed Garcia too much. It was as if there was an irreplaceable void in the music. Most of us Garcia diehards eventually came around to enjoy these bands and embrace the mission: reinforce and spread the legacy of the Grateful Dead's music. These guys had paid their dues, and they deserved to make the paydays coming their way for as long as they wished to tour. Compared to Grateful

Dead shows, these performances had little historical significance, but they turned a younger generation on to Jerry Garcia while keeping a thriving counterculture movement alive.

Guitarist Charlie Sexton joined Dylan's band in 1999. The lineup was now Sexton, Campbell, Garnier, and former Jerry Garcia Band drummer David Kemper. Many Dylan fans rate this the best band of Dylan's Never Ending Tour. Back in East Rutherford, New Jersey, playing a gig at the Continental Airlines Arena (formerly the Brendan Byrne Arena), Dylan played another legendary show. There were superb versions of "Song to Woody," "Ring Them Bells," "Blind Willie McTell," and "Tombstone Blues." Lesh joined Dylan for the last two songs of the set, "Alabama Getaway" and "Rainy Day Women #12 & 35." Knocked out loaded and down in the dumps thirteen years earlier, Dylan was riding high at the dawn of the new millennium.

TWENTY-THREE

TWISTED FATE WITH DYLAN AND THE DEAD

*L*ove and Theft was released on September 11, 2001, the same day hell was unleashed on New York City. I moved to Manhattan a year before *Time Out of Mind* came out. On the morning of 9/11, I emerged from a subway near Penn Station and headed south towards my office, where I worked as a sales rep selling office equipment. My first appointment of the day was to purchase *Love and Theft*, and then I'd head home and start digging into this album that had received rave reviews. Wearing a black suit and purple Jerry Garcia tie, I skipped along Seventh Avenue listening to a Grateful Dead jam, and stopped to admire the sunny and cloudless sky. I looked in the direction of the World Trade Center, but I didn't pay it any mind.

I punched in on an old-fashioned time clock at 8:23 a.m. I remember the time because I'd never punched in that early before. I usually rolled in around nine. My manager, Dave, would be accompanying me on my first appointment because he was a Dylan fan. After discussing the previous night's baseball games in his office, we were about to head over to Nobody Beats the Wiz in Herald Square to score *Love and Theft*. Suddenly, our secretary opened the door and in a Brooklyn accent sighed, "You guys ain't going to fuckin' believe this. A goddamn plane just flew into the fuckin' World Trade Center."

Everybody in the office gathered around the one small TV in the copier showroom. Dave suggested we head toward The Wiz because there was a great view of the towers by Herald Square. We stood on the corner of Sixth Avenue and 29th Street and saw the black smoke billowing out of the top of the North Tower as fire trucks, police engines, and ambulances raced to the tip of the island. It was more terrifying watching this unfold on the streets than it was viewing it on TV. I didn't see the second plane hit the South Tower, just the ensuing fireball explosion that seemed to engulf half the tower. My pounding heart tried to escape from my chest. Dave suggested we go to The Wiz, where we could buy the album and watch the news on their TVs. We actually purchased *Love and Theft* as President Bush declared that the nation was under terrorist attack.

I never got around to listening to *Love and Theft* on 9/11, but the following morning I opened the CD and went for a stroll with my Walkman. The second song stopped me in my tracks—*Every step of the way we walk the line. Your days are numbered and so are mine.* Hearing that after 3,000 people unexpectedly perished was unbelievable. Dylan wrote "Mississippi" for *Time Out of Mind*, but as if it was part of some master plan, it showed up in the second spot of his new album. The lyrics of *Love and Theft* were as strong as anything on *Time Out of Mind*, but the performances were louder and bolder. By design, the last album had a mysterious/weary vibe. *Love and Theft* is self-assured, with a masculine sound. There's swagger in the way Dylan sings, "Walking through the leaves, falling from the trees. Feeling like a stranger nobody sees." He was content in the role of being a stranger that nobody sees. "Mississippi" is an elite composition. Every line is worth pondering, and every line could be the start of a new song. It's Dylan's modern-day "A Hard Rain's A-Gonna Fall."

Under the pseudonym Jack Frost, Dylan produced *Love and Theft* and utilized his touring band in the studio. Essentially, he was looking to capture a live sound as the Dead had on *In the Dark*, except these were songs that Bob's band had never played before. The results are fabulous. "Tweedle Dee and Tweedle Dum" opens with a rollicking beat, and tasty guitar leads accentuate Dylan's vocals. This is musically more sophisticated and rewarding than Dylan's recent rockers, like "Everything is Broken" and "Wiggle, Wiggle." Dylan and his band crush the blues on the fifth track, "Lonesome Day Blues." Garnier's a thumping beast on bass as he lays down a thick foundation with Kemper. Dylan isn't singing the blues as much as he's hammering the blues with authenticity.

"Summer Days" is a rockabilly-styled '50s throwback with attitude, a tune that could easily be expanded for jamming purposes in concert. There's a piece of dialogue from *The Great Gatsby* in there, and a roaring '20s celebration is in the air. It took me a little while to enjoy this piece because when I first heard it, I was breathing in the nauseating fumes from Ground Zero, and hearing Dylan sing "Summer days and summer nights are gone," always brought me back to that moment, and that smell, for a while. "High Water (For Charlie Patton)," a tale that goes back to the devastating Mississippi flood of 1927, features crisp banjo strumming by Larry Campbell. "High Water" also speaks of America's ability to cope with and overcome disasters, making the content of the song topical in the aftermath of 9/11.

Love and Theft borrowed from many sources; even the title was inspired by Eric Lott's book *Love and Theft: Blackface Minstrelsy and the American Working Class*. There was much discussion of what Dylan may have pilfered, or borrowed, and the ethics of it. Dylan's approach to songwriting in this period paid tribute to the past by using bits of existing work as springboards for his own creations. It was also Dylan's wittiest album in years, with clever lines sprinkled into strong numbers like "Po Boy" and "Honest with Me."

"Bye and Bye," a Bing Crosby-style jazz number, swings with a finger-snapping groove—music to soothe the soul. As the crooner breathes a lover's sigh and paints the town, he's still spooked by self-reflections: "Well I'm scufflin' and I'm shufflin' and I'm walkin' on briars. I'm not even acquainted with my own desires…Well the future for me is already a thing of the past." Repeated listens to this album challenged me to question the way I was living my life. I wasn't sure if I was acquainted with my own desires either.

Dylan returned to Madison Square Garden on November 19, 2001. This was my first appearance at a major live event since 9/11, and I imagine it was the first for many New Yorkers on hand that night. Dylan wore a flamboyant pink suit, and outside of a wide-stance corkscrew twist during a harp solo in "Just Like a Woman," Dylan's performance was respectfully reserved. But before "Rainy Day Woman," he said the words we longed to hear: "Most of the songs we're playing here tonight were written here, and those that weren't were recorded here. So no one has to ask me how I feel about this town." It was an emotional night and a twenty-two-song performance, typical for this amazing leg of the tour. The following night, Dylan played "Mississippi" at the Mohegan Sun Casino. Based on the tapes, I liked that show better. It was as if Dylan was relieved to be done with the enormous burden of the MSG show. The fear in New York City was thick and heavy.

A sense of normalcy had returned to New York by the time Dylan returned to MSG for a pair of shows on November 11 and 13, 2002. After all the shows I'd seen, there were still plenty of firsts at these shows. Bob was now performing most of his songs from behind a Yamaha keyboard. The iconic image of Dylan holding a guitar at a jaunty angle with a harmonica rack around his neck had to be altered. Yet, Dylan was still super-cool as he stood and twisted while playing the keys. In the 1959 Hibbing High Yearbook Dylan's ambition was "To join Little Richard." And now at the age of sixty-one, with his bouffant hairdo and fancy clothes, Dylan carried on in the tradition of Little Richard.

The second song of the night was familiar, but I couldn't place it until Dylan sang the title, "Yeah Heavy and a Bottle of Bread." It was the surprising live debut of this ditty from the *Basement Tapes*. Three quick verses were sung against an exotic calypso beat. Bob turned his back to the audience, shuffled to his equipment rack, grabbed a harmonica, and hustled back to his Yamaha and unloaded a few shrill blasts. The music magically faded as if an engineer was turning down the volume. Dylan backpedaled from the mic and continued to play. He took two strides east and four strides west. I was there, but even as I watch this on video, it appears Dylan's floating. Is it a parlor trick or transcendence? Tony Garnier, who'd been playing with The Maestro for thirteen years, had a stunned smile upon his face. When the music faded to silence, the crowd erupted with a thunderous ovation. Dylan stopped time in the city that never sleeps.

The fourth song of the night was Don Henley's "End of Innocence." Dylan is a gracious man, a trait that's best expressed in the tunes he plays as opposed to things he says. This song said what he needed to say about America in the aftermath of 9/11. Dylan likes to downplay the significance of his songs, but this is the man who tells us, "I find the religiosity and the philosophy in the music…The songs are my lexicon, I believe the songs." Dylan enjoys turning his fan base on to lesser known legends from the past, but on this tour, he paid tribute to his contemporaries. At most of the shows he played the Rolling Stones' "Brown Sugar" and Neil Young's "Old Man." Perhaps the best of his covers on this tour was "Mutineer," a beautiful ballad by Warren Zevon that he played near the end of his sets. His Zevon tribute was particularly poignant considering Warren was suffering with pleural mesothelioma, a terminal cancer that would take his life in less than two years. Dylan debuted three other Zevon compositions on this tour: "Accidentally Like a Martyr," "Boom Boom Mancini," and "Lawyers, Guns and Money."

The climax of these Garden shows were spectacular renditions of "Summer Days" fueled by dueling guitar solos from Sexton and Campbell. Unlike the empty, superfluous jamming of 1993, these jams would impress anyone. On the second night, Dylan served a moving rendition of Van Morrison's "Carrying a Torch." On a nightly basis he also added "Things Have Changed," the song that earned Dylan an Oscar for Best Original Song at the 2001 Academy Awards. On November 13, after twenty songs and two encores, I headed for the exits thrilled by two of the best Dylan shows I'd seen.

Suddenly, there was a sonic eruption. Dylan came out with the band and played "Something" as a tribute to George Harrison, who had passed away a year earlier. Dylan sang it as best he could, and the band's recreation was flawless.

Sometime around 2000, I embraced modern times and purchased my first personal computer. The impetus behind this acquisition was Jerry Garcia. I was turned on to Internet sites where you could download Grateful Dead shows and then burn them onto disc. Record shops that carried bootlegs charged $50 for a double CD. Suddenly everything was free if I was willing to hunt. Finding various downloading sites and building a Grateful Dead CD archive became an obsession. There was one rogue site were you needed a password to get in, and once you downloaded a show, if you didn't select a new one to download within ninety seconds, you would be logged off. Getting on this site wasn't easy, and when I did get in, I would stay on all night. It took about ninety minutes to download a show, so I would set an alarm to constantly wake me up throughout the night. After a few weeks of this, I had a budding collection of fabulous Dead shows that I'd never heard before, and I was also on the verge of being checked into a mental institution due to sleep deprivation.

Through downloading sites and daily packages arriving in the mail from folks I met online, I acquired almost ever Grateful Dead show from the years 1969–1989, as well as several hundred Jerry Garcia Band and Never Ending Tour shows on CD. I was a main contributor on a website called the Dewboard, which was an offshoot of the *Morning Dew* Radio show on 99.5 WBAI, New York. We passionately discussed and debated the best versions of "Morning Dew," "Dark Star," Scarlet > Fire…etc. We would break down which sections of the different songs were better during certain months of a given year. There were thousands of Grateful Dead discussion forums popping up on the Internet. It was crazy, but by 2003, I was more into the Grateful Dead's music than ever before. The archives of music generated by Garcia and Dylan are now accessible, eternal, and there's more than enough there to keep any fan engaged for as long as they live.

In 2003, the remaining members of the Grateful Dead, except for Vince Wellnick, reunited for a tour, and added Jimmy Herring, Jeff Chimenti, Rob Barraco, and Joan Osborne to their lineup. Dylan and

Dead fans had another opportunity to cross-pollinate when Dylan opened for the Dead at Darrien Lake Performing Arts Center on August 8, 2003.

Bob Weir sat in with Dylan for a few songs and Dylan returned the favor, joining the Dead on "Tangled Up in Blue," "It Takes a Lot to Laugh, It Takes a Train to Cry," "West L.A. Fadeaway," and "Alabama Getaway." Dylan's voice was werewolf rough during this tour. A few nights later, Bob kicked off a three-night run in the Hammerstein Ballroom on August 12. On opening night, Dylan was joined by Nils Lofgren, best known as the lead guitarist of Bruce Springsteen's E Street Band. Dylan and Nils had great stage chemistry. Lofgren was more assertive and demonstrative than any guitarist I'd ever seen play with Dylan. Most guests proceed with caution on Dylan's stage.

The third night was postponed due to a major blackout that left New York City without power all night. It was a peaceful night with a lot of block parties, as opposed to the rioting and looting that took place during the blackout of 1977. Dylan made up the final date in the Hammerstein Ballroom a week later on August 20.

The Hammerstein shows were high-quality performances despite the wolfman growling and the departure of Charlie Sexton from the band. Sexton was lured back into the band in 2009, and has remained there as of the publication of this book. George Recile, who replaced David Kemper at the start of the 2002 tour, has been Dylan's only drummer since. As the Never Ending Tour grinded on with the consistency of the Grateful Dead's tour, Dylan has kept the core of his band intact. The members of the band certainly don't have the freedom that the musicians did within the Grateful Dead, but they provided Dylan a reliable framework so he could explore and expand musically. After the Hammerstein shows, Dylan, and the music world, mourned the death of two legends. Warren Zevon died on September 7, and five days later, Johnny Cash passed away.

He not busy being born is busy dying. Dylan's latest film project, *Masked and Anonymous*, premiered in early 2003. The critics ridiculed this production, which was written by Larry Charles, an essential staff writer for the TV series *Seinfeld*, and Dylan, whose writing pseudonym for this venture was "Sergei Petrov." Chalk up another box office disaster for Dylan, however, this was no *Hearts of Fire* or *Renaldo and Clara*. The movie featured an all-star cast including John Goodman, Jeff Bridges, Jessica Lange, Penelope Cruz, Luke Wilson, Angela Basset, Ed Harris, and Val Kilmer. Dylan plays Jack Fate, an old-school rocker who is bailed out of jail to play a benefit concert. The plot is scattered and vague, but the scenes, dialogue, and acting are captivating. It's not the type of film that the average movie-goer can digest. *Masked and Anonymous* is like a Dylan album that invites you to make what you will of it.

Jack Fate's band in the movie was his NET band consisting of Garnier, Campbell, Sexton, and Recile. The soundtrack has a diverse collection of Dylan covers, including Jerry Garcia Band's "Senor" and a Grateful Dead "It's All Over Now, Baby Blue." If you look at the current-day civil war in Syria, and you're not sure who's fighting whom, and who's on whose side, then you'll find this flick compelling.

On October 4, 2004, Simon & Schuster published *Chronicles*. It spent nineteen weeks on the *New York Times* nonfiction best seller list, peaking at No. 2. We all want insight into Dylan's genius, but if he told us who Mr. Tambourine Man or Mr. Jones were, that would be the ultimate let down. *Chronicles* gives us a ton of insight as it builds even more intrigue. We're getting closer to Dylan, but were still a million miles from the man. That keeps us salivating for more.

The twisted fate of Dylan and the Dead continually shows up in my life. One night near the end of 2004, a friend from the Dewboard website sent me an email informing me that I should be teaching a course called Discussing Dylan 101 at The New School in Manhattan. I immediately enrolled. After discussing Dylan for a semester, and seeing six Dylan shows in the spring of 2005, I decided to write a book on the Never Ending Tour. On May 2, 2005, I went to a Starbucks and started writing. I decided to finish getting my four-year degree, which I abandoned in New Paltz when *Oh Mercy* was released.

I took a class called Old Weird America. Greil Marcus was my instructor. In the Discussing Dylan class I met Robert Polito, who was a guest speaker that week. We talked about Dylan's performance in Fishkill that summer, and I mailed him a copy of the show. I swear, at the time, I didn't know he was the director of the New School MFA Creative Writing Program.

After graduating and being accepted for the MFA program in Creative Writing, I took a literature course with Robert Gates, who had interviewed Dylan in 1997 for *Newsweek*. In 2012 I published my memoir, *Tangled Up in Tunes: Ballad of a Dylanhead*. I later wrote *Positively Garcia: Reflections of the JGB, Volume 1* (2014), and *Grateful Dead 1977: The Rise of Terrapin Nation* (2015). I found my calling in an email. *Once in a while you get shown the light in the strangest of places if you look at it right.*

Dylan's follow-up album for *Love and Theft* took five years, but *Modern Times* was worth waiting for, and it was the perfect finale for the trilogy that began with *Time Out of Mind*. Released on August 29, 2006, *Modern Times* came out seventy years after the movie with the same title starring Charlie Chaplin. The opening track, "Thunder on the Mountain" has a dramatic fanfare instrumental opening and ending. The narrator sings of longing for Alicia Keys, and sucking the milk out of 1,000 cows. In the first three lines it's biblical, scary, and optimistic— *Thunder on the mountain, fires on the moon. There's a ruckus in the alley and the sun will be here soon. Today's the day, gonna grab my trombone and blow.*

"Workingman's Blues #2" is a sentimental anthem that speaks to the blue-collared American worker. The song title was a nod to Merle Haggard, who also toured with Dylan in 2006, although the feel and pace of Dylan's version is entirely different. There are four resplendent verses, and each one tugs at the heart. Dylan's voice carries the weight of every work-weary American as he croons the last verse: "Got a brand new suit and a brand new wife. I can live on rice and beans. Some people never worked a day in their life. Don't know what work even means." In

"Nettie Moore," Dylan sings of being the oldest son of a crazy man and being in a cowboy band. It's a desperate tune of yearning adopted from a traditional arrangement, and there's a dose of biblical references. The last track, "Ain't Talkin'," is another Dylan epic, wonderfully designed, and perhaps, the most distinctive song on the album.

Radio mesmerized Dylan as a kid in Hibbing; the music, the hosts, and the programming. Music radio shows are a dying craft in modern times. On March 3, 2006, the initial episode of *Theme Time Radio with Bob Dylan* aired on Sirius XM Satellite Radio. The show lasted for almost three years as Dylan turned his audience on to hour-long shows revolving around themes, dreams, and schemes. It was an eclectic mix of old-timey tunes with some contemporary surprises. Dylan's banter was funny, charming, and informative, as he broadcast from a mobile studio on the road. No book, radio show, or movie project could derail the Never Ending Tour.

In another odd twist of Dylan/Dead fate in my life, I had a conversation with Lance Neal, longtime host of the *Morning Dew* show on WBAI 99.5 FM. I nonchalantly mentioned something about how WBAI should do a Dylan show. Lance thought I was the right cat for the job, and he put me in touch with the program director. Next thing I know, I'm calling up my friend, Jim Kerr Jr. (son of Jim Kerr, famous classic rock New York DJ), and we're making a demo tape. I created my own theme time radio show called *Visions of Dylan*, and about ten two-hour episodes were aired on Monday nights on WBAI. Prior to this I had no radio or broadcasting experience. Dylan had a history with WBAI, appearing in the studio twice. In 1962, he was interviewed by Cynthia Gooding, and in 1966, he had a long rambling appearance on the *Radio Unnameable* show hosted by Bob Fass.

The eternal power of the Grateful Dead's music was confirmed when Sirius XM Radio hosted a permanent 24/7 Grateful Dead Channel in 2007. That channel's still raging today. Like most satellite radio, much of the channel was pre-programmed. Yet, there was a show called *Tales from the Golden Road* on Sunday afternoons, where Deadheads called in to reminisce about their glory days. Some calls were from knowledgeable fans, and some calls were from fried Deadheads who couldn't remember a note they heard, but they named their firstborn Althea and the family pet China Cat. Luckily, the hosts, David Gans and Gary Lambert, are gracious men with patience, and a lot of valuable insight. They usually managed to book an interesting guest or two every week. On November 11, 2012, ten years after the great Dylan show at Madison Square Garden, they had *Tangled Up in Tunes* author Howard Weiner on the show.

Together Through Life was Dylan's next album in 2009. It wasn't as strong as the music from his previous trilogy, but it was a new batch of originals that ranged from mediocre to good. David Hilgado of Los Lobos gave the songs a fresh feel with his accordion playing. The best numbers were "Beyond Here Lies Nothin'," "Forgetful Heart," "These Dreams of You," "If You Ever Go to Houston," and "I Feel a Change Comin' On." These were the songs that made it into his lineup with the Never Ending Tour.

After a decade of service with the Never Ending Tour, Larry Campbell left in 2006 to play with Levon Helm and Phil & Friends. When they open the Bob Dylan Hall of Fame, Larry Campbell will be inducted on the first ballot. When Larry split, Denny Freeman took over on lead guitar for a spell, and Donnie Herron filled the multi-instrumentalist role. Donnie's still a member of the band today.

Bob Weir and Phil Lesh joined forces again in 2009 and formed a band called Furthur that included Dark Star Orchestra guitarist John Kadlecik and Jeff Chimenti, Ratdog keyboardist. The band announced limited tours over a four-year period and the shows sold out at venues like Madison Square Garden. It's an incredible testament to the staying power of Grateful Dead music, especially considering Furthur ticket prices were five to ten times higher than the cost to see the Grateful Dead. There were a lot of old Deadheads attending these concerts, and there was a significant number of newbies who had never seen the Grateful Dead.

Furthur featured longer jams than the Grateful Dead did during their final years, and they broke out several songs from the band's formative years, songs that had been buried and left for dead long ago. I saw Furthur at Madison Square Garden, Radio City Music Hall, and a Minor League Ballpark in Coney Island. I enjoyed the music, but with all the tremendous Garcia music at my disposal, listening to these tapes again would be frivolous.

Dark Star Orchestra has been instrumental in spreading the legacy of Jerry Garcia. One of the founding members, Rob Eaton, was a renowned taper of the Grateful Dead in the day. The DSO concept is to perform a Grateful Dead show as faithfully as possible. If they're recreating the May 7, 1977, show from the Boston Garden, they'll play the exact set list from that night. They even have a female singer on stage recreating Donna's vocals, and they try to replicate the band's '77 sound. They've been doing a remarkable job for a long time, and like the Grateful Dead, they're always on tour. Currently, Jeff Matson is the guitarist, and he may channel the spirit of Garcia's playing better than anyone on the planet.

According to *Deadbase*, the statistical bible of Deadheads, the Grateful Dead played 2,318 shows during their thirty years of existence. Dylan's April 26, 2011, performance on the MoJo Stage at Byron Bay Bluesfest in Australia was concert number 2,319 of his Never Ending Tour. How crazy is that? In the second half of his career he played more gigs than the Grateful Dead. During the second half of my touring career, which started after *Love and Theft*, I saw Dylan perform in Rotterdam, Amsterdam, Mexico City, Montreal, Las Vegas, New Orleans, Memphis, Little Rock, Boston, Portland, Hartford, Allentown, Bethlehem, Wilmington, Cooperstown, and various other cities and cowtowns across America.

Martin Scorsese's 2005 documentary *No Direction Home* is the definitive historical testament of Dylan's sensational dash to fame ending with his 1966 motorcycle accident. On January 12, 2002, Dylan had the opportunity to perform for Scorsese, who was being honored with a

Critics Choice music and film award. Using expressive hand gestures as he sang "Blind Willie McTell," it appeared as if Dylan was auditioning for a part in one of Martin's gangster flicks. Dylan's voice was somewhere between a gargle and growl as he pranced around the stage with a mic and unleashed a few harp solos. It was a concise and moving performance, and when Scorsese thanked Bob during his speech, he referred to him as "The Great One."

It had been fifty-one years since Dylan arrived in New York City, and fifty years since his debut album was released by Columbia Records, but Dylan was too focused on the future to be celebrating the past. The Resilient One was recording a new album in Jackson Browne's Groove Masters Studio in Santa Monica between January and March. These sessions resulted in *Tempest*, which was released on September 11, 2012, exactly eleven years after *Love and Theft*.

Tempest is a return to the *Time Out of Mind* trilogy template. The first seven songs of Dylan's darkest work are intense. "Duquesne Whistle" is a traditional train song in which the singer and the song invite you into a time warp, memories and sounds of the past. The Grateful Dead are back in play on "Duquesne Whistle" as The Noble Bard, Robert Hunter, collaborated on the lyrics with Dylan. "Soon After Midnight," a lilting lullaby with attentive Sinatra-like vocals, rockets Tempest into arcane American weirdness when Dylan croons "Charlotte's a harlot. Dresses in scarlet/ Mary dresses in green/ It's soon after midnight and I've got a date with a fairy queen." I can't imagine Old Blue Eyes singing that verse.

Dylan's voice is an angry bark during "Pay in Blood," and the forceful rhythm and vengeful lyrics match the phlegm-filled growls of the singer. On the heels of this rocker comes "Scarlet Town," an immense composition based on the melody of "Barbra Allen." But just as the Grateful Dead created their own genre and sound, Dylan, in the second half his career, has done the same thing. It's hard to think of "Scarlet Town" as a folk ballad; it's a Dylan song along the lines of "Ain't Talkin'" and "Highlands." Donnie Herron plays some ghostly banjo, complemented by David Hidalgo's violin. It's as if Dylan can invoke his songs with the spirit of Edgar Allen Poe. Simple lines are rhymed with brilliant lines: *The evil and the good living side by side/ All human forms seemed glorified.* And Dylan concludes this minor masterpiece with convincing simplicity, "The black and the white, the yellow and the brown. It's all right there for ya in Scarlet Town." The attitude and strong cadence of Dylan's voice is triumphant, packing urgency into the lyrics.

"Early Roman Kings," the seventh track, is a standard blues number. The delivery of these intriguing lyrics make it an unforgettable tune and performance. At first, the song sounded like Dylan simply took Muddy Waters' "Mannish Boy" and swapped out lyrics, yet there's wonder and awe in every verse: *All the early Roman Kings in the early, early morn'/ Coming down the mountain, distributing the corn.* And how could you not think of The Great One when he sings, "If you see me coming and you're standing there. Wave your handkerchief in the air. I ain't dead yet, my bell still rings. I keep my fingers crossed like the early Roman kings." From ancient Rome to modern-day Detroit, the song is packed with evocative images reeled off in an unrelenting performance—perfect for a Scorsese soundtrack.

A week before the release of *Tempest,* Dylan played the Grand Reopening of the Capital Theatre in Port Chester, New York. The Grateful Dead played seventeen shows in this intimate theatre between 1970 and 1971, and Garcia stated it was one of his favorite places to play. The venue was renovated by Deadhead Peter Shapiro, and it's become one of the premier touring stops for bands within an hour of New York City.

Opening night with Dylan was a hot ticket, which I didn't have, but I boarded a train and headed to Port Chester anyway. I wasn't prepared to spend more than a hundred dollars to get in, so I figured I'd be shut out. I arrived at the right time because the box office opened and a small amount of tickets were released. After I got my ticket, I went to peek inside the theatre door. The entrance door suddenly swung open and the usher hollered, "We're open for business!" Dylan was the first performer at the grand reopening, and thanks to a simple twist of fate, I was the first fan in the theatre. Dylan played a solid show that night, but it wasn't on the level of the dazzling performance I saw him turn in at the Bethel Woods Performing Arts Center two nights earlier.

The Capitol Theatre has become the East Coast hub for live Grateful Dead/jam band-related gigs. It's become a home for Phil & Friends in recent years, as Lesh has chosen to play long runs in Port Chester as opposed to going on tour. Weir and Kreutzmann have appeared at the Cap in various configurations, and Melvin Seals and the JGB are frequent guests, keeping the music of the Jerry Garcia Band alive. Dark Star Orchestra and Joe Russo's Almost Dead are the top-shelf Dead cover bands that sell out the theatre year after year, and the adjacent bar, Garcia's, has a stage and hosts smaller gigs. Melvin Seals, Larry Campbell, and Jeff Matson have performed in Garcia's, and almost every week there's a new quality Dead cover band in there. In the United States, no other band has inspired more cover bands than the Grateful Dead. And even with the inevitable passing of the remaining members, the music will never stop.

Dylan side-stepped celebrations commemorating his fifty years of public service. With the fiftieth anniversary of their heroes nearing, Deadheads willed a Grateful Dead reunion. Any issues or artistic differences were to be cast aside for this mega-event, Fare Thee Well: Celebrating Fifty Years of Grateful Dead. Lesh, Weir, Kreutzmann, and Hart were back together with Bruce Hornsby and Jeff Chimenti on keyboards, and after wild speculation, the role of stepping into Jerry's shoes went to Trey Anastasio of Phish. For the first and only time since Jerry's death, the band was billed as the Grateful Dead, and three concerts were announced for July 3, 4, and 5 at the site of the band's last show, Soldier's Field. The hysteria for tickets was similar to the Dylan/Band tour of 1974. Due to the overwhelming demand, two warm-up celebration dates were announced for June 28 and 29 in Levi's Stadium, Santa Clara.

The sold-out shows were attended by 363,933 fans, and the ticket revenues were $52,232,414. Fifty-two million for five shows! The

400,000 pay-per-view subscriptions for the Chicago shows set a record for a music event. As Deadheads peacefully invaded Chicago, these shows were covered as major events by the news broadcasts and the media—without a doubt, this was the biggest Grateful Dead story since Jerry's death.

Trey put in a lot of practice time with the band, and he did a commendable job. I missed the thrill of being there, and wasn't blown away listening to these shows on radio. The music was sufficient for a celebratory gathering, but not the type of thing worth listening to again if you have a healthy collection of Grateful Dead tapes. Regardless of critical appraisals, it was the mother of all parties and reunions, and it continued to propagate the legend of Jerry Garcia and the Grateful Dead. Those officially involved with the concert profited heavily, and an obscene amount of money was spent out in the parking lot on Shakedown Street (independent vendors). The Grateful Dead economy stepped into overdrive once again.

On Halloween 2015, the most vibrant and popular post-Garcia Dead configuration was born in Madison Square Garden. A few years earlier, blues guitarist John Mayer stumbled upon Grateful Dead music on Pandora, and the Dead switch in his brain was activated. Mayer formed a band with Weir, Kreutzmann, Hart, Jeff Chimenti, and Oteil Burbridge (bass) that was called Dead and Company. The shows were enthusiastically received, and they toured during the summer of 2016. Mayer's guitar playing was fabulous. He played in the spirit of Garcia, without falling into the trap of trying to imitate him.

Most of the guitarists who have taken on this role were peers of Jerry, and had known the Dead's music for many years. Mayer still has that first-love enthusiasm for the music, and it comes through in his vibrant playing. Dead and Company have another major summer tour scheduled for 2017. With younger guitarists like Mayer keeping the tradition alive, enthusiasm for the Grateful Dead will be passed on to future generations, and the legend of Garcia will continue to propagate.

In 2015, Dylan released *Shadows in the Night*, a CD consisting of ten ballads that Frank Sinatra recorded back in the '50s and '60s. The performances by Dylan and his touring band were attentive. Dylan followed this effort with *Fallen Angels* the following year, and every song on this CD, except for one, was once recorded by Sinatra. Dylan playing nothing but covers for an entire album doesn't excite me. I prefer when Dylan creates his own Sinatra-like ballads such as "Bye and Bye," "Beyond the Horizon," and "Soon After Midnight." If he mixed a few originals into these albums, they would be more appealing.

Dylan followed this effort with *Fallen Angels.* The third in his series of classic American covers, *Triplicate*, came out in 2017. Upon the release of *Triplicate*, Dylan stated, "I am finding these great songs to be a tremendous source of inspiration that has led me to one of my most satisfying periods in the studio. I've hit upon new ways to uncover and interpret these songs that are right in line with the best recordings of my own songs, and my band and I really seemed to hit our stride on every level with *Triplicate*."

Dylan has mellifluously slipped the songs from this recent trilogy of albums into his shows, mixing them in with his recent compositions. The only downside of his shows lately has been his reliance of a fixed set list. As a Deadhead and Bobcat (one who follows the Never Ending Tour), the replicate set lists kill off the desire to follow him on tour. But Dylan's offering up a quality show that he believes in. It would be foolish to write Dylan off as someone who has nothing left to say, or is moving towards retirement. I predict we're due for a new album of originals no later than 2019. But as Dylan said in a 1991 interview with Paul Zollo, "The world don't need any more songs… They've got enough. They've got way too many. As a matter of fact, if nobody wrote any songs from this day on, the world ain't gonna suffer for it. Nobody cares. There's enough songs for people to listen to, if they want to listen to songs. For every man, woman and child on earth, they could be sent, probably, each of them, a hundred records, and never be repeated. There's enough songs. Unless someone's gonna come along with a pure heart and has something to say. That's a different story."

Dylan has had every accolade, award, degree, and honor that can be bestowed upon a songwriter. For many years, fans have been lobbying for Dylan to win a Nobel Prize in Literature. This appeared to be something that would never happen, but on October 13, 2016, it was announced that Bob Dylan was awarded the Nobel Prize in Literature "for having created new poetic expressions within the great American song tradition." Dylan was the first recipient from the world of music, and the Nobel committee expected an overjoyed Dylan to respond by flying to Sweden to receive the award and his $900,000 prize and deliver the required lecture. Dylan didn't return their calls, and Patti Smith was Dylan's stand-in at the ceremony on December 10. Dylan finally met with the Nobel committee in private the day before Dylan kicked off the 29th year of his Never Ending Tour in Stockholm, Sweden, on April 1, 2017. Dylan's perceived snub touched off an uproar of discussion and debate. Dylan's always been uncomfortable with these types of ceremonies. As prestigious as the Nobel Prize is, it's just an award. Dylan's works speaks for itself.

On the night Dylan became a Nobel Prize winner, he was performing at The Chelsea, The Cosmopolitan of Las Vegas. On the same day twenty-seven years earlier, Dylan debuted "Man in the Long Black Coat" and walked out into the crowd and split through the side exit of the Beacon Theatre while the band was still playing. A year later, on October 13, 1990, as the United States was on the brink of the first Gulf War, Dylan was playing "Masters of War" in front of ten rows of Cadets in West Point. He learned his lesson well from the Grateful Dead: "You're either a player, or you're not a player." Dylan's work is far from finished, but if his musical oeuvre is combined with the live performances of the Grateful Dead and the Jerry Garcia Band, and all the influences and innovations within are considered, this body of work is a profound representation of the history of American music in the 20th century.

IF YOU GET CONFUSED,
LISTEN TO THE MUSIC PLAY

The combined and complete archives of Dylan and Garcia contain more than eighty years of music. With all the bootlegged and officially released material available, it's tough to narrow down listening suggestions for someone unfamiliar with either of these artists. There's no way to condense and properly evaluate their canons for easy consumption, so I've elected to focus on the abundance of officially released music.

The plethora of live Grateful Dead releases since 1991 are difficult to keep track of, even for aficionados. It started with the band's vault releases, and continued with the Dick's Picks series, courtesy of band archivist Dick Latvala. This series became the gold standard for live releases that focused on specific shows, and the band continued to release retrospective collections and concerts on a yearly basis. Latvala passed away in 1999, and the band's new archivist, David Lemieux, continued the Dick's Picks series until 2005. After that, Lemieux launched his own Dave's Picks series.

In addition to that, there's the Road Trip series and the Download series, mixed in with various other official releases. Just putting these retrospective releases into perspective is tough for fans who are obsessively committed. But within this jungle of live material lies the best Grateful Dead music, so I did my best to pick out the top fifteen of this batch.

I ranked the best official studio and live Grateful Dead albums that didn't fall into the retrospective category together as one without commentary, since I'd already discussed them in the book. Since Jerry Garcia's solo projects had a different sound and feel from the Grateful Dead, I suggested five albums from his studio and live releases. In both the Dylan and Dead listening suggestions, I eliminated any releases that were more than four CDs, because those issues are more along the lines of box sets.

The Dylan recommendations consist of two lists. There are the studio albums, which I only ranked since they were already discussed. The other list is of his best live albums and previously unreleased material. After carefully considering the candidates, everything came up Bootleg Series. Dylan's live albums never matched the majesty of his studio output until the Bootleg Series began to correct that imbalance.

Retrospective Grateful Dead Releases

1. *Cornell 5/8/77*: Transcendent versions of "Dancin' in the Street," Scarlet > Fire, and St. Stephen > Not Fade Away > Drums > St. Stephen > Morning Dew, make this the most popular Grateful Dead concert—beyond perfection.

2. *Sunshine Daydream*, August 27, 1972, Old Renaissance Faire Grounds, Veneta, Oregon: The Dead blazed three sets of music on this sunny, 100-degree day. "Playin' in the Band" is twenty minutes of intense seismic psychedelic activity. There's a superb mix of jamming and song execution on "Dark Star," "Birdsong," and "Greatest Story Ever Told," as well as a poignant version of "Sing Me Back Home."

3. *Dick's Picks Volume 2*, October 31, 1971, Ohio Theatre, Columbus, Ohio: The best single-CD release in the Grateful Dead archive kicks off with a tight, 23-minute "Dark Star." Not Fade Away > Goin' Down the Road Feelin' Bad > Not Fade Away is the ultimate rendition, and the band's definitive rock and roll statement.

4. *Dick's Picks Volume 31*, August 4–5, 1974, Philadelphia Civic Center, Philadelphia;

August 6, 1974, Roosevelt Stadium, Jersey City, New Jersey: This fabulous three-night compilation features a sensational "Eyes of the World." Erasing boundaries between musical genres and removing time constraints, the Dead fully explore China Cat > Rider, "Weather Report Suite," and sandwich "Scarlet Begonias" inside of "Playin' in the Band." From a gorgeous "Pretty Peggy O" to a bawdy "Big River," the band's diversity is unrelenting.

5. *Steppin' Out with the Grateful Dead: England '72*: A unique four-CD collection of performances from seven of the band's eight shows in England is a stellar representation of this tour. The extraordinary fourth CD features a rare Pigpen composition, "The Stranger (Two Souls in Communion)," and the brilliant Dark Star > Sugar Magnolia > Caution segment from the Empire Pool in Wembley on April 8.

6. *Dick's Picks Volume 33*, October 9–10, 1976, Oakland Coliseum Stadium, Oakland, California: The first night in the coliseum was the show of the year, highlighted by exquisite song selection and sequencing. Set two is a rhapsody of fused music highlighted by the St. Stephen > Help on the Way transition—classic anthem shakes hand with new masterpiece. The performances from the second show are on par with the energy of the first one.

7. *Dick's Picks Volume 36*, September 21, 1972, The Spectrum, Philadelphia: The band's debut in the Philly Spectrum was epic. The mojo was rollin' as the Dead unveiled an abundant set list that included Dark Star > Morning Dew, and an electric "Friend of the Devil."

8. *Dave's Picks Volume 12*, November 4, 1977, Colgate University, Hamilton, New York: Before set two, Lesh introduces the band as the Jones Gang, and then the Jones's go off on a rampage. The Eyes of the World > Estimated Prophet > The Other One combo is wildly inventive.

A sprawling, jazzy, "Let it Grow" ends the first set. This is an impressive display of the band's raging command in 1977.

9. *Dave's Picks Volume 5*, November 17, 1973, Pauley Pavilion, Los Angeles: Deadhead Bill Walton was king of the collegiate basketball world at UCLA when the Grateful Dead played this loaded show. "Here Comes Sunshine" and China Cat > Rider rocked the first set. The undisputed highlight of this show is the Playin' in the Band > Uncle John's Band > Morning Dew > Uncle John's Band > Playin' in the Band—a loop inside of a loop.

10. *Dick's Picks Volume 4*, February 13–14, 1970, Fillmore East, New York City: The Dead introduce their flock to new tunes from *Workingman's Dead*; "Casey Jones," "High Time," and "Dire Wolf." And they unleash their primal psychedelic power on the Fillmore East with scorching versions of "Dark Star," "That's It for the Other One," and "Turn On Your Love Light." "Mason's Children" is a charming rarity.

11. *Red Rocks 7/8/78*:This was the second night of the Dead's debut stop at the sanctified amphitheatre. It's a strong outing all the way through, but the final two segments rule. Set two concludes with Wharf Rat > Franklin's Tower > Sugar Magnolia—ridiculous "Sugar Mag." The triple encore of Terrapin Station > One More Saturday Night, and "Werewolves of London" had Denver Deadheads howling.

12. *Dick's Picks Volume 15*, September 3, 1977, Raceway Park, Englishtown, New Jersey: Another legendary '77 performance featuring a distinctive "Mississippi Half Step" masterpiece. In front of a gathering of 150,000, the Dead deftly manuever between hammering stadium rock and elegantly playing with sophistication as if they were at a supper club . . . high-octane versions of "Eyes of the World" and "Not Fade Away."

13. *Live at Cow Palace*, December 31, 1976, Cow Palace, Daly City, California: 1977 began with this second set, and it was a great omen

for one of the most important years in Dead history. "Sugar Magnolia" gives way to "Eyes of the World," and the set ends with "Morning Dew."

14. *Road Trips Volume 2 Number 3*, June 16, 1974, Iowa State Fairgrounds, Des Moines, Iowa; June 18, 1974, Freedom Hall, Louisville, Kentucky: This road trip packages sublime selections from consecutive shows. The China Cat > Rider from Iowa contains an expansive, action-packed jam, and the "Morning Dew" encore from Louisville is legendary.

15. *Road Trips Volume 4 Number 4*, April 6, 1982, The Spectrum, Philadelphia: An outstanding 1982 performance with precise yet plentiful jamming. This is the only show in Dead history where they played "Shakedown Street," "Terrapin Station," "Morning Dew," and "Sugar Magnolia."

Grateful Dead Albums

1. *Europe '72*
2. *Live Dead*
3. *Reckoning*
4. *American Beauty*
5. *Grateful Dead (Skulls and Roses)*
6. *Aoxomoxoa*
7. *Blues for Allah*
8. *Steal Your Face*
9. *Workingman's Dead*
10. *In the Dark*

Jerry Garcia Albums

1. *After Midnight: Kean College, 2/28/80*: This bare-bones configuration of the Jerry Garcia Band was a quartet featuring John Kahn on bass, Ozzie Ahlers on keyboards, and Johnny De Foncesca on drums. The

rarely played After Midnight > Eleanor Rigby > After Midnight is the finest JGB improvisation/creation. Garcia tees off on "Sugaree," "That's What Love Will Make You Do," "Tore Up Over You," and "Mission in the Rain." Robert Hunter joins the band for two tunes, helping to make this a one-of-a-kind JGB experience.

2. *Cats Under the Stars*: This is the only studio album credited to, and created by, the Jerry Garcia Band. "Reuben and Cerise," "Cats Under the Stars," "Rhapsody in Red," and "Gomorrah" are among the most beloved JGB originals. This may be Jerry's finest moment of all in the studio.

3. *Live at Keystone*: The music world is turned on to the magic of Merl Saunders and Jerry Garcia thanks to this record, featuring selections from their shows at the Keystone, Berkeley, on July 10 and 11, 1973. Garcia cooks the blues on "It Takes a Lot to Laugh, It Takes a Train to Cry," and performs a poignant "Positively 4th Street." Released in late 1973, this iconic album features Jerry exploring varied genres: blues, jazz, reggae, and R&B.

4. *Legion of Mary: The Jerry Garcia Collection, Vol. 1*: At times, Legion of Mary could head off into realms of superfluous jamming with the sax and flute contributions of Martin Fierro, but this compilation captures the best of times for this short-lived configuration. This "Tough Mama" might be Jerry's best-ever cover of a Dylan tune. Other alluring performances include "I Second That Emotion," "That's a Touch I Like," and "Money Honey." This collection is all cover tunes, but Jerry had that way of making them his own.

5. *Pure Jerry: Warner Theatre*, March 18, 1978 (Pure Jerry #6): The Pure Jerry title fits this performance, as Jerry pours his virtuosity into "The Harder They Come," "Mystery Train," "Simple Twist of Fate," and

several numbers from the recently released *Cats Under the Stars*. The elegant backing vocals of Donna Jean Godchaux and Maria Muldaur cushion and enrich Garcia's crooning. A sparkling 19-minute version of "Lonesome and a Long Way From Home" makes this CD a must for any fan of the Jerry Garcia Band.

Dylan Studio Albums

1. *Highway 61 Revisited*
2. *Bringing It All Back Home*
3. *Blood on the Tracks*
4. *Blonde on Blonde*
5. *Desire*
6. *The Freewheelin' Bob Dylan*
7. *Love and Theft*
8. *Oh Mercy*
9. *Time Out of Mind*
10. *Planet Waves*
11. *Infidels*
12. *Modern Times*
13. *Another Side of Bob Dylan*
14. *The Times They Are A-Changin'*
15. *Slow Train Coming*

Dylan Bootleg Series

1. *The Bootleg Series Volumes 1–3 (Rare & Unreleased) 1961–1991*: Thirty years of Dylan leftovers gives us insight into another level of brilliance. The chronological sequencing makes each volume seem like a cohesive album. The sensational highlights are the *Blood on the Tracks* outtakes, "Blind Willie McTell," "Series of Dreams," "Mama, You Been on my Mind," "She's Your Lover Now," and "Let Me Die in my Footsteps."

2. *The Bootleg Series Vol. 8: Tell Tale Signs: Rare and Unreleased 1989–2006*: The first seventeen years of the second half of Dylan's career produced a treasure trove of unreleased gems, reinforcing the power of Bob's later works. This was released as a double album, and a limited-edition triple album. The extra CD has the third, and best, rendition of "Mississippi," as well as a definitive live "Cold Irons Bound." The most noteworthy composition that didn't previously make it to an album is "Red River Shore," a haunting and beautiful ballad of yearning from the *Time Out of Mind* sessions. In addition to all the alternate versions, this collection offers eight live performances, and wonderful covers of "32-20 Blues" (Robert Johnson), and "Duncan & Brady" (traditional).

3. *The Bootleg Series Vol. 6: Bob Dylan Live 1964, Concert at Philharmonic Hall*: Dylan has a sellout crowd hanging on his every syllable. Troubadour, raconteur, and comedian rolled into one, Dylan entertains his devotees with an eclectic mix of originals featuring talkin' blues songs alongside lyrically rich jingles. The songs are thought-provoking and deep, but Dylan lightens the mood with sly vocal improvisation and humorous between-song banter. Dylan was moving towards visionary music, yet this extraordinary concert features gripping performances of his *Freewheelin'* songs: "Talkin' John Birch Paranoid Blues," "Talkin' World War III Blues," and "Don't Think Twice It's Alright."

4. *The Bootleg Series Vol. 7: No Direction Home: The Soundtrack*: Side two of this bootleg adventure is a classic album in its own right. It contains the iconic electric "Maggie's Farm" from Newport '65, and the "Like a Rolling Stone" with the infamous "Judas" shout. Mike Bloomfield's guitar is outrageous on "It Takes a lot to Laugh, It Takes a Train to Cry." With the addition of a live 1966 "Ballad of a Thin Man," an electric outtake of "Visions of Johanna," and a funky early version of "Stuck Inside of Mobile with the Memphis Blues Again," this is an essential edition of the bootleg series.

5. *The Bootleg Series Vol. 5: Bob Dylan Live 1975, The Rolling Thunder Revue*: A solid compilation of songs sequenced to resemble an evening on tour with Dylan and his cast of barnstorming performers. Any album with live performances of "Hurricane," "Isis," "Romance in Durango" and "Sara" is a godsend.

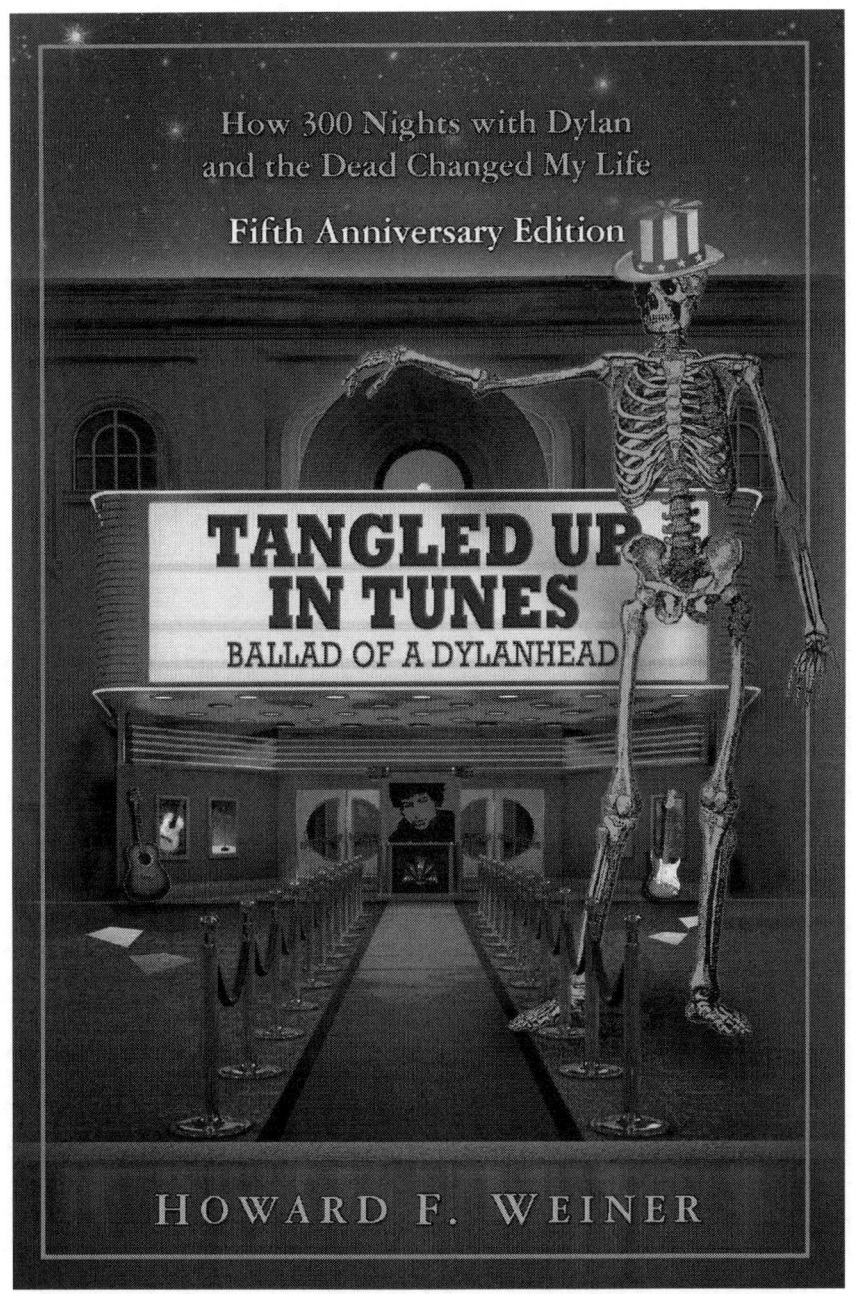

Books by Howard F. Weiner @ www.tangledupintunes.com

GRATEFUL DEAD 1977

THE RISE OF TERRAPIN NATION

HOWARD F. WEINER

Books by Howard F. Weiner @ www.tangledupintunes.com

10012623R00164

Printed in Germany
by Amazon Distribution
GmbH, Leipzig